REPORT FROM SPAIN

REPORT FROM SPAIN

BY EMMET JOHN HUGHES

NEW YORK: HENRY HOLT AND COMPANY

FOR MARIFRANCES

CONTENTS

When foreign affairs were ruled by autocracies or oligarchies, the danger of war was in sinister purpose. When foreign affairs are ruled by democracies, the danger of war will be in mistaken beliefs.

The world will be the gainer by the change, for, while there is no human way to prevent a king from having a bad heart, there is a human way to prevent a people from having an erroneous opinion.

That way is to furnish the whole people . . . with correct information about their relations to other peoples, about the limitations upon their own rights, about their duties to respect the rights of others, about what has happened and is happening in international affairs, and about the effects upon national life of the things that are done or refused as between nations; so that the people themselves will have the means to test misinformation and appeals to prejudice and passion based upon error.

Elihu Root

Foreign Affairs, New York, I. 5 (September 1922)

THE REGIME OF FRANCO

1 GENERAL FRANCISCO FRANCO AND HIS ARMY

SPAIN is a totalitarian country and its Chief is His Excellency the Caudillo, Generalissimo of the Armies on land, sea and in the air, and Chief of the Government, which is made up of twelve ministries."

Or . . .

"The Spanish State, born under the sign of the unity and greatness of the Fatherland, is a totalitarian instrument at the service of the Fatherland: National-Syndicalist in character in everything which signifies a reaction against liberal capitalism and Marxist materialism."

Curt, clear, and comprehensive, these definitions of the present Spanish regime, with their eager emphasis on the totalitarian character of the Spanish government, appear in the *Curso Completo de Primera Enseñanza*—the standard elementary school textbook used throughout Spain today. A wretched, retrograde educational system has endowed Spain with classrooms which are among the less noble monuments of a traditionally great nation: classrooms which only a favored few can enter, they suffer the neglect of a government busy with more glamorous affairs than the education of its people. Yet, in a grim sort of paradox, it is in these rooms that political truth is spoken in stark simplicity. Gaudy drama, in sharp contrast, is reserved for the momentous occasions of state

3

gatherings, especially public appearances of the Caudillo. Here,
in surroundings of official pomp, the Chief of the Spanish State,
speaking for the benefit of people more sophisticated politically
than the children of Spain, uses a different vocabulary. He
speaks of "Christian democracy." He talks of "organic democracy." He exultantly extols "Evangelical democracy."

Obviously no authority on semantics, but endowed with a
keen taste for irony, the Caudillo has developed a delicate device which needs to be more widely appreciated: to speak the
truth to the adolescents of Spain and to save the mocking lie
for the adult peoples of the world.

2

Francisco Paulino Hermenegildo Teodulo Franco Baha-
monde has presided over the destiny of Spain for eight dictatorial years. In that period of time—already considerably longer
than the life of the Spanish Republic—he, his army, his judi-
ciary, his government departments, his police and his Party
have enjoyed a political and punitive power subject only to
such limitations as have been imposed by their consideration
of their own interests. For these leaders, the sweet taste of martial triumph in 1939 has never proved sickening: Spain still
lives officially under martial law.

The man and his regime, in true totalitarian fashion, are
one and inseparable. He is Commander in Chief of all armed
forces. He is the Chief of the Government. He is the Leader
of the Party—the only Party. *His* parliament, the Cortes, boasts
only one incontestable right: to approve his decrees, if he sub-
mits them for approval. To the indefinite enjoyment and perpetuation of this power, only nature opposes a limitation—that
of mortality.

Paradox, of which Spain has always been so fond, is the key
to the regime of General Franco. For it is an important truth
that the dictator of Spain utterly lacks any such mass personal
following as to support his exercise of power and, in the final

analysis, is entirely dependent upon an alliance of old, historic political forces which might at any time destroy him by their betrayal. And yet these forces—Army and Church—depend upon him for their own enjoyment of power to such an extent that without his individual presence the whole structure of the Spanish regime would fall.

This man is a Gallegan. By tradition these men of Spain's northwesternmost corner are striking prototypes of the Latin peasant character: they are stubborn, they are shrewd, they are cautious, they are adroit, they are tenacious. These adjectives not only apply accurately to the character of Spain's dictator, but also illuminate the whole nature and temper of his regime: its resolute clinging to power, and its sinuous, elusive capacity to reconcile the most flagrant contradictions, to rationalize the grossest inconsistencies.

I have seen Franco in the royal box in Madrid's bull ring: short in stature, with that abdominal curvature that delights caricaturists, smiling rather lamely, a bit like an unwilling and inarticulate toastmaster at a big banquet. He raises his arm in a gesture that might be a Fascist salute or might be a vague wave in slow motion. He nods agreeably and a bit nervously to the chants of *Franco! Franco! Franco!* which the multitude tries to make sound agreeable and not too nervous.

I have watched him in a more comfortable position: seated in his big open Mercedes, waving to the waving crowds along Madrid's grand sweep of the Castellana (which everyone forgets to call the *Avenida del Generalissimo*), surrounded with mathematical precision by a protecting screen of the Moorish guards, with their red and gold uniforms, their silk turbans, dark dull faces, lances glittering in the sun: in this martial world, he seems content and almost at ease.

And I have observed him at the official annual July eighteen reception for the diplomatic corps in the grand gardens of La Granja palace: appearing suddenly to greet his scores of waiting guests, moving with a sort of dogged dignity to shake hands and give a small jerky smile to all around him. At close range, despite the brisk neat uniform with its smell of new leather, he does not look very martial: in stature, gesture, and countenance, he suggests a moderately successful business executive. Sparse, gray hair betrays his years, but his swarthy face has few lines suggesting strain or fatigue. The deep brown eyes are not so much cold as impenetrable, with only a slight sparkle to accompany the quick smile. The small mouth and slightly receding chin give a suggestion of strength of will rather than strength of character.

The character of Franco is a compound of such contradictions and anomalies that they have often perplexed his close associates as much as foreigners busily trying to analyze it from a distance. He is intensely, devoutly Catholic; he and his family are scrupulously faithful to all the rites and disciplines of their faith. His advocacy of the Falange Party's radical social program is undoubtedly motivated by his conviction that it is a worthy political translation of Christian social doctrine. He most certainly views himself as the valiant defender and protagonist of Spain's Catholic traditions, which he sincerely believes were gravely threatened in 1936 and were saved only by God's grace and his own zeal.

Yet there exists not the slightest evidence that any religious sentiments qualified his admiration and affection for atheist Mussolini and pagan Hitler. In the entire bleak history of Naziism, not a single instance is known when the champion of Spanish Catholicism suggested, either publicly or through diplomatic channels, even a modest concern over the Nazi Party's persecution of the Church in Germany or its systematically vicious extermination of Catholic patriot leaders in occupied countries. As for relations with Rome, mounting evidence of the Vatican's coolness toward his regime apparently has failed to tarnish the shining armor of the mind of this "defender of the faith." At home, his religious zeal has conveniently stopped short of any such fanaticism as might induce him to modify Spain's cynical and sanguinary judicial and penal system, with faith only in the efficacy of punishment, with hope and charity for none. Nor has the steadfast hostility of Catholics of the Basque region ever impelled him to wonder whether his devout pretensions were not exaggerated.

In temperament and tactics, other contradictions abound in the man's character. In some respects, like many of the men close to him, he lives in a medieval world. For him, complex political issues resolve themselves into simple, sharply defined shapes, either divine or demoniac. Political critics and opponents, who perforce must be either Communists or Masons, are "possessed" by satanic powers. To err politically is to sin grievously; and like denial of the Holy Ghost, for such a failing there can be no expiation, no adequate penance, only damnation. Probably with as much genuine fervor as a Charlemagne or a Louis IX or a Richard III, he sees himself as the custodian of a divine commission, believing that his power is born of a felicitous marriage of celestial and national will—and that in a last resort his God will protect him and his cause from the Kremlin, the United Nations, the Republican exiles, or the Spanish *maquis*. . . . Yet he bears the marks of no medieval prince but rather of a typical twentieth century dictator in his keen knowledge of the techniques of modern warfare, his respect for a smartly organized and well-armed police system, his appreciation of the power of the public press and the efficacy of the propaganda lie, his cunning capacity for dividing and confusing political enemies, his adroitness in the art of diplomatic deception. For, in his formative years, his were not monastic tutors laboriously explaining the rights and duties of the Christian prince. Morocco taught the gallant young soldier a different code. Here he fought with bravery and distinction, perceived that governorship in such an area meant constant warfare upon the governed. He learned the need of playing off one envious Moorish chieftain against another, allying himself with one, warring upon a second, betraying a third, preparing to betray the first. It was a relentless game of governing by conspiracy, cabals, caprice, conquest. This was what he

learned and this is what he has practiced, for this is all that
he knows.

The limitations of his mentality are firmly fixed. He utterly
lacks what may be called simply a sense of the times, a cosmo-
politan awareness of the driving currents in the flow of world
history. Quite literally, he does not *understand* the bases of
world criticism of himself or his politics, hence can so easily
(and without hypocrisy) accept the crisp cliché that such criticism is only the "agitation" of "Communists." Since "Communists" simply signify "enemies of the state," his political logic
is irrefutable. His political conduct implies the conviction that
he has founded an enduring as well as a decent government:
he appears perfectly impervious to the thought that, even without "interference" by foreign powers in the affairs of Spain,
the years of this regime can be no more than the years of his
mortal life. . . . Yet, despite this amazingly oblique vision, he
has a shrewd insight into the devious devices of practical politics—an unusual craft for elusive political maneuvering, for
surprising and well-timed cabinet changes, for appointments
and proclamations cannily designed to baffle his critics and
often to turn them upon each other. On the ward or precinct
level of politics in a big American city, he would be a shining
success.

This is the man who is dictator over the 25,000,000 people
of Spain. It is right and necessary that he be understood and
assessed as he is, not merely as professional caricaturists depict
him, with their artistic virtuosity so contemptuous of the harsh
limits of political fact and truth. It is, of course, more facile
(and more fun) for either dexterous cartoonists or prolific
columnists (with that treasured passport to the land of miraculous wonders known as "behind the scenes") to titillate their
readers with the idea that the last dictator in western Europe
looks like a penguin, struts like a peacock, has the brains of a
mare. Unfortunately, such merry reflections are not only false:
they seriously cripple the capacity of those who believe them
to do anything constructive (or destructive) about a situation

which, to a more sober observer, might look like the vicious vestiges of Fascism. In this instance, the facts about a man's character may not be flattering but they should be sobering to some of his more flippant detractors. A politically mature people should be able to understand and evaluate accurately, in a foreign statesman, a kind of intelligence that is crafty, a sincerity that is fanatic, a tenacity that is ruthless, an integrity that is cruel. A politically mature people should be unafraid to remember the nouns as well as the adjectives in that sentence—and should rebel against the cheap argument that any foreign political leader challenging or denying their way of life must, simply by virtue of his intransigence, be a pervert or a freak.

The simplest analogies emphasize the importance of this matter. In time of war, a sane general is more interested in his opponent's battle order than in the names and number of his mistresses; the opening of the second front was not perceptibly facilitated by the rumor that Hitler was a homosexual. Similarly, only a naïve and fraudulent statesmanship conducts the foreign affairs of a nation on the assumption that he who is wrong is weak, that he who is weak is a huge joke.

Since 1939, when the Spanish Civil War ended, the press, pulpits and public platforms of the democratic nations have bulged with enough predictions of the "imminence" of the fall of the Franco regime to convince even the most credulous that neither are the issues so simple nor the men so stupid as they have been depicted. Finally the realization has come that, with the regime of General Franco, the world has been confronted with nothing so simple as a Quisling government imposed upon the Spanish people by the German Condor Legion—but instead a deadly serious alliance of political forces whose persistence in retaining power, however exasperating, can no longer be denied. Consequently, serious understanding of those political forces can no longer be delayed.

3

What are the character, strength, and resources of the regime of Francisco Franco?

As with the various conflicting qualities in the character of Franco himself, the regime over which he presides embraces distinct, unassimilated political forces. In strict truth, there exists no such cohesive entity as *the* government of Madrid. Instead, there exists an alliance of individual political groups whose combined power is as overwhelming as its allied life is precarious. This alliance binds virtually the whole of the Spanish Army, the hierarchical mass of the Spanish Church, the Falange Party, impressive numbers of collaborationist Monarchists, professional political parasites—and a fretful, fugitive army of frightened conservatives and reactionaries.

Each of the Big Three—Army, Church, and Falange—has particular, independent origins, histories, and aspirations. Not one of them necessarily endorses the ambitions of the other two, but in fact usually views those ambitions with suspicion if not envy. They are not so much allies as cobelligerents.

Consequently, the character of the regime of General Franco can clearly be defined only in the answers to two questions: What is the nature of each of these political forces, and what factors hold them together in their present alliance?

The Spanish Army possesses that force and authority without which no government of Spain in modern history has been able to survive. It has defended governments, betrayed governments, created governments. The very function of government in modern Spain has seemed to reduce itself simply to the national exercise of civil authority as permitted or prescribed by the nation's standing army.

In the last three hundred years, no nation in the world has plunged from the pinnacle of world power into the gloomy abyss reserved for third-rate powers with the speed and dis-

patch displayed by Spain. At the same time, no once-great empire, now confined within its own national frontiers, has been
confronted with so many painful reminders of the dead days
of glory, so many living testimonies to its huge labor of conquest, exploration, and colonization. The continent of South
America, the little independent countries stretching along Central America, the islands of the Caribbean, large areas of the
United States, the islands of the Philippines: all these today
bear the special mark of the heritage of Spain. For passionately
patriotic Spaniards, these Hispanic regions are constant, mute
but eloquent suggestions of an imperial power which might
still be latent, immanent in Spanish character.

But in a practical sense, the material dissolution of the
Spanish empire meant that there no longer was the need at
home for such institutions as had been demanded by the responsibilities of imperial rule—institutions like an army to
stand guard over globe-encircling colonies. The humiliating
disaster of 1898 left an army geared for imperial tasks essentially unemployed—while among the intellectuals of Spain it
precipitated that critical, inquisitive study of their own national traditions and weaknesses which marked the great philosophical labor of "the generation of '98." Because the Spanish-
American War upset both the political and intellectual equi-
librium of Spain, it is probably true that no contemporary
Spaniards had so profound an effect upon their nation's history
as did McKinley, Theodore Roosevelt, and Admiral Dewey.

In those tragic years at the turn of the century, a Spanish
government equipped with political vision and courage would
have realized at once that the nation could neither need nor
afford a huge standing army. But such a government did not
exist. Instead, the statesmen of Madrid, with few exceptions,
busied themselves with the more immediate and lucrative task
of bolstering the national government's prestige in the face of
a bitterly disillusioned public opinion.

In this effort to salvage the Monarchy's reputation and restore its stability, the men of Madrid evaded the arduous work

of endowing the Monarchy with a spirit of farsighted leadership that would direct the efforts of the Spanish people toward the building of a new Spain. It was easier to fall back upon the expedient of buttressing the government by force. Moreover, Madrid had to confront not only the fact of its shattered national prestige abroad but also the challenge of those dangerous recurrent separatist tendencies within Spain, especially in Catalonia but also threatening throughout most of the east and north. These separatist movements always emerged to battle Castilian authority, situated in Madrid, at those moments when the national government was suffering some painful crisis or humiliation. Such regional loyalties could be subdued and overridden when imperial prestige was high, when a more glamorous and expansive destiny could evoke and capture the loyalties of citizens of the provinces. But after 1898, when these loyalties turned to disillusion and despair, the resurgence of regional allegiances, with their shrill indictments of national authority, was easy to foresee.

Thus it was also easy to foresee that the Spanish Army would survive its day of humiliation to continue life on its historically grand scale. The only change would be in the task commended to its care: instead of the guardianship of a grand empire, the protection of a weak, wary, and worried national government. In this building of what they expected to be an impregnable fortress, the men of Madrid apparently neglected to think that it might become an inescapable prison.

By 1917, the already apparent truth became plain to see for all but the willfully blind. In that year, starting in Catalonia and spreading fast throughout the Army of the nation, there sprang up the *Juntas de Defensa*. Strategically situated army officers banded together with the alleged purpose (often enough sincere) of reforming and strengthening the structure of the Army. But the more enduring character of these groups quickly crystallized simply as political councils through which the military could state their ambitions, and present their demands to the civil authorities. They became pressure groups in uniform—by the novel, revolutionary device of applying to the Army the labor-union concept of organization.

When General Primo de Rivera (whose son was to be the founder of the Falange Party) began his six-year dictatorship with his coup d'état in September of 1923, the Spanish Army proved once again that it was the decisive arbiter of Spanish politics. As Mussolini had done two years before with the House of Savoy, so in Spain did General Primo de Rivera proclaim his allegiance to King Alfonso XIII. This was not, however, a Fascist regime in twentieth century style. It was the Spanish Army, the same which had seemed so humbled and irresolute in 1898, now flexing its muscles, raising aloft its tattered but gaudy banners, loudly proclaiming its mastery in the only arena where it could defy all challenges—on its own soil. As Ortega y Gasset remarked many years ago, the Army had remained like a loaded pistol, deprived of any foreign target, turned and aimed against the authority it was pledged to uphold.

After Primo de Rivera's prestige even within military ranks had declined so sharply that Alfonso could dismiss him from office, the King and his advisers floundered and fretted through the remaining months before the 1931 elections decreed their own end and heralded the Spanish Republic. The King had emerged from his own prison-fortress only to learn that he was unwanted outside its gates. And from the King's jails came many of his political prisoners to take his place and their turn at governing Spain.

The Republic made valiant efforts to curtail the authority of a force in Spanish history which had made sovereignty a caprice of the military. But even in these heroic, tragic years, when there came the great Socialist uprisings in the Asturias in 1934, the Republican government (under Catholic Rightist Gil Robles) had to call upon the Army to down the rebels in the name of the Republic. Crack regular forces were aided by big contingents of Moorish troops, and it was General Francisco Franco who led them in the bloody, triumphant task of restoring order.

It was this same army which eighteen months later revolted under General Sanjurjo, passed under the leadership of the same General Franco three months later, played the decisive role in bringing the Nationalist victory in 1939, and has acted to the present day as the decisive guarantor of the Franco regime. Above all else, Francisco Franco, Chief of the Spanish Government, is Generalissimo of the armed forces—the forces which suffered their gravest disaster when he was a boy of six years of age, and which have risen under him once again to be the actual custodians of the sovereignty of Spain.

Traditionally conservative and Monarchist, this Spanish Army has bewildered some observers and dismayed many Monarchists by its apparent fidelity to a regime stubbornly opposing Monarchic restoration. The explanation is simple. More profound and venerable than any tradition of loyalty to the Monarchic institution is the military's tradition of securing its own collective interest by any political means available. The political education of the Spanish soldier in the past could never be called advanced and often could scarcely be considered elementary. Political judgments have always used a simple criterion: that regime is good which is good for the Army. Apart from this, certain temperamental tendencies and inhibitions characteristic of the Spanish military have harmonized nicely with the practices and policies of the present Spanish regime. It has been vehemently anti-Communist, reverent of the rights of private property (the bigger the property, the bigger the right), cynical of public opinion, and overwhelmingly convinced that society can suffer no greater evil than something called "disorder."

Now, for eight luxurious years, the Spanish Army has been preened and pampered by General Franco. Already dissolved is any threat to its hegemony which might have been launched by the revolutionary upstarts of the Falange Party. It suffers no important conflict of purpose with the Spanish Church. It is unchallenged. And it is lavishly endowed.

Typical evidence of the Army's endowment was publicly proclaimed in the government's budget for the calendar year of 1946. Under what is officially called the "regular" budget for all ministries, the Army received the sum of 2,104,300,000 pesetas. This figure, representing about 20 per cent of the entire budget, could fully be appreciated only when compared with allocations to other agencies of the government. The budget for the Ministry of the Army exceeded the *total* of the sums assigned to the Ministries of Foreign Affairs, Justice, Commerce, Treasury, Agriculture, and Public Works, the Spanish Cortes, and the Falange Party. Stated in different terms, the amount allocated to the Army is sixteen times the appropriation for the Foreign Office, more than twenty times that for Agriculture.

Significantly, there was but one government department that received a sum even remotely approaching (25 per cent less) that with which the Army was honored: the Ministry of the Interior. The substantial sum of more than one and one-half billion pesetas went to this ministry principally for the maintenance of the security police forces which serve throughout Spain as an auxiliary arm of the Army in the defense of the regime. The grand total allocated for all the regular armed forces (including Navy and Air Forces) and the security police amounted to forty per cent of the entire "regular" budget.

But this was not all. It is the practice of the Spanish government to supplement its "regular" budget with an "extraordinary" budget. With the exception of a small sum marked for the public debt, the Army in 1946 received more than fifty per cent of these "extraordinary" funds (over 900,000,000 pesetas)— while the entire balance went to the other two branches of the armed forces and to the ubiquitous Ministry of the Interior. When both the "regular" and "extraordinary" budgets are combined, we discover that, of a total projected annual expenditure of a little more than thirteen billion pesetas, almost six and one-half billions belonged to the national defense and security forces. It is not surprising that the Minister of Finance, addressing the Cortes on the subject of the budget which they perfunctorily endorsed, remarked laconically:

In the period following an internal war, with its consequent problems of criminality, of release of prisoners, and of constant subversive efforts supported from abroad, it is not possible for the expenses of public order to be the same as those in a normal period. . . . The guarantees which the order and integrity of the Fatherland demand cannot be abandoned.[1]

This revealing statement constitutes an obvious franchise for the military. Their responsibility and authority amount to much more than the simple function of national defense. They are primarily charged with the work of dealing with political opposition within Spain, *i.e.*, "problems of criminality."

Enjoyment of this franchise entails not only authority but those practical benefits of which the Spanish military are so fond. They are such benefits as: big German Tiger tanks, which look so massive and impressive in the Victory Parade every April 1; more and larger training schools for officers and raw recruits, whom it is useful, of course, to keep under arms, rather than be allowed to swell the ranks of the unemployed or the politically disgruntled; special food rations which make the military a highly privileged economic caste and which insulate them against any accurate conception of food shortages in the country at large; fast promotions and big salary increases for ambitious, politically loyal officers.

But Army opinion and sentiment are affected by more than these simple expedients, designed principally for generals and senior officers. Younger junior officers constitute a separate case. In their twenties or early thirties, these men have been trained and indoctrinated entirely in the eight years since the end of the Civil War. In the academies of Spain, they have absorbed without serious question or criticism the instructions

[1] *Arriba*, Dec. 30, 1945, from which the budget statistics also are taken.

of officers who (to the very bitter end of Naziism) were infatu-ated with German military prowess, who were passionately devoted to the Generalissimo of their Civil War victory, and who were at least careful not to voice public criticism of the creed of the Falange Party. Young men trained in such an environment lack even the sentimental attachment to a Mon-archic system which may yet linger wistfully on older military hearts. They emerge as the authentically stamped, approved, uniformed products of the only political regime they have known in their mature years. Their allegiance is genuine, un-questioning, and determined.

Naturally, there have been exceptions—some dissidents who doubt if the regime of General Franco, despite all its benefits to the military, can possibly qualify as a permanent political settlement. Monarchists have fondly looked upon a few leading generals, such as Kindelán, Varela, and the late Orgaz, as sure sympathizers whose political courage was conveniently coupled with a fairly wide popular following. But such white hopes have yellowed with age or inertia. Or they have been neatly frustrated by the alternate firmness and suppleness of the Generalissimo.

A few instances usefully illustrate General Franco's dexterity in dealing with recalcitrant military leaders. It was in July of 1943 that Monarchist generals, businessmen, and members of the Cortes signed and circulated a petition addressed to Franco and calling upon him to effect a Monarchic restoration with dispatch. When news of this treason reached Franco in his resi-dence at the Pardo before the petition could be formally sub-mitted, an acute case of nervous disorder afflicted all the sig-natories. Nonetheless, two generals and one admiral, none of whom had signed the petition but who sympathized with its objective, summoned their courage and arranged a Monday afternoon appointment to confer with Franco. They were re-ceived stiffly in Franco's office, seated themselves before his desk, explained with pained ceremony and deference that they personally favored restoration of the Monarchy and strongly opposed any sanctions against those who had signed the petition. Franco rose slowly from his seat, stalked around the desk to confront the men at close range, and with the most violent gesticulations delivered the shrill harangue: "You too! You do not understand that the Monarchy is *lo parcial*—and my regime is *lo total*. I represent the Victory and *la integridad española!* I am here to fulfill a divine mandate, and any contrary maneuver is an act against Spain itself!" Two generals and one admiral withered under this blast, left in mingled fear and dismay. The next morning the Falangist daily, *Arriba,* in an official editorial entitled "Loyalty to Franco," obediently repeated Franco's arguments for a wider audience.

A year later, another of the recurrent Monarchist attempts to make history with petitions met with a different kind of reception from Franco. Rumors reached the Generalissimo that a number of prominent Army generals might sign the forthcoming document. Each of the suspects received an individual invitation to call upon Franco at the Pardo. Solemn and unruffled, Franco received each separately, gave fulsome thanks to each for his services and loyalty to the regime, informed him that an appropriate increase in pay had been authorized as an expression of personal appreciation. There was not even a veiled mention of any projected petition. There was no petition.

Not long after this episode, the Generalissimo chose a pleasant summer night to stage still another kind of ceremony. From the Pardo came urgent telephone calls to the key generals stationed in and around Madrid. The message: they were to report to the Pardo at twelve midnight without fail or delay. When the generals assembled, Franco received them, pleasantly told them he was satisfied with their performance. He had merely wanted to be sure they were ready to answer any urgent summons. There followed a short but frightening dissertation on the "Bolshevik menace." The generals then retired for a haunted night's sleep.

With such brisk facility has General Franco managed his

Army—fortifying it as the supreme arbiter of Iberian political destinies, while converting it into the crucial bulwark of his regime. Its thirty-six divisions stand guard throughout continental Spain and the African possessions, most heavily deployed in Spanish Morocco and the area between the Ebro River and the Pyrenees. Its full strength of more than 700,000 men qualifies it as the strongest standing army in Western Europe.

In a country where a show of bayonets is more impressive than a show of hands, everyone knows who has the bayonets.

2 THE FALANGE PARTY—ITS HISTORY AND ITS GOSPEL

A COMPACT GROUP of young Spaniards today proposes to intervene in political activities in an intensive and effective manner."

This blunt statement was the first shrill battle cry of Spanish Fascism. In March of 1931, one month before the birth of the Spanish Republic, a curious political manifesto containing these words and called *The Conquest of the State* appeared on the streets of Madrid. It advanced these propositions:

"We direct ourselves to political action with the concrete purpose of projecting over the nation the outline of a new State—and of imposing it. . . .

"The State is the highest political value. . . . Nothing above the State! . . .

"In the face of the internal disintegration which we witness today, we raise the banner of national responsibility. . . . We proceed to the affirmation of Spanish culture with imperialistic ambitions. . . .

"The first clear vision of the character of our industrial and technical civilization belongs to Marxism. We will fight against the limitations of Marxist materialism and we must overcome it—but not without recognizing the honors due it as the now dead and exhausted precursor in the first clashes. . . .

"We do not seek votes, but rather valiant and daring minori-

20

ties. We seek young militant groups who will not flinch at facing a gun nor at the discipline of war. . . .

"We head toward victory, and we are the truth of Spain. . . . The world needs us—and we must be at our posts!"

In 1931, not the world, not Spain, not even Madrid sensed any acute, overpowering need for the authors of this manifesto. Even *Madrileños,* more accustomed than most to the spectacle of bizarre political parties and the hyperbole of impassioned political rhetoric, probably made little sense out of this exuberant language. Nonetheless, the movement which burst forth at that time with such infantile babblings grew in the next eight years to emerge, by the end of the Spanish Civil War, as totalitarian Spain's unique political party: *Falange Española.*

Another eight years have passed since that day of "Glorious Victory." For most of these eight years, the victory has been glorious for the Falange: the one-party syndicalist state gave it a monopoly on the enjoyment of political power, a virtual monopoly of economic power. But the latter years—and especially the months since the destruction of Naziism—have been less fruitful. The Chief of the Spanish State, who so ardently had adopted the Falange's men and principles as his own, has been busy with cruel political shears—snipping one after another of the ties connecting him with a group which, in the post-World War II era, seems a grotesque anachronism and a heavy liability. In slow but systematic succession, Francisco Franco has shorn the Falange of many of its most valued prerogatives. Prestige and power equally have been taken from the blue-shirted men: the Fascist salute, their post in the cabinet, their own organized militia, their control of national press and propaganda. This is the process which has been carelessly called "liberalization" of the Spanish regime.

Yet the Chief of the Spanish State continues to be the Chief of the Falange Party. The Falange continues to be the unique political party in Spain. And precisely in the very diminution of its power—*because* of its very decline in prestige—the Falange continues to serve the political purposes of General

Franco. It never has failed to serve as one of the three great pillars upon which the present Spanish State is founded.

2

Although the political party formally known as the Falange was not born until October of 1933, the true beginnings of Spanish Fascism go back to earlier years.

During the twenties, in the time of the dictatorship of General Primo de Rivera, there appeared for the first time in certain of Madrid's intellectual circles an interest in Italian Fascism which was something more than academic. The young man who stimulated this interest, who was the first active apostle of the new gospel in Spain, was Ernesto Giménez Caballero. Today a National Counselor of the Falange, Giménez Caballero is a tall, angular man, with unruly dark hair and a black mustache, bulging brown eyes, excitedly gesticulating hands; sallow in complexion, voluble in speech, nervous in movement. Holding undisputed title to the role of the Spanish D'Annunzio, since 1929 he has ranked as the foremost poet-philosopher of the Falange movement.

The philosophical aberrations of Giménez Caballero have pursued a breathtakingly dizzy course from left-wing Socialism (he started as an ardent admirer of Fernando de los Rios), through various shades of a kind of Jesuitical reaction, to simple totalitarianism. His political odyssey began in Strasbourg, Germany. There he had gone to study in the middle twenties and there he married the sister of an Italian consular official. Married life carried him to Italy in 1928, where he became intimately acquainted with one of the enthusiastic young Italian intellectuals then inspired by Mussolini—Curzio Malaparte. Giménez Caballero absorbed the Fascist gospel from his friend, and upon return to Spain immediately translated one of his books (*En Torno al Casticismo de Italia*) expounding the urgent need for a Fascist-style renaissance throughout Latin Europe.

With this and a series of subsequent original writings, Giménez Caballero propagated in Spain a special, specific brand of Fascist doctrine which was to have important influence on political developments to come. Particular emphasis in this political gospel fell upon Rome as the home of the Catholic tradition, as the seat of Fascism, and as the symbol and protagonist of Latin Europe. This doctrine fumed with rage against northern Europe, against every historic development which had contributed to the decline in prestige of the Mediterranean nations. The fact that the center of political and economic gravity had moved north and toward the Atlantic, that the Mediterranean was no longer the center of world civilization—this was viewed as a tragedy for which every development in modern history was indicted: the Renaissance, the Protestant Reformation, liberalism, industrialism, capitalism, socialism, popular suffrage, the French Revolution! And in this fantastic doctrine of "Latinity," it is remarkable to see that this first exponent of Spanish Fascism viewed Germany as the enemy's citadel: having listed all the allegedly disastrous phenomena of modern history, he concluded, "in short—Nordism." How deftly were Falangist historians to revise their views after Adolf Hitler had laid the Weimar Republic to rest!

Even more curious, in view of subsequent history, Giménez Caballero (like Curzio Malaparte) never looked upon Russia as the "Bolshevik monster" of Fascist propaganda. Instead, he regarded Russia as a comrade and ally of the aggrieved, abused Mediterranean powers. Like Spain, Russia stood on the periphery of Europe, repeatedly attacked and victimized by greedy European powers. Both nations served as bridges to continents other than Europe—Russia to Asia, Spain to Africa. Traditionally and racially, both peoples had been stimulated and influenced by forces completely outside the European current of history. Hence the exultant call: "Italy against Europe. Spain against Europe. Russia against Europe."

They sound today like fantasy, these words from a man who

has been a National Counselor of the Falange for years, at one time Press and Propaganda Chief of the Falange, and a man of unique importance in shaping the Fascist mind in Spain. But it must be remembered that these first stirrings of Spanish Fascism came years before Hitler rose to German power; and even after that, years more passed before the ambitions of Rome and Berlin became welded into the Axis of mid-Europe.

These facts are important, for the entire course of Spanish totalitarianism is marked by the persistence of two distinct forces, two almost independent ideologies. Giménez Caballero propagated the first—looking to Rome for inspiration, passionately professing allegiance to Catholicism, shrilly proclaiming a wildly nationalistic appeal, completely lacking a social gospel or awareness of class struggle or economic issues.

The man who looked to Berlin, who saw something more in Fascism than Latin chauvinism, was Ramiro Ledesma Ramos. Son of a village schoolteacher, poverty-haunted student in the University of Madrid with a flair for quoting Nietzsche and Kant, Ledesma Ramos was the guiding spirit of the group of youths who published *The Conquest of the State* early in 1931. A frank admirer of Hitler, whom he mimicked even to the extent of copying the famous Hitler hairline, a man of harsh temperament, steel-like intolerance, enormous passion for proletarian justice, Ledesma probably contributed more to the ideological growth of Spanish Fascism than any other Spaniard of his times.

He represented—or more accurately, developed and unleashed—four great currents in Falangist thought which, joined together, created an independent, distinct philosophy from that of Giménez Caballero. In the first place, Ledesma ranks as the most articulate and faithful expression of German intellectual influence—in everything from his academic fondness for the nineteenth century German philosophers and his personal reverence for Hitler, to his sustained effort to translate the social program of Naziism into the language of Castile.

This is his second distinguishing mark: propagation of a doctrine appealing explicitly to the urban proletariat and provincial peasantry. He viewed Marxism with none of the frenetic horror of later Falangists but looked upon it rather as the gallant vanguard in the battle for proletarian justice—a vanguard now misguided and bewildered but nonetheless valiant and venerable.

Thirdly, this stern Teuton in Spaniard's dress viewed Catholicism and the Spanish Church as the allies of reaction. They were enemies that must be fought as resolutely as the textile magnates of Barcelona, the bankers of Bilbao, the land-mad estate holders of Andalucía. So forthright and fervent was Ledesma's anticlericalism that an officially sponsored biography of him published in Madrid in 1942 could write of him: "He was not a Catholic and did not say he was. . . . Ramiro could not propound a Catholicism which he did not feel, but he offered instead a respect and comprehension which we frequently lack in our country. But the moneyed classes, sealed in their castles behind granite walls, preferred solutions like the ill-fated Popular Action [*i.e.*, the Catholic party under Gil Robles], which, even supposing it could have triumphed, had sufficient vitality only to delay the inevitable." [1]

Ledesma instilled this anticlericalism into the movement he founded and baptized as the *Juntas de Ofensiva Nacional-Sindicalista* ("Councils of the National-Syndicalist Offensive"), and it continued to be a powerful force within the JONS for two very sound political reasons. In the first place, leaders of the JONS were busily proselytizing Spain's passionately anti-clerical anarchists, mobilized in the CNT (*Confederación Nacional de Trabajo*—"National Federation of Labor"). In no country in the world had the Anarchist movement of Bakunin assumed such proportions as in Spain. Such a great proletarian force meant the existence of a working-class movement intensely anti-Marxist as well as anticlerical—hence a huge and

[1] Emiliano Aguado, *Ramiro Ledesma en La Crisis de España*, p. 53.

potentially fertile field for the crusading of the JONS, who rallied around the banner of social revolution at the same time that they declared war on Communism. To reassure its Anarchist audience that its anti-Communism in no way implied a disguised form of "clerical reaction," the JONS necessarily kept its political doctrine pitched on an anticlerical key.

The second consideration prescribing an anticlerical policy was this: during its entire history to the time of the rising in 1936, the Fascist movement found its most dangerous competitor not in the Communists but in the Catholic groups led by Gil Robles. The battle which the JONS and Falange waged against the Catholic right was fought not only in the conviction that the social program of Gil Robles was utterly barren, but also under the compulsion of the political need to win converts from the rightist forces who also were battling Communism and Socialism. Exactly as Communists feared and fought against Socialists with even greater desperation than against reactionaries, so also did the Falange always find itself threatened more by Catholics with a moderate program of social reform than by Marxists. The peril which most plagued these early apostles of Iberian Fascism was the danger of finding themselves viewed as just "white terror" agents in the employ of clergy or aristocracy, and consequently of being swallowed up by the numerically larger conservative ranks ranged under Gil Robles in *Acción Popular*. This explains the meaning of that remarkable scene in Madrid in May of 1931, the time of great church burnings throughout Spain, when the youthful revolutionaries of the JONS happily watched from their offices the crowds setting fire to the Jesuit convent of La Flor just across the Avenida de Eduardo Dato . . . watched, never interfered, and contentedly concluded that others were saving them the trouble of perhaps doing the same thing later.[2]

This movement known as the JONS—in addition to the attributes of Germanic influence, proletarian appeal, and anti-

[2] Ramiro Ledesma Ramos, *¿Fascismo en España?*, p. 69.

clerical orientation—had a fourth and final mark distinguishing it plainly from the Latin Fascism of Giménez Caballero.
It was passionately revolutionary. It believed in the efficacy of
"direct action," of gunfights in the streets, of squad raids on
leftist clubs, of heckling in political meetings until bottles and
clubs could be invoked to demonstrate the vitality of the new
Movement. While the sporadic leaflets issued by the JONS
reiterated demands for such vagaries as "imperial expansion"
and "a new social order," actually no full, coherent political
program or even political objective was envisioned. Tough,
intolerant, fanatic youths of the JONS simply viewed themselves as a kind of vanguard fighting against "decadent liberalism" and "corrupt capitalism": shock troops in a war in
which there was not even an accepted commander in chief, in
which even the enemy was a blurred, indistinct figure, and in
which the only victory was to win more battles. There is not
the slightest evidence to demonstrate that Ledesma Ramos or
the JONS gave either aid or sympathy to the abortive coup
d'état led by General Sanjurjo in August of 1932. Strictly reactionary in political character, Sanjurjo's rising was subsequently denounced by Ledesma for this very reason.

It seemed that the commander in chief which the Movement
so desperately needed, did emerge in the youthful person of
José Antonio Primo de Rivera, the handsome, widely respected
and popular son of Spain's late dictator. But like Ledesma and
so many other pioneers of Spanish Fascism, he died before a
Republican firing squad in 1936 after the outbreak of Civil
War, leaving the Movement without the leadership of the two
men who most contributed to its formation.

Since 1939, official propagandists have exalted the name and
personality of José Antonio to the highest rank in the Falangist
hagiography: he is "The Founder" or "The Martyr." Yet many
of the men who in recent years have penned such adulatory
phrases were among his most bitter opponents when he was
emerging as the leader of Spanish Fascism. The angry debate

which raged around him sharply brought into focus the most critical problem in the history of the Falange.

To his supporters, Primo de Rivera stood for a rare combination of intelligence and character. Certainly he was excellently educated; he read in many foreign languages and spoke English impeccably, studiously ranged the fields of political thought from Trotsky and Lenin to Rosenberg and Farinacci. He was devoutly Catholic, yet deplored the political medievalism which infected the Spanish clergy. He was physically courageous and morally above reproach. As a human being, he was respected and liked not merely by his political companions but also by men as far removed as Indalecio Prieto, Sanchez Roman, and the great Anarchist leader, Angel Pestaña.

Yet, in the eyes of those who desperately battled against him (especially Ledesma Ramos and his immediate cronies), this young son of the famous general was merely a political dilettante. Despite his admitted intelligence and integrity, his political life was simply a pale shadow cast by his father's career, and the only objective of his political enterprise was to vindicate the name of Primo de Rivera. He was an immature aristocrat, a *señorito,* who might speak eloquently on nationalistic themes but who could only sound ridiculously patronizing when he mentioned the proletariat or social revolution. Surely and fatefully, Ledesma believed, Primo de Rivera would betray the Movement into the hands of Spanish reaction.

In taking his first important political step, young Primo de Rivera tripped and fell unhappily. It happened in March of 1933 with the ill-fated attempt to inaugurate a new publication called *El Fascio.* In this abortive enterprise, "The Founder" was joined by some stray intellectuals interested in Fascist theory, including Giménez Caballero, Juan Pujol, Rafael Sanchez Mazas—all under the beneficent auspices of the Royal Italian Ambassador, Sgr. Guariglia (caustically known as "the widow of the Dictator," for his undisguised mourning over the political death of General Primo de Rivera). Police

seized and destroyed all copies of the first number of the publication before it could be distributed, and the project was
abandoned. I have the only copy I have ever seen of this rare
and bizarre journalistic venture. It is a faithful, uncritical
translation into Spanish of both Nazi and Italian Fascist doctrine, with several commendatory columns devoted to the
JONS.

Seven months later, at a rally attended by several thousands
in the Theater of Comedy in Madrid, the movement known as
Falange Española was formally baptized and launched. Ironically, it was the freedom of speech allowed by the Republican
government during the electoral period of this autumn of 1933
which provided the opportunity for young Primo de Rivera to
initiate a movement resolutely opposed both to free speech
and political elections. The men around him on this occasion
were, in a political sense, not very prepossessing figures: his
two associates in this *acto de fundación* were Julio Ruiz de
Alda whose only claim to fame was accompaniment of Ramon
Franco (the General's brother) on his famous flight to Buenos
Aires; and Alfonso Garcia Valdecasas, a Republican deputy in
the Cortes whose heart was with the Monarchy, to whose followers he fled a few months later. To Ruiz de Alda goes the
dubious credit for the last-minute invention of the Party's
name (it had been scheduled for baptism as the "Spanish Syndicalist Movement"), with the neat initials of "FE" to remind
Party members of the "faith" they should hold in Spain's
syndicalist future.

Few of the speeches of Primo de Rivera are worth reproducing individually, either as examples of political analysis or of
Spanish literature. Yet the essential ingredients of his doctrine
are fairly simple and coherent. His primary axiom was that
"España tiene una revolución pendiente." This "pending revolution" which Spain allegedly would have to experience was
political—an Iberian equivalent to the French experience of
1789. Yet this historical problem was posed: if Spain now were
to undergo such a revolution, she would emerge only on the

threshold of the liberal parliamentary experiment, where the
rest of Europe had stood at the start of the nineteenth century.
This would mean adoption by Spain of the very political con-
cepts being challenged most radically in the year 1934.

The second axiom in Primo de Rivera's doctrine came from
a rather loose interpretation and acceptance of the Marxist
argument that the proletariat was being driven relentlessly
into an utterly hopeless economic position. From this proletarian despair, there could come only violent revolution and
a division of society against itself. Thus, in addition to her
"pending" political revolution, Spain also faced the threat of
economic and social explosions which challenged the whole
contemporary world.

In terms of these arguments, Spain's national problem resolved itself into this: to effect a political revolution so radical
as to allow Spain to leap over the entire experience of the
liberal parliamentary age; and through that revolution to
develop a political machinery strong enough to negotiate the
imminent and inevitable social upheaval. It must be conceded
that such theorizing—however dogmatic, arbitrary, and de-
batable were its postulates—took fair account of the desperate
dilemmas confronting Spanish leaders. In many respects (as
Primo de Rivera often admitted in private conversation) his
analysis and formula differed little from that proposed by
Spain's leftist intelligentsia. His was a specific, reasoned concept of the peculiar needs of Spain—and not a fumbling effort
merely to raise another national swell on the "wave of the
future."

In February of 1934, four months after its formal founding,
the Falange officially merged with the JONS movement. The
new organization (*Falange Española de las Juntas de Ofensiva
Nacional-Sindicalista*) adopted a triumvirate of directors
(Primo de Rivera, Ledesma Ramos and Ruiz de Alda) and
officially espoused most of the social revolutionary argument
of the JONS and the JONS organizational symbols: red-and-
black flag (the traditional Anarchist colors), and the yoke-and-

arrows seal. At the same time there also joined the main stream of Spanish Fascism a fairly important group led by Onesimo Redondo, who had developed a Fascist-style organization in Valladolid that had already joined forces with Ledesma's group. Though Onesimo Redondo is usually placed beside Ledesma and Primo de Rivera as one of the "Big Three" of Spanish Fascism, he contributed little in either doctrinal content or popular strength. The only distinctive achievement of his publications was the first translation into Spanish of texts from *Mein Kampf*. But his organization did have one particular significance: they had grown up in Valladolid under the direct inspiration of the Jesuits, who viewed the Party's program as possibly a convenient way of taking the edge off some of the angry proletarian sentiment which so often threatened to destroy clerical as well as capitalist privilege. As a result, political disciples of the Jesuits joined hands with scores of ex-Communists and hundreds of ex-Anarchists to shape the course of a movement which already needed nine words to state its aggregate name!

Such a political party inevitably suffered from a chronic conflict of irreconcilable tendencies within itself. By the end of 1935, important fragments on both the left and right wings fell away from the Party. On the left, neither Ledesma's personal ambition nor his proletarian belligerence allowed him any longer to tolerate the rising personal prestige of Primo de Rivera. When the Party's triumvirate leadership proved patently inefficient and Primo de Rivera was named Chief of the Movement, Ledesma angrily voiced his suspicions of the new leader's intrigues with Monarchists, Republicans, priests, and generals. He bolted from the Falange and engaged in a series of newspaper philippics against Primo de Rivera, depicting him as a crass, corrupt agent of rightist reaction. Almost simultaneously, the Marqués de Eliseda (one of three Falangist deputies who had managed to win election to the Cortes) publicly announced his withdrawal from the Party on the grounds of religious conviction. He declared that, as a Catholic, he could not subscribe to a totalitarian program which failed to recognize the omnicompetence of the Catholic Church and threatened to convert it into a mere tool of the state. While neither of these defections involved great numbers of rebels, they badly damaged the Party's prestige and gave to the press of both the Catholic right and the Socialist left a rich opportunity to rejoice editorially over Fascist internal strife.

During the last two years of the Republic preceding the revolt of July, 1936, the history of the Falange means the history of its relations with the traditional rightist forces. It is a subtle and complex story, which can only be briefly sketched here, but it was of crucial importance in shaping the future character of the regime of General Franco.

It had actually been the rightist victory in the elections of November, 1933, which compelled the Falange and JONS to join forces, regardless of the personal predilections of their respective leaders. This triumph of Gil Robles and the CEDA (bloc of rightist parties) directly threatened the very existence of the two extremist-Fascist political movements. The latters' only real claim to popular support had been their pretension that they alone could stop the onward march of Communism. Such a claim seemed fatuous, so long as traditional rightist parties could still win elections under the Republic: the very peril, which the Fascist movement claimed it alone could destroy, seemed no longer a danger. Hence political exigency, more than ideological affinity, dictated the merger of Ledesma's party with Primo de Rivera's. Divided, they could only flounder and defeat each other; united, they might survive.

In the months that followed the merger, it is a known fact that a substantial percentage of the small financial resources of the Falange came from conservative and Monarchist sources —even while Falangist leaders were delivering their harangues in city slums and poverty-ridden villages on the coming "social revolution." Primo de Rivera's wide contacts in rightist circles were inherited from his father and from the days of his youth;

it was inevitable that he turn to some of them for help. One of the most important contributors at this time was none other than José Felix de Lequerica, who in the year 1944-45 was to become General Franco's Foreign Minister. This fact is confirmed by the written testimony of both the official biographer of Primo de Rivera, Ximenez de Sandoval, and of Manuel Aznar, formerly in the Spanish Embassy in Washington.[3] In 1945, it was Giménez Caballero who told me that the progressive rightist drift in the history of the Falange could be dated from the time of Lequerica's financial contributions.

Yet the same Giménez Caballero related that one of Primo de Rivera's favorite remarks to Ledesma was, "It is necessary to be bribed . . . the better to deceive the bribers." Obviously, more important than the question of who furnished funds for the Falange is the question of the extent to which acceptance of those funds compromised the political doctrine of the Party. It is significant that nearly always the Party treasury was close to bankruptcy and, in the first weeks of 1936, could not even pay the rent for its own headquarters in Madrid.

It is beyond doubt that the leaders of the Falange were determined to stick to their peculiar revolutionary principles—to the absolute limit of political possibility. Not any political hypocrisy but true conviction led Falangist leaders publicly to condemn, again and again, the barrenness and futility of such a program as Gil Robles and the Catholics proposed and which amounted to little more than retreat into reaction, under the cover of a few rhetorical flourishes addressed to the working classes. This Falangist conviction was faithfully expressed when ex-Monarchist Calvo Sotelo (Minister of Finance in General Primo de Rivera's government) asked to be admitted to the Falange in 1934: he was coldly refused, despite the fact that his name might have been an exploitable political asset. And young Primo de Rivera could not have been more clear

[3] Manuel Aznar, *Dolor y Memoria de España en el II Aniversario de La Muerte de José Antonio*, pp. 190-191; Ximenez de Sandoval, *Biografía Apasionada*, p. 199.

and emphatic than in a press interview in the same year, when
he declared in a statement published in *Ahora:* "I do not believe that in the face of one revolution (*i.e.,* Communism), one
can merely raise the arm of an elementary instinct of defense,
but rather must we have another revolutionary aspiration, another enthusiasm of the same poetic force. . . . The role
which is going to belong to Gil Robles is going to be that of
acting in the face of revolution with the instruments of power
at hand. . . . Against this assault of the revolutionaries, he
will be able to oppose machine guns and armored cars. But this
is not a clash of two revolutionary tendencies, but merely of
one revolutionary tendency against an arsenal."

Another fundamental difference stood between the Falange
and the traditional right. The latter was playing its political
game within the framework of the Republic, submitting its
cause to the electoral test and fairly confident (until the end
of 1935) that it could hold its own, politically and economically. Long before the elections of 1936 turned the right from
power with the Popular Front victory, the Falange had denied
that any electoral procedure could be trusted to prescribe
Spain's future. "Spain is going to be what the electoral slips
say," exclaimed young Primo de Rivera. "And if they again
speak blasphemies and ferocities, as they have done so many
times . . . ? In that case, will Gil Robles accept the triumph
(of the left) as legitimate?" This was precisely the issue which
Gil Robles' CEDA refused to face and hoped it would never
have to decide.

And a third basic conflict with the right arose from the fact
that so many rightist leaders under the Republic were suspected (with good reason) of working for a Monarchic restoration. This change was repeatedly leveled against Gil Robles by
the Republican left, and it was certainly true of a fair number
of voters who endorsed the CEDA program. On this question
of Monarchic restoration, Primo de Rivera was unequivocal:
"We understand that the Spanish Monarchy finished its cycle,
remained without substance, and gave way like a dead shell on

April 14, 1931. . . . We cannot direct the fresh impetus of the youth who follow us toward the recovery of an institution which we regard as gloriously dead." Thus we see that the Falange, in battling any possibility of Monarchic restoration for the last three years under the Franco regime, has been fighting not only for its own existence but also for the same political principles expounded by its leader more than ten years ago.

Despite all these important points of difference between the Falange and the traditional right, the two were allied in one respect: both were dedicated to fighting Marxism to the death, and either would accept or attempt any alternative rather than suffer defeat at the hands of the left. Hence, from the Falange point of view, rather than face annihilation in righteous political solitude, it would in the final analysis accept an alliance with the right in the hope of becoming, through adroit political maneuvering, the dominant member in the partnership.

Similarly, from the viewpoint of the right, so long as it felt that its economic and social prerogatives could be defended within the framework of the Republic, this was the simpler, safer course. Why get tarnished with the Fascist brush if it could be avoided? If the political machinery of the Republic, however, should fall into the hands of men prepared to attack the estate of the right, then some other recourse than political campaigns would have to be sought out. The first alternative, of course, would be the traditional one: the Spanish Army. And only secondarily, there would come the occasion of testing the still untried power of the Falange. The Army, that today, buttresses the Spanish regime, was the white hope of Spanish reaction in the dark days of 1935.

It is impossible to assess precisely the strength of the Falange as 1935 drew to an end and bloody '36 approached. Of what the Falange called true "militants," probably a total of 25,000 in the whole country would be a generous guess. Primo de Rivera himself did not believe that the Falange would be able to assume political power for at least five and probably ten

years. Late in 1934, on the eve of the great Socialist uprising
in the Asturias, he had taken the bold step of addressing a
secret letter to General Francisco Franco in which he implicitly
had confessed his fear that his movement could not gain
strength rapidly enough to head off a Socialist triumph. In
that letter, he protested that "any nation won by Socialism
falls into the category of a colony or protectorate" (*i.e.*, a Russian colony). He implored the young general to take appropriate precautionary steps. It was a remarkable confession of
Primo de Rivera's own lack of confidence in the potentiality
of his Party. The occasion was noteworthy for two other reasons: first, when the Asturian rising actually did occur, it was
Franco whom the Gil Robles government summoned to direct
the suppression of the rebels. Secondly, it was the first and only
political contact directly made between *el Fundador* and *el
Caudillo*. And General Franco never answered the appeal.
Gallegan patience and caution paid dividends then, as they
have many times since then. It is one of the many strange
paradoxes of the "Glorious Movement" that, while Falangist
propaganda has exalted both Franco and Primo de Rivera to
twin political pedestals, their paths crossed but once, for a
moment, then proceeded on in different directions.

The victory of the left which came in the famous elections
of February, 1936, perfectly fulfilled Falangist prophecies. The
Party organ *Arriba* gloatingly, bitingly taunted the followers
of Gil Robles in this, their "penitent hour," with the words:
"They had eyes and they saw not, they had ears and they did
not understand. . . . They are the same ones who today
shiver in their homes with their teeth chattering. . . . They
wish now that the Falange were ten times what it is—and they
do not understand that if it were a thousand times its size, it
would never be at their service."

Immediately after the victory of the left, Falangist propaganda turned itself to the task of not only flogging the bat-
tered CEDA but of extolling the victorious Popular Front
forces under Manuel Azaña! Strange as this may appear, this

was sound political strategy. Primo de Rivera knew perfectly well that disillusioned, frightened rightists were going to desert their old parties in the thousands: hence they needed no encouragement or editorial fondling. On the contrary, what was necessary from the Party viewpoint was to maintain the firmness of the Party program, to prevent the Party from being deluged by reactionaries eager to convert it into their refuge and their arsenal. Between February, and July, 1936, more than 50,000, perhaps as many as 75,000 new recruits rushed into the Falange. Accordingly, confidential instructions were delivered to all Falangist centers that no position of responsibility within the Party was to be entrusted to new members until they had proved their allegiance to the Party program and its "revolutionary" content.

It was at this time, when the forces of reaction were fleeing frantically in search of some new political haven, that a slight but revealing episode occurred. Young Primo de Rivera one day received in his office a personal visit from Eduardo Aunós —the man who later was to become General Franco's Minister of Justice.[4] One of the most dexterous and nimble political straddlers for twenty-five years of tumultuous Spanish history, Aunós came to warn the Falangist leader to flee to Portugal before the Azaña government began a campaign of arrests against the Party. To this, Primo de Rivera tartly replied that Sr. Aunós apparently did not understand that "the Falange is not an old party of romantic conspiracies with all its leaders abroad." [5] The incident excellently highlighted the contrast in temperament and disposition, as well as ideology, which separated the Falange from the traditional right.

In the final weeks before the military rising of Generals Sanjurjo and Mola, the nation seethed with expectation of

[4] In 1946, Aunós was named Spanish Ambassador in Rio de Janeiro, but was refused acceptance by the Brazilian government following the State Department's Blue Book on Argentina, which implicated Aunós in wartime negotiations with the Germans in Buenos Aires.

[5] Ximenez de Sandoval, op. cit., p. 521.

imminent battle, and certainly Falangist leaders knew what was going on. Yet, down to a mere three weeks before the armies of rebellion would be marching against the Republican government, the Falange's confidential circular instructions to their provincial leaders emphatically warned against allowing the Party to become a tool in the hands of the old-line military. "We will be neither the vanguard nor the shock troops nor the invaluable ally of any confused reactionary movement. . . . We are not a vanguard but an entire army in the single service of our own flag. . . . The participation of the Falange in one of these premature and naïve projects . . . would precipitate its total disappearance even in the event of victory." [6]

Perceptive and even prophetic as those words were, they expressed a policy impossible to defend in July of 1936. Down to the last, Primo de Rivera and leaders close to him, like Fernandez Cuesta and Manuel Hedilla, saw clearly the grave peril for themselves in an alliance with the Spanish Army, traditional protagonist of national reaction. Yet, what alternative was there to accepting such an alliance? For years, the Falange had been calling for the overthrow by force of the existing form of government and all its economic practices. Now that challenge for the use of force was being answered— and the Falange could not declare itself in favor of a policy of "nonintervention." The extraordinary truth was that the Falange was unprepared for what took place in 1936. It was being deprived by the Army of exclusive right to the role of "defender of Spain" against the Marxist "threat." It was itself too weak to play that role alone. So, in his final manifesto to his Party, dated July 17, 1936, Primo de Rivera had to deny his own convictions, capitulate in principle, summon his followers to join in revolt with the military: "Workers, laborers, intellectuals, soldiers, sailors, guardians of our Fatherland: shake off your lethargy in the face of the nation's downfall and come with us, for a Spain one, great and free! ARRIBA ESPAÑA!"

[6] These documents can be found in Francisco Bravo's *Historia de la Falange.*

This last manifesto of the leader of the Falange, who was to die before a Republican firing squad four months later, does not contain even the word "revolution," nor the word "empire," nor the word "youth," nor "National Syndicalism," nor even "Falange" itself. With that document the Falange, supposed to be the proud protagonist of the proletariat, submitted to becoming a political instrument in the hands of a Sanjurjo or a Franco.

3

I have sketched the outline of the Falange's history preceding the Spanish Civil War because only in such perspective can one appreciate the specific, innate character of this Party which, since 1939, has existed and persisted merely as one of several distinct forces mobilized by the Franco regime. And only with this understanding of its historical character can one appreciate the supple dexterity with which General Franco has used the Falange, manipulating and maneuvering it as one of the mobile defenses of the government over which he presides.

From the first blood-filled moments of the "Glorious Movement" in July of 1936, leaders of the Falange knew that they faced the danger of becoming nothing more than helpless political agents of the Army. This danger existed even if the war lasted only a few weeks or months, as most of the insurgents boldly believed and predicted. But the danger multiplied every month that the war dragged on. Military authority could brook no competition in such times, and the Army could invoke the "exigencies of war" to assert full authority and to justify any political act.

In only one respect did prolongation of the war bring political comfort to the Party: it brought constantly heavier German and Italian participation. As the special propagators of the totalitarian gospel in Spain, Falangists naturally were blessed with the enthusiastic backing of Berlin and Rome in any maneuvering for preferential position among the various and disparate groups identified with the Nationalist cause. These groups included Monarchists sure that Franco would restore their king; Carlist traditionalists happy to battle for their special brand of reaction; Catholic groups seeking revenge for (and safety from) the vicious excesses recently inflicted on them; simple, old-fashioned men of landed and capital wealth anxious to save what they had and earn a little interest on it whenever possible; and army generals anxious for a taste of power served on any dish.

In such an aggregation, the Falange (which failed conspicuously throughout the war to earn any distinction as a military force) was pitted against political forces vastly more prestigious and of incomparably greater experience. This blurred, clouded political future made the inexpert Falangist leaders nervous and fearful. A combination of their nervousness and of clumsy Nazi intrigue, designed to secure the Falange's ascendancy, produced a strange crisis which almost destroyed the Falange in early 1937. The circumstances were the following.

After the nation-wide outbreak of hostilities, the Falange had set up office in Salamanca (the Nationalists' temporary "capital") under a provisional *Junta de Mando* ("Command Council"). It was necessary to establish this emergency *Junta* because virtually all prominent Falange leaders had been executed, jailed or caught behind the Republican lines. In these circumstances, Party leadership fell to one Manuel Hedilla. He had been the Falangist provincial chief in Santander. He was an uneducated dock hand whose political enemies scoffed that he could not even write his own name. A belligerent believer in proletarian redemption through the gospel of the Falange, Hedilla was tough, tactless, intemperate, and politically naïve.

Upon recognition of General Franco's "government" by Nazi Germany on November 18, 1937, there arrived in Salamanca as German Ambassador the renowned General Wilhelm von Faupel, since 1934 head of the Ibero-American Institute of Berlin. He brought with him two German agents, Kohn and Krueger, fresh from propaganda triumphs in Brazil. Charting out Germany's highroad to Latin America, von Faupel and his associates set themselves to the task of not only securing the fidelity of the Falange to Nazi aims but also discovering and equipping a leader who might serve as a sort of Spanish Quisling: a man raised to power by the direct application of German pressure. The man they chose for this role was Manuel Hedilla.

The conspiracy inspired by Nazi-Falangist ambitions implicated so many highly placed figures and revealed so shockingly the concealed conflicts within the Franco forces that it has been hushed in the most solemn official secrecy to the present day. Complete details probably will never be known, but the essential outline of the intrigue is clear. Hedilla was moved by a genuine fear that General Franco was ignoring all the revolutionary content of the Falange program and seeking to create an amalgamated political party of his own embracing the most conflicting and irreconcilable elements, among which the Falange would be only one. Hedilla was joined by other Falangists, eager to assure the establishment of the "New State." Outstanding among them was José Luis Arrese—the same who was to reappear officially in 1942 as the head of the Falange under the Franco regime. These men gathered substantial quantities of arms from German sources in Salamanca (as well as aid and encouragement from Finns headed by Karl Von Hartman, the famous Finnish soldier of fortune who later became Military Attaché to Finland's Legation in Madrid). They proceeded to attempt a coup d'état by surrounding and overwhelming Franco's headquarters.

The plot was discovered and smashed. Hedilla was sentenced to death, but his sentence was commuted to life imprisonment at the urgent requests of both German and Italian officials. After 1939 he was released. He works today as an obscure dock hand in Mallorca, eccentric, still illiterate, regarded by his fellow workers as slightly mad—a brash, bizarre figure who made only one daring, urgent entry on the Spanish scene before becoming a fugitive from history. Arrese was sentenced to seventeen years in prison, later was pardoned and appointed the first Falange chief in Malaga, later to rise to second in command of the Party under Serrano Suñer, finally to supplant Suñer in 1942. Exactly how relations developed henceforth between Franco and the first German Ambassador accredited to him is not known but is scarcely difficult to guess. Either because General Franco demanded it, or because Berlin knew how gravely von Faupel had become implicated in an abortive undertaking, both he and his misguided colleagues were recalled to Berlin. A curious ending for the mission of Naziism's first representative to their friend in Iberia!

The fate and function of the Falange were officially sealed and defined by General Franco's first official proclamation giving the Party recognized status in the new Spanish regime— the Act of Unification of April 19, 1937. This Act (which was the immediate provocation for Hedilla's revolt) performed by fiat the political miracle of merging the Party with the Carlist Traditionalists, a group whose reactionary politics know no parallel more modern than life on the feudal manor, whose militant Catholicism crystallizes in the belief that their rifles may yet serve as the spearhead for a new counterreformation. The resultant amalgamation bore the name of *Falange Española de las JONS y Tradicionalista,* officially described as "a single national political entity, liaison between the State and Society." And the cautious Generalissimo and Chief of the new Spanish State added these convenient and significant clauses: "The movement which we lead is precisely that rather than a program. It will not be a rigid or static thing, but subject in all events to the work of revision and improvement which reality advises." Thus, in a single stroke, General Franco forcibly wed the Falange to its political antithesis and made it subject to the personal caprice of his own definition of "reality."

The remaining Civil War years brought compensation to the

Falange with its official and emphatic endorsement as the cornerstone of Spain's new order. In August of 1937, General Franco officially promulgated the statutes of the Party and recognized the Party as "the inspiration and basis of the Spanish State." In March of the following year, some real recognition of Falangist social doctrine came with the publication of a labor Bill of Rights (*Fuero del Trabajo*), describing the new State as "a reaction against liberal capitalism and Marxist materialism." In June of 1939, at the first post-Civil War meeting of the National Council of the Falange, General Franco publicly espoused the whole Falangist program and promised the construction of a true National-Syndicalist state based on the principle of "Fatherland, Bread, and Justice."

At this point, an important question arises from the complicated history of these times: Why did Franco bother to adopt the Falange in 1937? Certainly the Falange's military contribution to victory in the Civil War was negligible. With equal certainty it can be stated that, at that time, Franco had suffered from no indoctrination of Falange or Fascist ideology. Probably he understood them only vaguely.

One important factor, of course, was the influence of Germany and Italy. This means more than the direct application of pressure by the two Fascist powers to see a regime akin to their own installed in Spain. The Fascist countries were Franco's great sources of strength in a generally hostile world. Logically, he must have looked ahead to beyond the immediate exigencies of his own civil war and must have perceived that any future government of his would have to count heavily upon the comfort and co-operation of these powers. There could be no escape from his alignment with them in a world already sharply cut by ideological cleavage. To turn that alignment into a productive alliance, the Falange would be a convincing asset.

But the real explanation lies in the curious fact that when the military rising began, none of the insurgents were quite sure where it was going to end politically. The original Na-

tionalist manifesto designed to vindicate the rising spoke
blandly of restoring order within the Republic. This became
patently preposterous when the job of "restoring order" assumed the dimensions of a civil war. At the same time (for
reasons still not completely clear) Franco never accepted the
prospect of a Monarchic restoration as his ultimate goal. If his
beliefs then coincided with those of a later date, he may have
been convinced that the Monarchy was too moribund and
discredited an institution to thrive in Spain. Personal enmities
with individual Monarchist leaders affected his decision. Personal ambition could not have failed to play its own part.

Yet the war could not be fought simply *against* a Republic:
it had to be fought *for* something constructive. And among the
various political groups ranged under his leadership, the
Falange was the only one which could even lay a serious claim
to some popular appeal. It should also be remembered that
the lines of battle in 1937 were so drawn that Nationalist territory essentially amounted to the northwest of Spain; and it
was precisely this territory where Socialist influence traditionally has been weakest and where the Falange (with its Anarcho-
Syndicalist converts) had the most substantial popular following.

Thus the Falange, minority faction that it was on the day
the standard of rebellion was raised, came to serve an essential
role in the Nationalist scheme. While the Act of Unification
spoke pedantically about the Falange as a "liaison between the
State and Society," the simple language of political necessity
called for a link between the generals directing the war and
the popular masses to whom they had to appeal to vindicate
their cause. This was the function of the Falange: to convert
a military cabal into the New State.

4

Born of such history, the Falange, in eight years' enjoyment
of its monopoly as Spain's single political party, has usefully

served the army general who raised it to power. This service has been rendered not merely in the form of an ideological crusade, but in the more tangible form of practical political functions. Most important of these functions are the following:

1. It has provided General Franco with the men to run the governmental machinery of his nation, not only in certain cabinet posts but more importantly in provincial and municipal governments.

2. It has served as a reservoir of manpower which General Franco could confidently regard as loyal to him—for the simple reason that, without him, the Falange's life-expectancy would be dismally short.

3. It has organized and maintained the 22 syndicates through which all of Spain's economy is vertically organized, effectively controlled by the state, and made to serve what are euphemistically called "the interests of the Fatherland."

4. It established and (until 1946) operated, through the Vice-Secretariat of Popular Education, a control of press, radio, cinema, and propaganda, exploiting all such channels of communication to exalt every action of the Franco government, and employing every device of a totalitarian propaganda machine to bewilder, confuse, deceive, and disillusion all men who doubted that Spain was happy.

5. It served, from the outbreak of World War II to the darkening days of 1944, as the symbol and testimony of alliance with the Fascist nations whom General Franco expected to conquer the democracies; and it thereby seemed to secure Spain's respected role in a New Order.

6. It seized upon educational institutions and organized the youth of the nation into such bodies as the *Frente de Juventudes* and the *Sindicato Español Universitario,* thereby working to achieve the fidelity of the young to the New State and bequeathing to the next Spanish generation, if a free one, a problem of incalculable proportions.

7. It propagated a social doctrine, conducted social activities through such agencies as *Auxilio Social,* pressed for advanced social legislation and lavish public works programs—to an extent which has made perceptible inroads into some proletarian ranks.

8. It developed a special militia and secret police whose viciousness

and vengefulness were of great assistance to the regular security
police in hunting down men who "rebelled" in 1936 to defend the
Republic, or who engaged in such treasonous practices as reading
the American Embassy's news bulletin and listening to the BBC.
9. It has served, since the end of World War II, as a superb scapegoat whose punishment by Franco could be advertised to the world
at large as evidence òf "liberalization" of the Spanish regime.

These have been the most important uses to which the
Falange Party has been put by General Franco. Virtually all
of them suggest characteristic attributes of a typical Fascist
State.

And yet here the picture must be kept in clear, true focus.
It becomes easily blurred, easily misunderstood, by careless acceptance and use of an adjective like "Fascist." The
loose language of political invective in recent years has not
helped the Western democracies to understand the Spanish
regime clearly or deal with it intelligently.

Although the fateful marks of a Fascist regime are plain for
all to see in the government in Madrid, this government never
has been, nor is it today, completely, faithfully Fascist in either
the Italian or German sense. We need not dwell on the esoteric
questions of Spanish temperament which make even Spanish
Fascists a special brand, but need only note a few points of
paramount and striking significance:

The Spanish Fascist movement at no time possessed a leader
who had risen from the proletariat or even lower middle-class:
the man acclaimed as its founder, the son of a famed former
dictator of Spain, inherited the noble title of the Marqués de
Estella.

This one potential "Führer" figure whom the Spanish movement possessed was dead even before the real battle for power
was well under way; and from the Movement's earliest days,
far from being inspired by the peculiar genius of a single pre-
eminent figure, it had to fight through a series of organizational confusions and conflicts involving even direction under
a triumvirate.

The Falange could attain power only after a civil war of three years' duration, only then through curious and devious political maneuvering, and only by inheriting the legacy of disaster and bitterness engendered in those years. These were circumstances never paralleled in Italy or Germany.

The Falange, despite all its official resources, propaganda, and punitive powers, never developed a popular following even remotely comparable with that evoked by the movements under Hitler and Mussolini.

The Falange (though it might have welcomed the opportunity) never committed its own existence, as well as the nation's, to an imperialistic policy involving international war. Hence it never had the chance even momentarily to offer a discontented populace foreign gains or glories to compensate for domestic ills.

Similarly, the Falange movement never passed through such a purge as the Nazi extermination of the radical wing under Ernst Roehm. Therefore, its radical social program has persisted as the core of Falangist philosophy and action, without interruption and without digression into foreign ventures.

Finally, the Falange rose to power only under the auspices of an army general and only as a subordinate ally of the traditional military forces of the nation. Whereas the German *Wehrmacht* operated as an instrument at the political direction of the Nazi Party, such a relationship has never remotely or momentarily prevailed in the Spain of General Franco, who himself is the official head of the Party.

April 1 is the anniversary of the official end of the Civil War—the day of "Glorious Victory." Each year it is celebrated with an elaborate military parade along Madrid's broad, stately Castellana. This last April I watched the march of the trim thousands of soldiers and marines, the score of superbly trained cavalry units, the tight chugging ranks of the motorcycle corps, the mobile antiaircraft guns with their huge barrels aimlessly pointing skyward over the crowds, the gaudy Moroccan guards, the lumbering tanks and trucks.

But in this march past General Franco's reviewing stand there appeared not a single Falangist unit in their solemn, sleek black uniforms. It was the first time since the Civil War's end that the men of the Party failed to appear in the government's grand annual display of power.

The times and political expediency were changing. This year General Franco was content to be surrounded by crack contingents from his army of three-quarters of a million men— and by the sweet aroma of incense. . . .

3 THE CHURCH OF SPAIN

SPAIN, traditional land of color, often seems to speak of herself in colors, thus revealing herself to the world. It is easy to think of a kind of Spanish spectrum.

When I left Spain early last summer, the colors seemed brightly alive, warmly vivid. The wide Castilian plains and fields, dull, dread brown through harrowing months of drought, at long last had been blessed with rain. A green that almost seemed to glow covered the fertile country: smooth, velvet green in the valleys and hills of Guipúzcoa and Vizcaya; thick, lush green in the fields and orchards on the plains around Aranjuez.

In hundreds of churches, in great cities and tiny villages, golden yellow flames danced deliriously from thousands of candles lighted happily by men and women grateful to God that the saving rain had come. It had come from Spanish skies as gloriously blue as always—that sheer, shining blue, unmarred by a single careless cloud, that seemed almost to protect the earth with its magnificent mantle.

But on the streets of Madrid and other cities of the land, a different kind of blue was less popular than it had ever been. The coarse, dark blue of swaggering men in uniform was not often seen. The political weather was changing too.

And there was red. There was the festive red-with-yellow of

the national flag that draped all buildings on special holidays
. . . the red-with-gold glittering on the uniforms of the Moorish guards . . . the frightening, exciting red that aroused
every Spaniard as it spilled upon the sand of the bull ring.

But red, that glittering color so imbued with sharp political
meaning, so electrically charged with insinuation and invective, had acquired a new meaning. Within the Pardo, palatial
residence of the Chief of the Spanish State, it had won sudden,
overwhelming popularity . . . the ecclesiastical red of the
bishops of Spain, who came to the Pardo to swear their allegiance to the Caudillo of Spain.

2

The Falangist organ *Arriba,* in its special edition of April 2,
1946, commemorating the "Glorious Victory" of the Civil War,
flashed these headlines across the entire back page:

THE CATHOLIC VICTORY OF FRANCO

SPLENDID PUBLIC UNITY OF RELIGIOUS IDEAS, THE
VOICE OF THE CHURCH HIGH AND FREE, CONSE-
QUENT WIDESPREAD VITALITY AND PROGRESS TO-
WARD THE FULLNESS OF CATHOLIC LIFE AND ACTION

Because they believe in the existence of this "splendid public
unity of religious ideas" in the Spain ruled by General Franco,
the great bulk of the Catholic clergy, seconded by a great if not
major part of Spanish Catholic Action, have accepted the role
of defenders of the present Spanish regime.

The world knows that, from the time of their Collective Pastoral Letter of July 1, 1937, the bishops of Spain, while deploring the tragedy of civil war, also accepted it—to use their own
unfortunate phrase—as "an armed plebiscite." By that phrase
and accompanying praise for the Nationalist cause, the Spanish
hierarchy called upon all Catholics to concur in their judgment that force of arms, at a time when the ranks of the pro-

fessional army were massed on one side, constituted a fair test of the will of a people.

The world also knows—although conveniently elastic memories seem to have allowed some to forget—the savage persecution and vandalism to which the Spanish Church was submitted in the last months of the Republic. Partly to refresh such poor memories, the Primate of Toledo, in his pastoral letter of September 1, 1945, recalled that in the diocese of Toledo alone some 300 priests had been killed—more than half the priesthood of the entire diocese. Primarily in the anxious hope of escaping such suffering, of finding defense against such attack, Church leaders had rallied to the cause of General Franco and solemnly pronounced the Nationalist revolt a "crusade."

But it would seem obviously sensible for men passionately dedicated to the welfare of their own Church not to be satisfied merely with a defense against attacks: they should also be seeking seriously and earnestly to discover and cure the *cause* of those attacks. In the course of the four years that I spent in Spain, I met and talked at length with innumerable lay readers and prominent prelates of the Church. I am sorry to say that I found very few who were bothering with any such inquisitive effort. The great majority were satisfied with dismissing such mass demonstrations of hate and distrust merely as the vicious work of a few Communist agents. Ironically and tragically, if one asked how to account for the wide popular participation in this grim work of a few Communist agents, the answer sounded like a Communist's equally miserable explanation for the Catholic devotion of millions of the world's workers: just the credulity of the masses. In this fashion, the majority of the Spanish clergy came to think and to act as if church burnings were a vicious practice never indulged in Spain before 1936 or even before the First Internationale. Some of the clergy, too, seemed to have elastic memories.

This attitude is generally characteristic of the demeanor and disposition of the Spanish Church throughout modern history.

In its essentials, the considered conduct of the Church in political affairs has been indistinguishable from that of the Army. At any given moment of decision, both have made their political choices on the basis of a simple, uncomplicated, uncritical judgment of the best method to secure their own interest and welfare.

It might reasonably be observed that this is scarcely shocking or abnormal. Such institutions are not expected to commit political suicide. Their leaders are charged with precisely the responsibility of defending their institution's welfare and interest. This is true, but the special mark of the Spanish Church's political conduct is that, despite the fact that it has been vehemently indicted for confusing politics and religion, the attitude of the Spanish clergy, in the deepest sense, is thoroughly *apolitical*. It is the habit of the Spanish Church, not to seek out or think out a specific political program for propagation to the people, but rather merely to identify itself with some convenient independent political force. That identification is made not from any affinity for a special political doctrine but from the pragmatic desire to effect a useful political alliance that will guarantee the privileges and prerogatives of the Church.

The Spanish clergy's endorsement of the Nationalist cause in 1937 followed this general pattern. The clergy reasoned and believed that only a Nationalist triumph could secure public order, rescind the Republican Government's legislation on religious and educational questions, and protect traditional Church privileges. In taking their firm stand, the bishops of Spain were not subscribing to any particular political or economic program. They could not have done so, even had they so wished. No such program existed. Nor does there appear, either in the famous Collective Pastoral Letter or in the subsequent writings and addresses of then-Primate Cardinal Gomá y Tomás, even a mention of the word "Falange." Except for some specific references to Communism and Marxism, the texts of these documents would have been just as appropriate on the occasion of any military uprising in the early nineteenth century as they were in 1937. Then, as so often, Church and Army were natural allies bound by their common purpose of destroying political forces which had threatened to destroy them.

When the armies of "the Crusade" triumphed in 1939, the Spanish hierarchy, if it could freely have prescribed its own political settlement, would have elected a Monarchic restoration. Traditional sentiment would have been the least important reason. More important was the fact that the Monarchy was an institution tried, tested, and found to be fully compatible with the principles and purposes of the Spanish Church. It was a known quantity, at a time when the political equation of Spain seemed to be composed mostly of unknown quantities. Of these unknown quantities, the most doubtful, perhaps most dangerous, for the leaders of the Church was the Falange Party. Well-informed members of the clergy knew perfectly well the dangerous conflict which had arisen between the Catholic Church and the totalitarian parties in Italy and Germany. They also knew that within the Falange, besides the numerically large but politically inexperienced group of young Catholics, there were formidable blocs of ex-Anarchists and ex-Communists.

For the Spanish Church, the circumstances of the victory of 1939, full of both promise and danger, dictated a dual political task: to help perpetuate a regime which promised security, and to maintain within that regime a favorable balance of power with other contending political groups. The execution of these tasks has not been the work merely of a few outstanding, astute prelates, nor of all the bishops of Spain. It has also been the work of the largest, least publicized, and best organized aggregation of men and women allowed to carry on political functions in contemporary Spain: the 350,000 militants of Catholic Action.

3

"It is the most powerful and, for Franco, the most dangerous organization in Spain today."

That was in late 1944. The man who described Catholic Action to me in those words was himself one of its most prominent leaders. But it was only a little more than six months later that General Franco, in one of the most surprising and adroit political moves of his rule, named a new Foreign Minister: Martín Artajo, the secular head of Catholic Action. A few weeks later, when I saw my friend again, the lyrics were the same but the words had changed:

"It is the most powerful and, for Franco, the most useful organization in Spain today."

The confession was sadly made, but the strength of Catholic Action remained beyond question. Even with generous allowance for Spanish hyperbole in either statement, the important truth is that the pattern of power in Spain is vitally affected by this movement which, in so many respects, is unique on the Spanish political scene.

While vaunting a power and prestige of huge political dimensions, the organization of Catholic Action in Spain officially professes to be wholly nonpolitical in character. According to its spokesmen, it has a single function: mobilization of the Catholic laity, under their traditional insignia of "soldiers of Christ," in the cause of translating into reality the ideals expressed by the encyclicals of the Popes. In the words of the eminently official *Guide of the Church and of Catholic Action,* "Catholic Action, in its broad meaning of a secular apostleship at the orders and at the service of the Church, is as old as the Church itself."

In the sweeping terms of this tradition, Catholic Action claims among its vanquished foes such diverse and formidable enemies as the Roman Emperors, the Moors and the Protestants. But modern history (according to the *Guide of the*

Church) brought the special, urgent challenge of "the liberal and demagogic doctrines, spreading materialism." In fact, the first battles of modern Catholic Action came in the early and middle nineteenth century with the two-front war waged by the Church against the social evils of industrialism, on the right, and against Marxist efforts on the left to propagate proletarian solutions to these evils—a war led by such honored men as Ozanam, such distinguished organizations as the Society of St. Vincent de Paul. In 1848, under the fervent (and extreme rightist) political benediction of Pius IX, "Catholic Associations" were formed among the laity of most of the countries of Europe. These organizations expanded and continued through successive pontificates into the twentieth century, when Pius XI emerged as special patron of this lay movement with the familiar title of "the Pope of Catholic Action." It was he who worded the classic definition of the work of Catholic Action: "participation of the laity in the hierarchical apostleship."

In view of the role played by Spanish Catholic Action since the end of the Civil War in 1939, it is interesting to note that the earliest foundations of the movement were laid in a similar era of Spain's turbulent history—following the civil strife which ended in 1876. The man who set these foundations was Cardinal Moreno, Primate and Archbishop of Toledo. He proposed (in the words of the *Guide of the Church*) "to repair the spiritual ruins" brought by the civil wars, which were "the ominous work of rationalists, liberals, and Masons." His goal was "to unite all Catholic forces in a powerful bloc."

More than half a century was needed to fulfill the work begun in the 1870's. Internal strife wrecked the organization founded by Cardinal Moreno within five years, but by 1894 the distinguished figure of the Marqués de Comillas came forward to direct a new *Junta Central de Acción Católica,* which he continued to do until his death thirty-one years later. Even more significantly, in the same year of 1894 there came the founding of the National Council of Catholic Workers' Corporations, from which there shortly evolved the Catholic *sin-dicatos* of urban workers and similar organizations among agrarian laborers of the countryside. In theory and often in practice, the Church's war against the evils of industrial capitalism was to be prosecuted with as much *élan* as the war upon Marxism.

From the turn of the century to the end of the Civil War, Catholic Action maintained a steady forward progress despite the violent political vicissitudes and upheavals afflicting Spain. In 1903 its ecclesiastical leadership was sharply defined by a letter from Leo XIII instructing the Cardinal Primate of Toledo to assume the title of "Pontifical Director of Catholic Action." Twenty years later Cardinal Reig y Casanova wrote the first coherent, complete "principles and bases of Spanish Catholic Action." In 1929 Cardinal Segura—vigorous foe of the Republic soon to be born, equally vigorous foe of the Falange since 1939, today Cardinal of Sevilla—summoned the first national congress of Catholic Action. In 1939, Cardinal Gomá y Tomás waited only a few weeks after the end of the Civil War before drawing up new "bases" for Catholic Action, submitting them to the Vatican for an approval quickly given, and thereby defining the structure of the organization as it has functioned under the rule of General Franco.

The structure of Catholic Action provides the key to its whole character and purpose. It is based upon skillful solutions to three distinct problems of internal relationships: first, the relationship between ecclesiastical and secular membership; secondly, the problem of developing a united national organization which at the same time can reach down effectively to provincial and municipal levels; and thirdly, the problem of maintaining four independent "branches" necessary for the different age and sex groups (men, women, young men, young women), while also securing their close co-ordination within a single organization.

Ecclesiastical authority is assured in Catholic Action on the top level of national direction through two bodies: the *Junta*

Suprema and the *Dirección Central.* The first is merely a special name for a conference of all the bishops of Spain convened under the presidency of the Primate of Toledo—the supreme authority of Catholic Action and its direct liaison with the Holy See. Since it is patently impossible for all the bishops of Spain to sit in continuous session, the authority of this body is effectively delegated to the *Dirección Central,* of whose six members five are ecclesiastics (including the Primate as president) and only one is a layman. This lay member is the Director of the *Junta Técnica Nacional,* the third of the triumvirate of national bodies.

The transition from the *Dirección Central* to the *Junta Técnica* is, first, from a predominantly ecclesiastic to a predominantly secular body; secondly, from a policy-making to a policy-implementing level of activity. But this distinction does not diminish the truly decisive importance of the secular *Junta Técnica.* For this supreme secular council of Catholic Action spells the difference between what otherwise would be merely an overgrown diocesan convention and a national force of firm popular strength and influence. The thirty-one men constituting the *Junta Técnica* include only one ecclesiastical representative.

Here the precarious balance between secular and ecclesiastic authority must be most skillfully maintained. How is an organization like this to escape the charge that it is merely a group of laymen who have tried to wrap themselves in the robes of priests in order to grace their personal political opinions with a specious, sanctimonious air of religious authority? To meet this problem, the basic laws of Catholic Action have adopted the simple device of investing the *Junta Técnica* with what is theoretically only "executive" authority, as distinct from the "policy-making" authority retained by the bishops. This distinction protects Catholic Action's lay leaders from the charge of usurping ecclesiastical authority for their own purposes—whether the charge be made by critics outside the

Church or bishops within the Church jealously guarding their own diocesan authority.

Under this neatly defined national leadership, the four "branches" or "associations" which make up Catholic Action run in four vertical lines from the national to the parochial level. The most interesting politically, the Association of Men was not founded until March of 1940, since which time it has won an enrolled membership of more than 32,000. The Association of Women, founded in 1919, has an enrollment of 91,000 and operates more than 60 diocesan centers. The Association of Young Men (unmarried and in the age group of 17 to 30) is the largest of the four associations with an enrollment of 124,000. The Association of Young Women was organized in 1926 with an initial membership of a meager 1,000; 20 years later, its membership has passed the 117,000 mark.

Each association extends in a vertical line from the national to the diocesan and parochial levels. On the national level, a Superior Council directs each association's activities under a dual ecclesiastic-secular presidency to which appointments are made directly by the Primate of Toledo. Precisely similar patterns exist on the diocesan level, where each of the four associations has its own Diocesan Union (whose officers are appointed by the local bishop) and the four Diocesan Unions are co-ordinated in a *Junta Diocesana* under the personal presidency of the bishop. And the parochial level carries through the same procedure systematically: each association has its parochial center, the four centers are represented on a joint parochial *Junta,* and the local priest takes the place of the bishop in exercising ecclesiastic authority on this lowest level.

Thanks to the sturdy symmetry of this structure, Catholic Action can penetrate into the provincial and municipal life of the nation without ever abdicating its truly national character; and on every level of action—parochial, diocesan, and national—there prevails the same careful balance of power between secular and ecclesiastic representatives.

Toward what purposes are these impressive resources of

Catholic Action mobilized? The official *Guide of the Church and of Spanish Catholic Action,* alluding to the final revision of the basic statutes of Catholic Action made in 1939, makes this sweeping statement:

The historic evolution of events and the new circumstances of the social life of our Fatherland, after the great National Crusade, demanded . . . the reorganization of Catholic Action before undertaking the great pacific battle for the rechristianization of Spain.

To wage a "battle for the rechristianization of Spain" may seem like the assumption of a huge labor by an organization whose specific franchise is supposed to be only the propagation and implementation of the Catholic ideals expressed in the encyclicals of the Popes. But since Vatican pronouncements range over the field of possible discussion from censurable films, birth control, and religious education, to Communism, strikes, and anti-Semitism, such a franchise clearly carries an authority vastly larger than the usual claims of either a political party or a religious society.

Concretely, how does this extraordinary organization expend its energies? The list of functions seems endless. It operates a Central Institute of Higher Religious Culture, where devout intellectuals can explore the deeper implications of their faith. It gives to all Vatican pronouncements the widest possible distribution—whether or not the pronouncements are always palatable to the political regime in power. It publishes *The Church* and *The Sign,* the two most powerful publications of their kind in Spain. Local and diocesan centers hold conferences and "assemblies" for discussion of such subjects as "Social Charity," "Capital and Capitalism," and "The Foundations of International Order." The national leadership directs periodic "campaigns" which reveal repeatedly the size of the organization's resources—as when, in the autumn of 1944, it swiftly raised no less than 27,000,000 pesetas in response to a Vatican call to help war victims.

In the big, politically significant field of social welfare, a permanent "Secretariat of Charity" performs a huge labor. Allied with it are such affiliated agencies as the Society of St. Vincent de Paul. To co-ordinate its work, it maintains an elaborate *fichero de pobres* ("file of the poor"), containing (in 1944) some 60,000 names of men and women receiving regular assistance. Under the secretariat (which counts upon more than 1,400 workers), a total of 318 local offices carry on the national work of charity.

Philanthropy is scarcely more important than propaganda for the leaders of Catholic Action. The "Secretariat of Publications and Propaganda," working on the same grand scale as the "Secretariat of Charity," is concerned with thousands of books, pamphlets, leaflets, and magazines which often carry serious political impact along with their religious instruction. Thus the weekly *The Church* earned itself deserved fame in December of 1944 when it editorially extolled the antitotalitarian substance of the Pope's Christmas message: official censors, stunned by political treason from such a quarter, hesitated several days before they suppressed this issue of the Jesuit-edited publication. Subtly but closely linked to this official activity of Catholic Action is a private corporation known as *Editorial Católica:* proprietor of a chain of six of Spain's best newspapers, including the morning Madrid daily, *Ya.* Spokesmen for Catholic Action solemnly deny any connection with this chain of papers. Yet, by a curious coincidence, the head of *Editorial Católica* is also a distinguished member of the *Junta Técnica* of Catholic Action.

But the most striking evidence of the inescapable political character of Catholic Action rests upon a negative fact: the Association of Men was not founded until 1940. The significance of this fact is that, while the other three associations were functioning for years, it was not found necessary to rally this particular group earlier. Why?— For the sound reason that Catholic men had their sphere of political action in the Catholic party under Gil Robles, *Acción Popular,* which served as the nucleus of Gil Robles' vast rightist bloc, the CEDA. During the stormy days of the Republic, Catholic men in politics knew precisely where their massed weight should be thrown.

All this was changed by the end of the "Glorious Crusade" of General Franco in 1939. The men and women of Catholic Action, the great majority of whom had supported or fought for the Nationalist cause, had not thought too carefully about the kind of political settlement for which they were struggling. Some had dreamed, wistfully but vainly, of Monarchic restoration. Their awakening was rude and unpleasant. The Catholic bloc, whether liberal (mildly) or conservative (extremely), seemed to find itself holding aloft a cross to which five Falange arrows had been crudely nailed. This was not the banner for which they had fought. There seemed still to be a major battle to be waged. And before many months had passed, the Association of Men had been mobilized as the vanguard of Catholic Action.

In making a summary assessment of Catholic Action's strength and importance, one fact needs emphasis: an elaborate political machine that really works efficiently is a rare commodity on the Spanish political market. The machinery of Catholic Action possesses efficiency, among other qualities almost equally scarce. It has the public and firm allegiance of 350,000 people. It has a machinery of organization which is not satisfied with any extravagant display of power confined to the nation's capital, but which reaches into the lives of the provinces and the cities of all the country. It has been saved by the virtual political immunity that comes from the word "Catholic" in contemporary Spain and protects it against the capricious, vicious assaults of the Falange Party which have wiped out so many possible centers of future political growth. It boasts extraordinary financial resources—probably greater than all that could be mustered by the Falange itself. Its leaders generally have a knowledge and sense of public opinion which comes only from years of experience in trying either to sell, borrow, or indoctrinate. It has an educated leadership and a rank and file with a high percentage of literacy—a far from insignificant factor in weighing the strength or durability of any political force in Spain.

But perhaps of greater meaning than any of these attributes, Catholic Action is favored by a tradition and continuity of consistent effort which, in the ruthless political arena of Spain, are qualities left to very few organizations. It was born in a Spain only recently rent by civil wars. Its structure survived successive periods of constitutional monarchy, absolute monarchy, military dictatorship, left Republic, right Republic, a three-year civil war, and a totalitarian state. Throughout such a history, it has successfully endured both the painful tragedies of persecution and the vitiating, enervating influence of a too beneficent state-and-church patronage. In terms of individuals, the human beings who have been the strength of Catholic Action generally have been the kind of humanity who, like Abbé Sieyès, manage to survive. They have tended to be the kind of men and women whose professional training, experience, or inherited talents mark them for continuing roles in the social and economic ordering of a country, however abrupt or drastic may seem the shock of changes in the political façade. As in a grand theater, they may be likened to the directors, technical advisers, costumers, or electricians whose services are continuing and indispensable—although the show itself may change frequently, although others stand in the glare of the footlights, and although they themselves may thoroughly dislike the latest production. Besides, in some cases, they may own the theater itself.

In view of all this, it is not difficult to understand how, in 1944, when Catholic Action seemed studiously remote from the political scene dominated by General Franco, one could speak of Catholic Action as a powerful and "dangerous" organization in Spain. It is equally easy to understand that, in a political alliance with the Generalissimo, it could serve him perhaps more usefully than any of his other allies. The Generalissimo himself understood this when—only two months after the triumph of the United Nations, at a moment when many thought that his regime could not survive that triumph—he chose as his foreign minister the head of Catholic Action.

4

When one July afternoon in 1945, young, energetic Martín Artajo sped in his car from Madrid to Toledo to ask the Primate of Spain whether he should accept Franco's offer to appoint him Spain's Foreign Minister, and when the Primate said that he should do so, one chapter in the history of the Spanish Church's relations with the Franco regime came to a decisive end. With equal decision, a new chapter was begun.

In that first chapter—the five years that followed upon the Nationalist victory in the Civil War—the Spanish Church devoted its concentrated, almost exclusive effort to the work of its own reorganization. Enjoying a sense of security denied it for many years, the clergy undertook "the great pacific battle for the rechristianization of Spain" by efficient re-establishment of its old functions: religious schools opened and expanded, seminaries were created or reorganized, hundreds of parish vacancies were filled, special charitable and propagandistic societies resumed their work with renewed vigor. There were also many new posts to be filled, posts which had not existed before the war. For example, there had to be chaplains, many chaplains, assigned to prisons newly filled with tens of thousands of political prisoners. And there were so many executions, so many bodies that had to be buried, so many last rites to be said.

The clergy studied the activities of the Falange with frequent approbation but constant care. It needed no encouragement to accept the Falangist thesis that the Party and the regime constituted impregnable bastions against the Communist forces threatening so much of Europe. But clerical eyes became coldly critical when they viewed the apparent preparations of the Falange to become the predominant power among the disparate forces allied with the Generalissimo. The government-subsidized work of the Falangist social welfare agency, *Auxilio Social* ("Social Aid"), promised dangerous competition in a sphere which the Church regarded as its own province. With sound justification, the fear grew that Falangist charitable work would be exploited as a powerful political weapon among the nation's poor. At the same time, a traditional Church prerogative seemed open to dangerous challenge by the Party: organizations like the *Frente de Juventudes* ("Youth Front") and the *Sindicato Español Universitario* ("Spanish University Syndicate") were striving for a mobilization of youth under Falangist banners. The Church had reason to fear the activities of these organizations—their influence on school curricula, their lusty emphasis on physical training and prowess, their attractive appeals through organized recreation and summer camps, their indoctrination of a crude kind of military ethics, their ill-concealed contempt for religious instruction or observances.

It was on this crucial educational issue that the hierarchy of the Spanish Church fought its most determined struggle and won its most decisive victory. And the manner in which the victory was won serves as a highly revealing example of the political tactics of a hierarchy unafraid to exact the full price for its collaboration with the regime of General Franco.

Precipitated in the summer of 1943, the battle began pacifically enough with a deferential visit to the Cardinal Primate of Spain, Pla y Daniel, by the Minister of Education, Sr. Ibañez Martín—an inept, vacillating man who had risen to prominence only because of his endorsement of the Falange and whose own education was a painful testimony to the shortcomings of the system which he said he was trying to improve. His visit to the Primate followed General Franco's instructions to obtain the endorsement of the highest authority in the Spanish Church for the draft of a new national law of education. The visit was cordial: the terms of the law agreed upon contained liberal guarantees to the Church that its own educational institutions would be fostered and religious instruction given in all schools.

A few days later, the Council of Ministers met to consider, among other matters, Ibañez Martín's proposed new education law. Quick, angry opposition arose from two quarters. The Falangist Ministers (led by Minister of the Party José Luis Arrese) heatedly denounced any categorical reaffirmation of the Church's control of the nation's school system. And the Foreign Minister, small, earnest General Jordana, although a resolute opponent of the Falange and a devout Catholic, opposed such concessions to the Primate for other reasons. He was in the midst of complicated negotiations with the Vatican on the terms of the new concordat, and his diplomatic bargaining position would be weakened by any such outright grant of authority to the Spanish Church. Accordingly, tentative agreement was reached in the Council on terms which left the authority of the clergy much in doubt. The Minister of Education, recollecting his conversation with the Primate, squirmed unhappily and waited for the storm to break.

Thunder from Toledo came quickly. The Primate, not slow in learning of the deliberations of the Council, wrathfully summoned the Minister of Education to come at once. The Minister came, only to receive a bitter denunciation of his failure to stick to his original agreement. The Primate wasted no time on the wretched Minister but promptly headed for the Pardo for an unsolicited personal encounter with Franco himself. The discussion that followed was heated, but the Primate brandished a weapon more powerful than rhetoric: if the inacceptable law were passed, he would resign from the Cortes and as head of the Spanish Church would publicly denounce the legislation. The Chief of State argued, evaded, pleaded, and finally yielded.

After great delay and prolonged Falangist attacks upon it, the Law of Primary Education of July 17, 1945, was finally passed. Containing a number of commendable principles (such as abolition of child labor and compulsory elementary education) which are wholly academic because there are not enough schools in which to apply them, the new law invested the clergy with even greater educational authority than it enjoyed under the Monarchy. To the Church was given full authority on all teaching involving faith or morals; official recognition was accorded to all certificates and diplomas issued under ecclesiastic authority; all teachers in State schools must receive a full course in religious indoctrination before they can practice their profession. The preliminary Statement of Principles defined the objective of the Law: "to form the will, the conscience and the character of the child with a view to fulfillment of his duty and his eternal destiny." Declares Article 5, Chapter II of Section I: "Primary education, inspired with a Catholic sense and consistent with Spanish educational traditions, will conform to the principles of the Catholic dogma and faith and to the prescriptions of canon law."

While the Church has won such important victories as this in its struggle with the Party, it has not overlooked smaller issues which, although not involving any basic laws of the land, also have had political import. An amusing and revealing issue of this kind arose in 1944. Each year the Falangist press and propaganda authorities has bestowed a "José Antonio" Literary Award upon a book selected as best expressing the ideals of "the Movement." This year the award went to an obscure work called *La Fiel Infantería* ("The Faithful Infantry"), a crude literary effort eulogizing the Nationalist soldiers of the Civil War and, with a rough realism, describing some of the coarser, bawdier aspects of military life. Decorated with the government's highest literary prize, the book came to the attention of the clerical censors. Shocked by some passages, they called the matter to the urgent attention of the Primate. The result: the Jesuit weekly *Ecclesia* excoriated the book, the Cardinal Primate denounced it publicly, ecclesiastic censors ordered it confiscated—and the Falange's prize book of the year disappeared from view. While the Primate's counselors undoubtedly felt that the book's contents warranted such drastic action, the action was taken with a special pleasure that came from the knowledge that it would be some months before the Party's public prestige recovered from this glancing blow.

But it has been unusual for conflicts between the Church and Party to become so open. On the contrary, both have always taken pains to pay public tribute to each other. Especially since the full power of the hierarchy has made itself felt within the Spanish regime, the leaders of the Falange have done their best to make gestures resembling genuflections. Thus a characteristic front-page editorial in *Arriba* in 1945 declared: "The Falange, from its first hour, placed in the very forefront of its creative activity affirmations based upon the purest Christian doctrine and morals. . . . To defend the Catholic meaning of Spanish life was one of the firmest postulates of our program. . . . Who is capable of denying so obvious a truth? Our enemies can boldly deny it, but no one will believe them." Even those stern words suggested plainly that the arm accustomed to the Fascist salute felt strangely muscle-bound when it tried to make the sign of the cross.

By the time such editorials were appearing in the Falangist press, the ascendancy of the Church over the Falange was visible to all. The period of reconstruction and entrenchment was ending for the Church: it could enter the public political arena with a sure sense of strength. It was at this time—in late 1944—that I had a conversation with one of the oldest, shrewdest leaders of the Falange on the subject of relation with the clergy. His words reflected the opinion of the most mature Party leaders:

"The Church has won—it has virtually taken over the Falange movement. It will continue to use the Falange (within limits set by itself) for so long as the Party is useful, then discard it—just as they will use Franco till his usefulness is at an end. I have told Franco precisely that. With all its wisdom from long experience, the Church has maneuvered around the Falange the way it has with all such 'redemption' movements— first watching it, then running closely alongside it, then flanking it on both sides, then absorbing it. . . ."

The moment in the spring of 1945, when the forces of Naziism were finally destroyed in battle, coincided with this time in Spain when the Spanish Church finished its work of renovation and of successful combat against hostile Falangist forces. But it was more than a coincidence. For the defeat of international Fascism in itself had profoundly affected the strength and prestige of the Falange, its Spanish counterpart: in truth, all the adroit political maneuvering of the Spanish hierarchy contributed less to the decline of Falangist power than did the course of the Second World War. And precisely the same military and international developments directly affected the attitude and policy of the Spanish clergy—for they made the threat of the Communization of Europe seem real and imminent. Thus the spring of 1945 simultaneously convinced the clergy that it had emerged predominant among the forces competing within the Franco regime—and that the Franco regime, more than ever, needed to be fortified as a bulwark against the advancing forces of Communism. It was this compelling set of circumstances which brought about the selection of Sr. Martín Artajo, the secular head of Catholic Action, as the Foreign Minister of Spain—with the explicit approval of the Primate of Spain.

This new chapter in the history of the hierarchy's relations with the Franco regime has not consisted of obscure political maneuvering remote from the glare of publicity. On the contrary, this chapter has been written explicitly by the hierarchy for the widest possible public consumption. The words of the hierarchy came in this sequence:

On September 2, 1945, the Cardinal Primate published a pastoral letter reiterating and defending the stand of the Spanish Church taken in 1937. The document included a denial that the hierarchy had ever endorsed a totalitarian program for Spain and a renewal of the frequent plea by the hierarchy for a policy of clemency toward political prisoners. Also, a stinging blow was struck at the Falange Party with these words: "It would be well that there be eliminated from the

Spanish State all that could serve even as a pretext for suspicions" (*i.e.*, suspicions of foreign critics among the United Nations). But the principal effort of the Primate was spent upon a defense of the legitimacy of the Franco regime and all its works. He flatly reasserted that the rebellion of 1936 was directed against nothing more nor less than "the peril of Communism." With a magnificent disregard of the Spanish clergy's own fiery indictments of the "error" of advocating religious freedom in any form, he justified the privileged position of the Spanish Church with this statement: "The Spanish Church . . . must be recognized as legitimate, as much according to the doctors of the Church as according to the principles of the Atlantic Charter, which propounds religious freedom." And for the religious policy of General Franco's regime, the Cardinal Primate spoke these words of praise and gratitude: "We must recognize that in general, for many centuries, neither theoretically nor in practice has the independence of the Church been so recognized as by the present government."

On September 14, 1945, the Bishop of Orense, Blanco Najera, released a pastoral letter which, in its categorical and partisan political character, sounded more like an election-campaign handout than a serious pronouncement from a dignitary of the Church. Sharply indicting the Potsdam Declaration's statement that Spain could not become a member of the postwar United Nations, the Bishop exclaimed that the United States, Great Britain, and Russia "are approaching the construction of the new international order with an odious partiality." Such a policy of "odious partiality" was attributed entirely to "Masonic and Communist forces," and the exclusion of the Franco regime from the United Nations displayed "unparalleled blindness" on the part of the nations which had crushed Naziism. The Bishop curtly dismissed the argument that the United Nations' quarrel was only with the Spanish regime and not the nation or people as a whole: this was "specious." According to the Bishop, "a supine ignorance" afflicted those who conceived of the Spanish regime as totalitarian in any respect: such critics were guilty of "a mental incapacity to observe the essential ideological differences which open an abyss between one regime and another." The Bishop concluded with a salute to the Franco regime uttered in a kind of tremulous rhetorical ecstasy: "a bulwark of the Catholic faith . . . and the only country which has resisted and defeated the hordes of the Godless."

On December 23, 1945, after two months and nine days of silence and reflection, the Bishop of Orense could not repress another pastoral letter—this time without even such provocation as the Potsdam Declaration had given. He denounced "foreign intervention" in Spanish affairs. He declared as axiomatic the fact that democracy had been and always would be a failure in Spain. But the Spain of General Franco had a heavenly future: "Spain, which always has been the bulwark of Christian civilization, will be the star to which all European nations again will turn their eyes."

The time was February 27, 1946. The scene was Vatican City. The occasion was his elevation to the College of Cardinals. Declared the Primate of Spain: "We must proclaim the voice of our Crusade. . . . In the face of a fact such as our Crusade, we cannot unsay today what we said yesterday."

All these declarations (by no means a complete list of their kind) were issued in the months that followed the end of World War II, after the initiation of the verbal offensive against the Franco regime by the diplomats of the United Nations, and (most importantly) after the elevation to the office of Foreign Minister of the ranking lay Catholic leader in Spain, Sr. Martín Artajo. All these pronouncements contained one crucial meaning: the decision of the Spanish hierarchy (at precisely the moment when most foreign observers seemed to believe that the Franco regime would fall under the overpowering weight of the Allied victory over Naziism) to mobilize its resources in defense of that regime. On July 21, 1945, on the

occasion of his taking of the oath of office, Sr. Martín Artajo
and his cabinet made this declaration to the press:

The Government which today begins its political life, under the
presidency of the Caudillo of Spain, represents a new stage on the
road to the spiritual and material restoration of our Fatherland.

If, however, some mad caprice had induced the new Foreign
Minister to make a public confession of the political realities
of that moment, his statement would have read something
like this:

The Government which today begins its political life constitutes
in itself a tribute to the political dexterity of the Caudillo of Spain.
He is now in the successful process of eliminating some of the more
flagrant displays of Falangist influence, and of eliciting the support
for his regime of the great weight of the heretofore relatively independent Catholic forces of Spain. Thus we have reached a new stage
in the work of fortifying this regime on the domestic scene and of
rebutting the charges directed against it from abroad.

A few weeks after the entrance into this "new stage on the
road" to Spain's "spiritual and material restoration," the sanctimonious spirit of the times was admirably captured in headlines which the outstanding Catholic daily newspaper in Spain
(*Ya*, September 30, 1945) blazoned across its entire front page:

TOMORROW IS THE DAY OF THE CAUDILLO:
A CATHOLIC RULER

FRANCO, KNIGHT OF THE ROMAN
CATHOLIC APOSTOLIC CHURCH

HIS LIFE, HIS THOUGHTS AND HIS WORKS ARE ADJUSTED
TO THE PRINCIPLES AND NORMS OF THE CHURCH.—
THUS HAS IT BEEN VALIANTLY PROCLAIMED
BY THE ECCLESIASTICAL HIERARCHY

5

For more than three hundred years, the intellectual traditions of the Spanish Church have been of a caliber and variety
that refute the arbitrary, vastly oversimplified conception of it
as an historic model of clerical reaction. On the contrary, in
that intellectual heritage there has been the evidence of a
vibrant tradition of progressive social thinking and of revolutionary social action. And it is precisely the greatness and nobility of this tradition which have made doubly painful and
tragic the failings and blindness of the Spanish Church in the
last fifty years.

This tradition—a passionate dedication to the welfare of the
poor and underprivileged—found its fullest expression in seventeenth century Spain. In virtually every social conflict of that
era, every protest against tyranny and expropriation, it was to
the monks that the people turned for leadership; and the
leaders they found were men of stamina and courage. In the
New World into which Spanish explorers and conquerors were
penetrating, the wise and humanizing influence of the missionaries was largely responsible for the success of colonization;
and from these colonial areas, after years of labor on behalf
of oppressed Indians of the Americas, men of the great monastic orders returned to take up the cause of the oppressed
peasants and workers of Iberia. The spirit of these men was
that of the Franciscan father Martinez de la Mata, who called
himself "the slave of the poor afflicted."

In the realm of political and social ideas, these experiences
and practices were translated into truly revolutionary social
theory. The Inca collectivist state made a profound impression
upon the thinking of the missionaries. Jesuits like Josef de
Acosta carried with them back to Spain an urgent appeal to
evolve such a collectivist economy in which men would strive
for "that high perfection of owning no private property." And
the first years of the seventeenth century found other Jesuits

busily developing their famous experiment in Paraguay—the earliest example of a completely socialized society established by Europeans. These were the days when theologians thumbing through their encyclopedic volumes for an authoritative discourse on "property" found their subject listed under "theft."

Much later, in the stormy Napoleonic era, when the people of Spain found no monarch or government to lead them in their battle against the French invaders, once again priests and monks appeared at the head of armed, angry masses. The wealthy and the titled took little or no part in these heroic days: most of them betrayed to the French, and those who did not do so usually found themselves flatly excluded from the patriot guerrilla bands who believed that theirs was a battle for the poor and the priests alone.

It has been only the last century that has made popular the terse Spanish saying that *el dinero es muy católico* ("money is a good Catholic"). The phrase aptly states the conviction of the Spanish people that their Church has become a constant accomplice of none but the rich. By the nineteenth century, once the heroic Napoleonic days had passed, the times and works of men like Mariana and Vittoria and Suarez—with their first modern definitions of a democratic ruler and the first principles of modern international law—seemed like a memory so vague and distant that it might have never been.

For all but the blind, the signs of the changed times were starkly clear during the Carlist wars of the 1830's. In 1834, a cruel cholera plague in Madrid was followed by the ugly rumor that the Jesuits had poisoned the city's water supply: frenzied mobs burned every church and killed every monk they could reach. The performance was repeated the following year on a grander scale, in an outbreak of systematic burnings of churches and convents throughout the country. Beyond the awful death and destruction there lay two other tragedies: the men and women who burned the churches and convents were earnest Catholics themselves. That was one tragedy. The second was that the clergy refused to believe this. Satisfied in their conscience that rumors such as the water poisoning were false and malicious, they did not pause to ask themselves: What has made our people so credulous as to believe such things? And is the fact that they believe them not more important than the fact that the rumors are untrue? But the intellectual temper of the nineteenth century Church was not such as to provoke, or even to condone, the asking of such questions. It was the temper of the University of Cervera expressed in its address to King Ferdinand VII: "Far be from us the dangerous novelty of thinking." Such novelties had to be sacrificed, of course, for the enjoyment of vast landholdings, virtual monopoly on all educational facilities, subsidization by a monarchy, majority stock-ownership of railroads, mines, shipping companies, orange plantations, and fish markets.

With a heritage of these contradictory and conflicting traditions from the seventeenth and nineteenth centuries, the Spanish Church emerged triumphant from the Civil War in 1939.

The older tradition has not died entirely. The eight years of the Franco regime have not been without their examples of the moral and intellectual fortitude necessary in Spain to deny both the government's claim to be a unique "bulwark against Communism" and the same claim advanced by all the Fascist powers during World War II. Cardinal Segura of Sevilla, in his dogged opposition to all Falangist officialdom, has displayed more courage than almost any of his fellow-conservatives and fellow-monarchists. This stocky, mild-mannered, ascetic prelate probably deserves most of the credit for the Spanish hierarchy's refusal to embrace the Party or publicly endorse its totalitarian gospel. And there have been a few others of similar stamina. The Archbishop of Calahorra created sensations in 1943 and 1944 with his eloquent denunciations of the Fascist threat to free religion, the Nazi tyranny in occupied Europe, and the blight of anti-Semitism. Less eloquent but equally firm has been the Archbishop of Valladolid: situated in the traditional birthplace and hotbed of Falangism,

he has refused to participate in any of the Party's lavish ceremonies with which the city is regularly afflicted.[1] And throughout Spain today are simple monks and priests whose names do
not figure in any list of the distinguished hierarchy but whose
lives are magnificent human dedications to the needs of their
flock. Poor, earnest and devout, these men have somehow kept
alive that seventeenth century spiritual tradition in material
surroundings that often seem like residues of the same era.

But when these men, their words and their works, are given
their full measure of respect, the sad truth emerges that they
are exceptions which only force out in bolder relief the predominant characteristics of the contemporary Spanish Church.
Those characteristics include: an overriding dedication to in-
stitutional self-interest; a tough, prideful imperviousness to
criticism; a profound suspicion of any intellectual inquisitive-
ness; a contempt for any kind of education that is not synony-
mous with indoctrination; a sharp distrust and hostility toward
any political or social movement that could be called "radical,"
"leftist" or "liberal"; and a respect that approaches reverence
for power in any form.

As a simple and typical illustration of one aspect of this intellectual outlook, I recall a luncheon I attended two years ago
in the home of an attaché of the French Embassy. Also present
was a widely known Spanish priest, Dean of the Law Faculty

[1] Although there were some conspicuous exceptions, the Spanish clergy
as a whole, more than any other group identified with the Franco regime,
avoided public identification with the Fascist cause in the World War.
Typically foolish German blunders helped bring this about. The worst of
these was Heinrich Himmler's, when, in the course of his tour of Spain, he
visited the famous Benedictine monastery outside Barcelona, Montserrat.
Himmler viewed the figure of the Virgin enshrined by the monastery, a
ninth century madonna, judiciously appraised it, and complimented the
monks: "Obviously, the Virgin and Child are of Nordic origin." In striking
contrast, Spanish priests and prelates found themselves won by the calm
personal charm and Catholic devotion of American Ambassador Carlton
J. H. Hayes. The latter's friendship with the monks of Montserrat became
so plain that in 1944, Falangist officials in Barcelona seriously circulated
the rumor that the Abbot of Montserrat was conniving with the American
Ambassador in planning an Allied military landing in nearby Rosas Bay!

of the University of Madrid and an intimate legal adviser of the Minister of the Interior (in charge of "public order"). A general political discussion following luncheon quickly turned itself into a discussion of Communism (as defined by the Dean of the Law Faculty). Both my French friend and I contended at some length that the strength of a Communist movement in any country depended directly upon the state of that country's social health; that such a movement was both a symptom and inevitable product of grave social injustice; and that a government which was constantly making a public confession of its fear of Communism also was confessing its own incapacity to establish a decent social order. This line of argument made not the slightest impression upon the priest. He dismissed it as "nonsense" and heatedly explained: "The threat of Communism that I am talking about is simply the threat of Russian armies reaching the Pyrenees if Germany ever collapses—because they won't stop at the Rhine. So far as conditions within Spain matter, we no longer have to worry about Communism. Thanks to the army the Caudillo has built up, we can crush any revolt of any kind within 48 hours." And he emphasized in happy redundance . . . "within 48 hours . . . within 48 hours. . . ." It was plain, from the words and the tone in which they were spoken, that a government's ability to strike quickly and effectively constituted an undisputable title to sovereignty. All discussion ended with the establishment of the efficacy of compulsion.

It is difficult to make fully plain the extent to which the thinking processes of the majority of the Spanish clergy are geared to this basic, profound satisfaction with force as an arbiter of all issues. No less difficult is it to describe the extent to which the Spanish clergy exploits its religious and educational authority to propagate a standard of political morality of the most violently partisan character. For the great majority of these men, the political issues raised by "liberalism" or "socialism" translate themselves into questions of faith and doctrine on the same plane as original sin, the Sermon on the Mount, the Trinity, or the Sacraments.

The classic Spanish catechism, used in all religious instruction in Spain, is the *Nuevo Ripalda*.[2] Of the volume's 112 pages, all except ten concern themselves with the essential doctrines of Catholic faith, and morals. The remaining ten pages engage in what is called an "Enumeration of Modern Errors." This section begins with the flat assertion: "The principal errors condemned by the Church are 13: Materialism, Darwinism, Atheism, Pantheism, Deism, Rationalism, Protestantism, Socialism, Communism, Syndicalism, Liberalism, Modernism, and Masonry."

In a brisk manner that probably would have stunned medieval theologians into utter insensibility, the catechism disposes of Socialism thus:

Q. What do Socialists teach?
A. That the State can dispose of private goods which are sources of wealth and distribute them among the workers as it judges convenient.

Q. What does the Church tell me of Socialism?
A. That it is an absurd system and above all unjust.

Q. Why?
A. Because it violates private property which is sacred and unjustly disposes of what is not its possession.

The indictment of "liberalism" is longer and more illuminating:

Q. What are the freedoms which liberalism defends?
A. Freedom of conscience, freedom of worship, and freedom of the press.

Q. What does freedom of the press mean?
A. The right to print and publish without previous censorship all kinds of opinions, however absurd and corrupting they may be.

2 17th revised edition, published in 1944, under ecclesiastical *imprimatur* by the *Casa Editorial de Arte Católico*.

Q. Must the government suppress this freedom by means of censorship?
A. Obviously, yes.

Q. Why?
A. Because it must prevent the deception, calumny and corruption of its subjects, which harm the general good.

Q. Are there other pernicious freedoms?
A. Yes. Freedom of education, freedom of propaganda, and freedom of assembly.

Q. Why are these freedoms pernicious?
A. Because they serve to teach error, propagate vice, and plot against the Church. . . .

Q. Does one sin gravely who subscribes to a liberal newspaper?
A. Yes. . . . Because he contributes his money to evil, places his faith in jeopardy, and gives others a bad example.

Q. What rules can be given to know liberal papers?
A. The following:
   1. If they call themselves liberal.
   2. If they defend freedom of conscience, freedom of worship, freedom of press, or any of the other liberal errors.
   3. If they attack the Roman Pontiff, the clergy, or the religious orders.
   4. If they belong to liberal parties.
   5. If they comment on news or judge personalities with a liberal criterion.
   6. If they unreservedly praise the good moral and intellectual qualities of liberal personalities or parties.
   7. If, in reporting the events concerned with the battle waged by Our Lord Jesus Christ and His Holy Church against their enemies today, they remain neutral.

Q. What is the rule to avoid error in these cases?
A. Do not read any newspaper without the previous consultation and approval of your confessor.

To comment upon "religious" teaching of this kind would be superfluous, but deserving of some mention is a man who

is a classic personification of it: the Bishop of Madrid, Eijo y
Garay. The bishop is variously known to Spaniards as the
"Bishop of the Falange" or, in recognition of the benedictions
he bestowed upon the Blue Division fighting on the Russian
front, "the Blue Bishop" (*el obispo àzul*). Unlike most of his
colleagues of the hierarchy, Eijo y Garay has displayed bound-
less enthusiasm for all the works of the Falange, especially the
Youth Front, in which he has held the office of "National
Counselor of Religion and Morals." His frequent public statements have been unique in their remarkable juxtaposition of
texts from Leo XIII's encyclicals and from the political dis-
courses of José Antonio Primo de Rivera. Perhaps the bishop's
most extraordinary single performance was his instruction in
1944 (first issued verbally, then made in writing) forbidding
use of the Catholic chapel connected with the French Embassy
for celebrating Mass or giving the Sacraments to any French
citizens who were not loyal to the Vichy regime!

Facts such as these help to explain the paradox in the
Spanish people's character which allows so many of them to
be at once profoundly Catholic and acidly anticlerical. It also
helps to explain why earnest, devoted workers from Catholic
Action's welfare agencies, visiting the sick and the impover-
ished in the Vallecas slums of Madrid, so often are spat upon,
cursed, and driven with pots and broomsticks from doors that
seal tightly with hate and distrust behind them. No instance
is known, however, of the bishop himself attempting such a
visit—certainly not in the sleek, black Daimler which he received as a personal gift from Adolf Hitler.

As for the millions of devout Spanish Catholics, no one—
certainly no foreigner—can presume to gauge or weigh their
thoughts and fears of the future. I believe that for them these
may be years of perhaps greater pain and anxiety than the
times of fanatical persecution in the past. Not unlike great
Catholic patriots of Ireland, in their soulful anguish at the
spectacle of dignitaries of the Irish hierarchy refusing the last
rites to men rebelling against the "lawfully constituted author-

ity" of British rule, so have millions of men and women of Spain been experiencing a wracking test of their faith.

And they are meeting that test. The churches of Spain are overflowing. I attended Mass every Sunday and Holy Day of the four years I passed there. I never saw an empty pew, rarely found a vacant seat, very frequently knelt on the sidewalk or even in the street, with the overflowing crowd all around me. I know, too, that numbers of Socialist and Republican friends of mine were in those crowds—while blue-shirted youths of the Falange almost invariably marched by in the street, on their militant way to some camp in the mountains, lustily bellowing bad Spanish translations of Nazi marching songs.

Perhaps it may be guessed that the resolute devotion of these men and women partakes more than a little of the spirit of Boccaccio's Jew of the fourteenth century. He had traveled all the way from Paris to Rome to see personally the life and men of the center of Christendom. He returned at length to his Christian friend in Paris who was so eager to bring about his conversion. He related to his friend that, so great and shocking was the decadence of the clergy, he was prepared to enter the Church. For only a divinely-inspired faith could continue to survive and prosper under such leadership.

6

One day in September of 1945, I received through the mail a letter addressed to the American Embassy. A glance at it showed that the provocation for it was a newspaper story, datelined from New York, which had been carried under striking headlines on the front pages of all the Madrid press. The published article merely had reproduced some fulsome eulogies of the regime of General Franco which had originally appeared in the Brooklyn *Tablet* over the name of Padre Juan de Diego. The letter I received was headed: "An Open Letter to Padre Juan de Diego."

The text of the letter was short:

In the New York weekly *Tablet,* there appears this week an article based upon a letter addressed to the newspaper by a Padre Juan de Diego, in which, among other things, he emphasizes "the Catholicism and democracy of the Spanish regime apparent in all its legislative actions."

As is natural, this article has been republished in the entire Spanish press (the State demands it) under the heading of DEFENSE OF SPAIN IN THE FOREIGN WORLD.

But you can be sure, Padre Juan de Diego, as can all Catholics of the world, that it has been published in Spain precisely because it does not conform to the truth.

Do you believe, Padre Juan de Diego, that in a Catholic regime and after seven years since the end of a civil war, it is logical that the prisons be full; and that, thanks to the "magnanimity" of the Caudillo and his modern prison laws, those who are doing penal labor earn 3 pesetas per day?

Does it also seem to you Catholic that the normal wage of a laborer is from 10 to 15 pesetas a day, a few centimos more than in 1936— while the costs of articles of primary necessity for living have risen more than 40 per cent?

Is the consequent rapid growth of tuberculosis also Catholic?

Does it seem to you to be an evidence of Catholicism that it suffices for any Falangist to denounce another person, merely as opposed to the regime, to have the latter arrested and punished and tortured by officials of the State?

And as proof that we are one of the "democratic" nations, may the fact suffice that the Spanish Catholic who has written these lines to you cannot sign his name—lest he too be imprisoned.

4 STRESS, STRAIN, AND STRATEGY

THE SPANISH STATE may have been born, as their textbooks tell the children of Spain, "under the sign of the unity and greatness of the Fatherland." But no one knows better than His Excellency, the Caudillo, that the price of that unity has been eternal vigilance.

Dependent for power upon an alliance of the mutually suspicious political forces which emerged victorious from three years of civil war, Francisco Franco has achieved a remarkable success. After eight years of dictatorial rule, he not only has prevented that alliance from tearing asunder but also has induced its several distinct elements to feel more than ever dependent upon him. As a result, the continuing rule of General Franco today finds itself supported by western Europe's largest standing army; by the power and resources of the Spanish Church; and by a totalitarian political party which still operates most of the nation's administrative machinery, whose state syndicates have a strangle hold on the economic life of the nation, and whose proletarian social gospel has made a vigorous appeal to the laboring masses. These are not feeble forces.

The apparent resilience and persistence of this alliance must be attributed, in large measure, to the consummate adroitness of the political tactics of General Franco. The alert, artful duplicity and dexterity with which he has manipulated the men and the groups around him provide one important answer to the crucial question: Why—despite the hostility of the great majority of his own people and of the nations of the world—has his regime been able to survive?

2

The explosive, boisterous Falange Party in 1939 presented itself to General Franco as his first major political problem. The Chief of State had incorporated it in the new regime as a "movement" rather than a "party"—"not as a static or rigid thing." This definition promised some assurance that the Falange would be a subservient member of Franco's grand political alliance, not permitted to assert its self-sufficiency, its own freedom from Army generals or Church prelates. The Falange's merger with the archconservative Carlists, militant apostles of reaction, had shifted the center of political gravity within the Falange toward the right. Otherwise, it might have drifted to radical extremes incompatible with the interests of other groups allied in the Nationalist cause. Entrance of Carlists into the Falange also promised to precipitate internal conflicts which would serve the useful function of keeping Falangist leaders busy trying to maintain order in their own house, with less time to concentrate on dictating to the nation their particular political and economic prescriptions.

These controls upon the Party, put into effect while the Civil War was still continuing, were clear forecasts of General Franco's political tactics after the "Glorious Victory." In August of 1939, the new basic statutes of the Party were proclaimed by Franco, confirming the Party's monopoly of political power; and this was emphasized further by awarding the Falange three ministries without portfolio in the first postwar cabinet. But while the Generalissimo thus seemed to be fulfilling the hopes of the *camisas viejas* ("old shirts"), revelation of his true purpose was made in the appointments to the key positions within the Party. To the Party's post of highest command, that of Secretary General, went a trusted career officer of the Spanish Army: tall, tough, independent General Agustín Muñoz Grande, who was to win international fame four years later as the commander of the Spanish Blue Division on the Russian front. For the second highest Falange office, President of the *Junta Política,* Franco made an equally safe choice: his own brother-in-law, Ramon Serrano Suñer, the slight, dapper, self-seeking opportunist who was shortly to win renown as Spain's fanatically Germanophile Foreign Minister. But at this moment in 1939 the striking fact was that, precisely when General Franco publicly endowed the Falange with the fullest recognition and authority, he firmly insured his own personal control over the Party. In this greatest day of political triumph, the Movement once inspired by daring radicals like Ledesma Ramos was placed under the immediate direction of one of the Army generals against whom all orthodox Falangists had been warned.

The pattern of relationships thus established was politically ideal. The Party could not dare to show displeasure over the controls established by Franco, much less fight back openly. To have done so would have served only to strengthen the positions of those very forces which the Party's oldest leaders knew to be their enemies—Army and Church. Both the latter would have rejoiced at any chance to suggest to Franco that the Party was disloyal. Either, without Franco's own restraining influence, would have turned its full fire upon the Falange. All this Franco knew and could delight in the knowledge that the Party, despite some of its wayward impulses, must remain loyal to him as its only possible protector.

There followed then the era of great German victories in World War II and of ascendant Falange prestige in Spain—the years from 1939 to 1942. Having cast itself in the role of agent and spokesman for international Fascism, the Falange could exploit every Axis military victory in Russia or Egypt as vindication of its own cause, as justification for greater political concessions in Madrid. In these circumstances, Falangists succeeded in ridding themselves of General Muñoz Grande as their Secretary General. To this post the Generalissimo appointed Serrano Suñer. Despite Suñer's ardent affection for Naziism, this was scarcely a triumphant moment for the "old shirts" of the Party. At a time when Falangist prestige should have been most compelling, the best the Party could have in the way of a leader was Franco's brother-in-law—a man who had not joined the Falange until a year after the Civil War had started, a political refugee from the shattered rightist CEDA of Gil Robles about which all good Falangists had been so scrupulously warned in 1936!

By late 1942, the peak of Falangist prestige had passed. Its loud promises of quick Nazi military victory had been proven vain. It had become the focal target of domestic discontent. Its wildly ambitious leader had carried his battle for personal prestige against the Army too far. Anti-Falangist pressure from the military upon Franco became irresistible. In one of the most critical political decisions of his rule, Franco ordered the dismissal of Suñer from the offices of both Foreign Minister and Secretary General of the Party. In September of 1942, to succeed his brother-in-law, as Party leader, Franco named none other than the José Luis Arrese whom he had condemned to prison in 1937 for complicity in the attempted coup d'état of Hedilla. Thus it was only when the Falange's prestige and power had declined sharply that, as a calculated compensation, Franco appointed as its head a genuine old-guard Falangist.

And so Falangist affairs stand until July of 1945. Now the European war has ended with the destruction of the Fascist powers. Falangist hopes to share in the spoils and beauties of a New Order have been shattered. But its loud boasts and promises from the past echo embarrassingly in the present. The problem is pressing. General Franco's solution: eliminate entirely the post of Minister of the Party within the cabinet, dismiss Arrese as Secretary General, and allow that office also to disappear by appointing no one to replace him.

But surely the sturdy old guard of the Party is not so entirely forgotten? No. For, despite their grand displays of power, their strutting and their shouting, they already have been sadly disappointed by their Caudillo's actions many times since 1939. How bitter had been the disappointment that had come even then, immediately after the Glorious Victory! To have had to accept the leadership of such fake Falangists as Serrano Suñer and Muñoz Grande had been made doubly humiliating by the fate of the man who had been Secretary General—grave, handsome Fernandez Cuesta, true *camisa vieja,* life-long friend and colleague of Primo de Rivera, a true hero of the revolutionary days under the Republic. What had happened to him in 1939? The Caudillo had shipped him out of the country in diplomatic exile as his Ambassador to Brazil.

So what shall be done now, in July of 1945, when the Falange is being expelled from the highest offices? Summon Fernandez Cuesta. Pay due political respect to the "old shirts." Bring him into the cabinet itself. Appoint him Minister of Justice. It is done.

But Fernandez Cuesta is not alone. Despite all the lavishly publicized "evolutionary" measures of the Franco regime since the end of World War II, despite all the apparent curtailment of Falangist authority in Madrid, General Franco has never given the slightest indication of any intention of purging his regime of Falangists.

The contrary is true, and the evidence is clear. It can be found in the Spanish Cortes. The *Boletín Oficial* of May 3, 1946 (almost exactly one year after the collapse of Naziism in Europe), published the names of all men appointed to the new session of the Spanish "parliament." The list was an admirable yardstick for measuring the pace and degree of "change" within the Franco regime. By an overwhelming majority, the "new" appointees were merely carry-overs from all the preceding sessions of the Cortes. The only significant change was the disappearance of leading Monarchist sympathizers, notably the Duke of Alba, Count Rodezno, and financial titan Juan Ventosa. As for Falangist representation, quick comparison with the Cortes of 1945 revealed that the latter had included a list of forty representatives who belonged not merely to the Party but to the intransigeant *camisas viejas* of the pre-Civil War era, all of them violently Fascist and Germanophile. Of this number, a grand total of three failed to be reappointed to the 1946 Cortes! [1] Since the Cortes is of course only an impotent and perfunctory ratifying body, membership in it offers old revolutionaries of the Party no opportunity to cause trouble for the larger political schemes of the Generalissimo. But there is startling irony in this fact: the Cortes whose chief political service has been to delude credulous foreign opinion into the belief that the Spanish regime is being "liberalized," in fact has served Franco on the domestic scene as the harmless refuge for loyal Falangists whose other political posts have been taken from them!

With regard to the continuing relationship between General Franco and his Falange, I have listed in a previous chapter certain of the obvious services which the Party renders. But beyond the discharge of the responsibilities delegated to it, there are three distinct and important ways in which the Falange, despite its appearance of a political liability, fits nicely into the *franquista* scheme of things.

First: a paradoxical key to the political strength of Franco's position has been the fact that, despite the primary importance of his role as a general of the Spanish Army, that role alone could not suffice to justify his elevation to the post of Chief of State. There are probably no Spanish generals who are not

[1] The list of those reappointed to the 1946 Cortes includes such familiar Falangist names as the following: Serrano Suñer, Ernesto Giménez Caballero, Gabriel Arias-Salgado, José Luis Arrese, Fernando Castiella, Wenceslao González Oliveros, José Antonio Elola, Pilar Primo de Rivera (sister of José Antonio), Augustín Aznar, Pedro González Bueno, Sancho Dávila, Antonio Correa, Antonio Riestra del Moral, Antonio Tovar, Juan Pradera, José María Areilza, David Jato Miranda.

personally ambitious, and there are altogether too many Spanish generals for the title in itself to vindicate, in the mind of any Spaniard, the pretension of any one of them to be a Caudillo. Hence the title of chief of Spain's single political party constitutes a useful distinguishing mark of authority.

Secondly: the existence and prestige of the Falange, in Franco's calculations, undoubtedly played a fairly significant role in diplomatic dealings with Germany during World War II. The Party could be advertised to the Germans as convincing evidence that Spain truly was a totalitarian state and deserved recognition of its territorial ambitions in North Africa. In similar fashion, when Franco so desired to use it, the Party's existence could be a strong argument in withstanding German pressure on Spain for fuller participation in the war. When German Ambassadors von Stohrer, von Moltke, or Dieckoff applied pressure for specific economic or military concessions, or when they complained (as they often did) that Spain was not contributing enough to "the common cause," Franco could (and often did) parry their concrete demands by pointing to the Falange as plain proof of Spain's loyalty to Fascist principles, her share in "the crusade against Bolshevism," and her eagerness to partake of the joys of the New Order.

Thirdly: the Falange as a party—like Serrano Suñer as an individual—has served to polarize discontent within Spain, while also drawing some of the fire of foreign critics away from the figure of Franco himself. Within Spain, while public indignation might flare over the rigorousness of Falange censorship, the brutality of its police, the graft of its syndicates, and the arrogance of its officials, Franco as an individual tended to be screened from such public attack. When Spaniards discussed such trials and outrages among themselves, the immediate question often asked in past years has not been, How can we depose Franco? but rather, How can we impel Franco to take action against the Falange? Even Republican and underground groups, in the years that immediately followed 1939, shrewdly reasoned that the Generalissimo was the only man who might check the wild fanaticism and brutality of the Falange; and a successful attempt to assassinate him could result only in leaving all opposition groups at the mercy of a Falange whipped into fierce frenzy by the chance to avenge another "martyr." As the political strategy of the Franco regime has evolved, the Generalissimo has been able slowly to turn the Falange into a political scapegoat whose punishment has been supposed to disarm all his critics: witness the abolition of the office of Minister of the Party, the prohibition (rarely heeded) of the Falangist salute, the disbanding (only partly effected) of the Falangist militia, and the removal of Falangists, in January, 1946, from the State's press and propaganda offices.

In these various ways, through all the political vicissitudes of his regime, General Franco has been able to exploit the Falange Party as a source of prestige, a punitive guarantor of security and "public order," a distracting target for his opponents to attack, and a victim of his sudden passion for "Christian democracy."

3

Curbing the Falange has been but one aspect of General Franco's larger problem of keeping the Party and Army from engaging in a fight to the finish.

While the Falange has viewed the Army as a formidable citadel of reaction, frightening in its stubborn strength, the Army has seen the Party as a less powerful but more provoking rival. Army officers still sneer at the recollection of the Falange's clumsy and inept military efforts during the Civil War. But this contempt did not lessen their anger when the Falange Militia was created: it seemed to them that military authority and privileges were being awarded as a prize for military incompetence. They could understand little of the Falange's ponderous rhetoric about "social revolution," and what part they did understand they did not like. Above all, they detested the man who emerged as the personification of Falangist ambition: Ramon Serrano Suñer.

Of all the strange, disturbing figures who have crossed the Spanish scene since 1939, none has been more detested, none has helped bring his country closer to the edge of disaster, than sleek Serrano Suñer. He is a small, trim man. His face and head are small, delicately shaped, almost like a woman's. His hair is prematurely white, as is his neat little mustache. His blue eyes have a look of bland remorselessness. His fretful nervousness shows itself in a chronic cough, quick and sharp. His notorious vanity displays itself in his fastidious dress, so precise as to seem precious.

He appeared on the scene of the Civil War in 1937 with few distinctions to boast. As a youth, he had studied at the Spanish College in Bologna. By profession, he was a lawyer. In politics, he had belonged to Gils Robles' Catholic, conservative CEDA coalition. But by marriage, he was the brother-in-law of Francisco Franco. Never knowing any loyalty except his own ambition, Suñer became a Falangist. His brother-in-law found him useful, and by the end of the war had elevated him over all the old, genuine *Falangistas* to the leadership of the Party.

This was not enough. He became Minister of the Interior. This placed at his orders the security police and all the prisons of Spain. He used the police and the prisons to inflict a fearful vengeance upon all suspected enemies of the regime. Personal grief sharpened his fanaticism almost to the point of madness: he himself had escaped from the Republicans in Madrid only by hiding himself in a tuberculosis sanatorium; his two brothers had been killed. This loss also inflamed his fierce hatred of England, for he always insisted that his brothers' deaths followed the refusal of the British Embassy to give them asylum. This Anglophobia helped to fortify his conviction that the Nazi armies were invincible: in the summer of 1940, he boasted frequently that he had accepted Hitler's invitation to taste "victory cocktails" with him in London before September 15.

At that time, Serrano Suñer's obsession with power conspired with a bitter personal enmity to dictate one overriding ambition: to oust Colonel Juan Beigbeder as Foreign Minister and to become Foreign Minister himself. The feud between the two men, though of obscure origin, was known to all Madrid, and the contestants soon emerged as personifications of the most basic, critical issues of the day: Army vs. Falange, neutrality vs. belligerence. Serrano Suñer possessed two formidable weapons: his closeness to Franco and the determined support of German pressure in Spain.

General Franco's decision in the conflict came in a manner typical of the silent, secretive methods which have become habitual with him. In October of 1940, Beigbeder was confident that he had beaten back Serrano Suñer's attack upon his position. His confidence was fortified by a long and friendly personal conference with Franco on the afternoon of October 15. The following day, the Foreign Minister chatted in jocular fashion with the British Ambassador, Sir Samuel Hoare, and confided in him his own assurance that Franco was prepared to rebuff his brother-in-law. The next morning, when Beigbeder glanced at his morning paper, he read that Serrano Suñer had just been named Spain's new Foreign Minister.

For the two years during which Serrano Suñer ran Spain's Foreign Office, it was difficult to tell whether the stately old red-stone building bore greater resemblance to an annex of the German Embassy or to a district center of the Falange. In terms of domestic politics, warily viewed by the Army, it seemed apparent that the brash, upstart Falange, thanks to German pressure and Serrano Suñer's own sinuous political maneuvers, had won the astounding victory of complete control over the nation's foreign policy. Perhaps principally because the detested Party had emerged as the fanatic advocate of Spanish participation in the Fascist war against the United Nations, the Army, in a sort of conditioned political reflex, came to represent a policy of temperance, caution, neutrality—so unlike the traditional mood and manner of Spain's acquisitive generals. And Army officers, who knew well their forces' unpreparedness and lack of equipment, must have shuddered visibly on that memorable February 14, 1942, when they gath-

ered in the fabulously beautiful Moorish Alcazar of Sevilla to
hear General Franco loudly proclaim: "If the road to Berlin
were open, not merely one division of Spaniards would participate in the struggle—but one million Spaniards would be
ready to defend it." In those luxurious months of grand Nazi
military victories and unlimited German influence in Spain,
Serrano Suñer treated Allied Ambassadors calling at the Foreign Office like a churlish housewife raucously berating
vacuum-cleaner salesmen who interrupted her floor scrubbing.

But the summer of 1942, in the heat which is supposed to
slow the tempo of Madrid's politics as much as the movements
of Spaniards themselves, a sensational series of unexpected
events profoundly altered the course of the Franco regime.

It began on August 15 at the little old church of Begoña,
not far from the great port city of Spain's mining provinces,
Bilbao. In all Spain it was the great Holy Day of the Assumption of the Blessed Mother. At Begoña it was the special occasion for the Carlists to attend a solemn requiem Mass in honor
of their comrades killed in the Civil War. Outstanding among
those present was the Minister of War, General José Enrique
Varela: a traditional Monarchist, an archenemy of the Falange,
a leader of all the forces within the government fighting the
impertinent rise to power of Serrano Suñer and the Falange.
As the Minister was leaving the church, a bomb was inaccu-
rately but unmistakably tossed at him, seriously injuring scores
around him. After a second futile bomb was thrown, a black
car sped away from the scene of the outrage.

While the Spanish press did not whisper of what had happened and the Generalissimo strove to apply the ointment of
smooth words, the wound was too deep. The Ministry of War,
foreseeing fully the results, insisted upon full investigation of
the crime. The inquiry swiftly proved that the attack had been
planned by Falangists in Valladolid; that one of its sponsors
was Dominguez Muños, employed by the German sabotage
organization in Spain; that another of its sponsors was José
Luna, one of the half-dozen leader Party organizers; and that

all the men involved were colleagues or personal protégés of Serrano Suñer himself.

The crisis could scarcely have been more grave. It seemed to demand inexorably that General Franco choose between the Army, crying for vengeance, and the Falange, screaming its innocence. For two weeks, daily and nightly, big official cars with their loud motorcycle escorts roared in and out of the gates of the Pardo—bringing generals wrathfully demanding that the wrong be righted, Party leaders shouting to the harassed Generalissimo that the military were trying to exploit a "regrettable accident" in order to destroy the Falange, the great "popular base" of the whole regime.

On September 3, in true Gallegan fashion, the Chief of State arbitrated and decided. He yielded to the Army: Serrano Suñer had to surrender his offices, both as Foreign Minister and as the leader of the Falange. And he yielded also to the Falange: General Varela could no longer be Minister of War. To compensate the Party for their loss in prestige, the Generalissimo went even further. To replace Serrano Suñer as Secretary General of the Party, he named José Luis Arrese, whose name brought a thrill of pleasure to the tough old guard of the Falange. And as Minister of War, Franco chose General Asensio: ardently pro-Falangist, for which he was despised by most of his military associates, and eagerly pro-Nazi. Indeed, the Army was forced to pay a high price for the head of Serrano Suñer.

A few days after his ignominious departure from office, Serrano Suñer learned something which made his defeat even more bitter. He had not been beaten merely by the military men who he had always known were his mortal enemies: they had been helped in their effort to destroy him by none other than some of the Falangists upon whom he had blindly relied! In his mad drive to power, Serrano Suñer had forgotten that when he had entered the Party in 1937, to exploit it for his own political ambitions, he had enraged earnest, sincere Falangists who condemned him as an unprincipled interloper. They were right, and they waited their chance. It came in those last two weeks of August. The two men who planned the Begoña incident were Minister of Labor José Antonio Giron—and José Luis Arrese. This time the ways of Arrese were more subtle and devious than they had been in the crude conspiracy of Hedilla back in 1937. Having planned the outrage, Arrese and Giron urged Serrano Suñer to defend the men arrested; and when Dominguez Muños was sentenced to death, they persuaded Serrano Suñer to protest violently to Franco. It was an example of such coldly calculated duplicity as could have been matched only by Serrano Suñer himself. This time, he was the victim.

But the day's greatest triumph did not belong to these cunning conspirators of the Party but to General Franco. His tactics successfully averted what at one moment had seemed to be an inevitable break within his alliance of political forces. But it is a special mark of his political tactics that they seek always more than one advantage or gain from any solution to a problem. In this instance, his secondary gain came in the fact that, although he had done nothing more than meet a critical domestic problem with its necessary solution, in the sphere of foreign affairs he could claim credit among the United Nations for having dismissed as his Foreign Minister the most dangerous Germanophile in his cabinet.

And it is a curious fact that, in making this decision which held such serious implications for Spain's foreign policy, Franco had the luck of being free from any foreign diplomatic pressure. From the Anglo-American side there had never been any attempt to undermine the position of Serrano Suñer. At that time, with Nazi military might dominating the entire European continent, the Allies' precarious diplomatic position would have made any such effort as ludicrous as it would have been futile. The truth is that, although every diplomat in Madrid anticipated some cabinet changes in the first week in September, the American Embassy was taken by complete surprise by the news of Serrano Suñer's fatal fall.

As for German diplomacy, Franco was spared any pressure from this source by an absurd little coincidence that had incalculable consequences. The German Ambassador at this time was Baron von Stohrer: tall, aristocratic, charming and persuasive. A talented diplomat and fine linguist, he knew Spain intimately. During World War I he had been a First Secretary of the German Embassy in Madrid, and his chief function had been the organization of German sabotage of those Catalonian industries whose products were being shipped to the Allies. But his mission ended unhappily: deeply implicated in a plot to assassinate the pro-Allied Prime Minister, Count Romanones, he was recalled to Berlin at the insistence of the enraged Spanish Government. The Nazis, with their fine faculty for selecting and assigning diplomatic conspirators wherever their particular talents bore promise of successful intrigue, had shipped von Stohrer back to Spain as Ambassador.

This time it was no rash murder plot but a mad freak of fate that helped to end von Stohrer's second mission in Madrid. When the fateful bomb exploded on the steps of the church of Begoña, the German Ambassador was sunning himself on the beach of Biarritz across the French border. The gravity of the ensuing crisis in Madrid was not apparent immediately, and two weeks passed before the news reached von Stohrer that the position of his loyal Serrano Suñer was in grave danger. The German Embassy advised him that his immediate presence in Madrid was essential to avert disaster. Von Stohrer sped from Biarritz in a German military car, because his own diplomatic automobile was not immediately available. That seemed unimportant. But when the Spanish border was reached, it was found that his military vehicle lacked proper documentation to enter Spain. The delay that followed was fatal: von Stohrer did not reach Madrid until Serrano Suñer had been out of the Foreign Office more than twenty-four hours.

Joachim von Ribbentrop never pardoned von Stohrer for his failure to save the Spanish Laval. A few weeks later, von Stohrer's second wartime mission to Madrid ended with peremptory recall to Berlin.

4

Since the end of World War II with the final destruction of the armed forces of Fascism, and along with the development of a remarkable political vocabulary in which all past allusions to "the New Order" are corrected to read as eulogies to a thing called "an organic democracy," the regime of General Franco has adopted a singularly simple political strategy. This strategy has been to force the Falange Party into a tactful retreat from public prominence and simultaneously to bestow that prominence and prestige, formerly enjoyed by the Party, upon the Spanish Church.

In executing this strategy, General Franco has himself discarded the role of architect of a new society and assumed the more fashionable pose of "Defender of the Faith." The transformation could scarcely be considered subtle, but subtlety is no accurate measure of its effectiveness. Today, the regime which in 1939 resoundingly extolled the Falange as "the basis and inspiration" of its very life has been able to dispense with such inspiration, extol itself as a "bulwark of Christianity," elicit laudatory pastoral letters from the bishops of the nation, and—in the event of any ultimate challenge—merely dare anyone to attack its Army.

Viewing this transformation in its outward character, one quickly perceives that the very nature of this regime as an uncertain alliance of distinct and unassimilated political elements (which seems at first examination to be such a grave weakness) has also been a characteristic which permits such flexibility as would be utterly impossible in any rigidly defined structure of government. Thus, in a manner that never would have been possible for the Nazi regime, General Franco has been able to speak softly of "evolution," thereby working strenuously for survival.

Pursuing a strategy almost painfully obvious, General Franco has employed political tactics often remarkably devious. One noteworthy instance of such tactics was his first important public address following the collapse of the Nazi armies in May of 1945. He chose as the site for this appearance the city of Valladolid, the cradle of the Falange movement. In his journey to Valladolid he selected as his companion the Secretary General of the Party, José Luis Arrese. And he delivered a speech (*Arriba,* May 22, 1945) which could scarcely have been excelled in its emphatic endorsement of all the principles and practices of the Falange. To a nation feverishly speculating on his reaction to the military triumph of the United Nations, the Generalissimo blandly declared: "The events which have come to pass in the world only confirm the clear sightedness of the Spanish Movement." Far from snubbing the Falange, the Chief of State applauded at length its social program and its political daring, which were bringing about nothing less than "the Spanish renaissance." Contentedly he concluded: "Spain has prepared herself for this moment and therefore she can view events with serenity."

None but the politically naïve dismissed this performance of the Caudillo as simply the mad posturing of a man totally ignorant of the world in which he lived. Rather were his words and actions shrewdly designed to achieve a definite psychological effect. First, he aimed to confound and confuse those great numbers of the Spanish people who had hoped, even assumed, that Allied victory in the European war would act like automatic political magic in precipitating the end of the Franco regime in Spain. Secondly, General Franco carefully chose his words to erase completely the hope of those Monarchist leaders who were exclaiming ecstatically to each other that the international position of the Generalissimo was now so embarrassing that his only recourse was to summon Pretender Don Juan to allow the harassed Chief of State to make a quick, graceful political exit. To all persons entertaining such sanguine expectations, General Franco firmly explained that he was in no haste whatsoever, that he was not seeking any political exit, and that were he ever to select one he would walk, not run.

All this was well designed for immediate, temporary psychological effect. It was scarcely a serious attempt to solve any of the political problems confronting the regime. Hence the next two months were spent in the more arduous task of re-laying the foundations of the regime.

Appropriate opportunity for explaining to the nation his general political intentions came with the Generalissimo's annual "Day of Victory" (July 17) speech to the National Council of the Falange. With this speech, General Franco protected himself against any charge of false modesty by passionately reiterating that his leadership of the rebellion of 1936 had resulted in nothing less than the re-establishment of Spanish unity, her traditional moral and political values, her domestic peace and dignity among the nations of the world. Speaking at a time when the Potsdam Conference was in session and for the benefit of public opinion abroad, he recalled with pointed deliberateness the pledge of President Roosevelt, on the occasion of the Allied landings in North Africa, that the United Nations would respect fully the sovereignty of Spain. He sharply reminded diplomats of foreign powers, now indicting the Spanish government for the cruel manner in which it had seized power, that virtually every one of these powers had recognized that government *after* the end of the Civil War, presumably accepting it as a sovereign equal in the family of nations. For his Spanish audience, General Franco tried out his new political vocabulary with the assertion that his Movement was "filled with popular and democratic content," while a just and "democratic" society for Spain was promised by such measures (*i.e.*, decrees of the Chief of State) as reopening of the Cortes, holding "elections" for the Falange syndicates, granting some autonomy to municipal and provincial governments, and "guaranteeing" personal liberties by the *Fuero de los Españoles* (subject to suspension at the discretion of the Chief of State).

But the sensation of this address came when General Franco raised "the problem of assuring my succession . . . without damage to the nation nor peril for the continuity of the work of the Movement." He declared that he had decided that this assurance could be given only by "the traditional Spanish system": the Monarchy. While the Councilors of the Falange before him gaped and squirmed miserably at these words, he drily remarked: "I am not unaware of the uneasiness which this so necessary measure may cause in some sectors." He firmly concluded: "It is not a question of changing the command in the battle nor of substitutions contrary to the interest of the country, but of defining the regime and assuring the succession. . . . The institution which we forge must be stronger and greater than the possible errors of individual persons; in it, there must be totally guaranteed the spirit of our Movement." These were words of little solace to disheartened Falangists—but the political circumstances were too critical for them to protest the fusion of the spirit of the Party with the flesh of the Monarchy. They could only be weak but willing. It was the price of survival.

Within one week of the delivery of this speech, General Franco effected the most fundamental change in his government since the end of the Civil War. He had to act quickly and decisively, not only because of the need to seek to accommodate his regime to the realities of a world of victorious United Nations, but also because his cabinet was torn by a division almost as grave as that of 1942. The protagonists in this latest struggle within the government were the Minister of the Party, José Luis Arrese, and Foreign Minister José Felix Lequerica.

I have already mentioned José Luis Arrese several times: the accomplice of Hedilla in the attempted coup d'état against Franco in 1937, the political prisoner sentenced to seventeen years of hard labor for that crime, but pardoned three years later, the Provincial Chief of the Falange in Málaga, Serrano Suñer's trusted lieutenant, the betrayer of Suñer, finally Suñer's successor. An ardent revolutionary, a shrill orator, a skillful pamphleteer, Arrese, appearing in person on an official occasion, looks disturbingly like the Caudillo's barber or tailor whose vanity has been humored by an invitation to a state function—coarse unruly hair, watery brown eyes, thick stubble across his chin and cheeks, wet sensuous lips shadowed by a long curving nose, extraordinarily long arms dangling at the sides of a short body, moist hands with dirty fingernails, clothes that bag at elbows and knees. He has been the pride and guide of the Falange.

José Felix Lequerica first won a dubious kind of fame as Spanish Ambassador to the Vichy French government in 1940. After the rout of the French armies, he had served as mediator between Marshal Pétain and the Germans in negotiation of the armistice. At diplomatic functions in Vichy the following year, he attracted comment and attention by his habitual sporting of the Falange Party uniform. At a diplomatic dinner in December he toasted his Japanese guests on the occasion of their entry into Manila. A Basque by birth, wealthy, and well-educated, Lequerica had made some substantial donations of money to the Falange in the early thirties, but his more habitual pose was that of a conservative Monarchist.

Lequerica was a surprise choice of General Franco to become Foreign Minister when General Jordana (who had succeeded Serrano Suñer) died in August of 1944 as the result of a hunting accident. Some of the reasons inspiring Franco's choice of Lequerica were typically fatuous, others typically sly. One factor was that Franco was earnestly playing with the idea of Spain acting as mediator between the Axis and the United Nations to achieve a negotiated peace: since Lequerica had had this kind of experience before, he might fit the role nicely a second time. In terms of domestic politics, Lequerica had flirted with the Falange enough for the Party to have no objection to him, while his allegedly conservative and Monarchist sympathies found favor with the Army. Finally, to appoint him Foreign Minister was a delicate way of withdrawing an ambassador from Vichy at a time when Allied armies racing through France would shortly make him an embarrassing diplomatic anachronism.

A gracious and charming man socially, Lequerica was undoubtedly just as much a political opportunist as Serrano Suñer. But any resemblance ended there: Lequerica was of vastly superior intelligence, efficiency, and personal honor. He understood the methods of diplomacy and the urgent need of Spain to trim its foreign policy close to any prescription made by the Western democracies. His predecessor, General Jordana, had been a man of unimpeachable integrity who had already begun the task of re-orienting Spanish foreign policy, who was certainly inspired by more spontaneous sympathy for the United Nations than was Lequerica. But Lequerica, moving in the same political direction with probably less disinterested motives, proved more effective and more alert than his earnest but slow-moving predecessor. Diplomats of the United Nations in Madrid found that he was capable of carrying through virtually every action that he promised, hammering it through the most intransigeant opposition of Germanophile and Falangist officials. Whatever may have been his political aberrations in past years, as Foreign Minister he found the persistent obstructionism of the Falange intolerable, and its personification in José Luis Arrese insufferable.

Lequerica's mistake seems to have been that he went too far—not in his firm redirection of Spanish foreign policy but in his desire (rightful enough) to claim for himself all credit for the change. He became so anxious to win favor in Allied diplomatic circles that he spent much of his conversational time tactlessly relating the obstacles which other Spanish officials placed in his way—officials who included the Generalissimo himself. In this courting of American and British favor, Lequerica was joined by another cabinet minister: Eduardo

Aunós, Minister of Justice. The two became firm allies in their battles within the cabinet against the stubborn Arrese.

Neither the brash boasting of Lequerica nor the split within the cabinet could be tolerated for long by the Chief of State. Diplomats and foreign correspondents in Madrid were confident that Arrese would be ousted, but few remembered the tactics which General Franco had employed three years earlier when he had dismissed Serrano Suñer, and therefore few anticipated the drastic scope of the changes which Franco would make in July of 1945. Arrese was dismissed. But Lequerica went also, to be replaced by Martín Artajo, and found unexpected company in his close official associate, Eduardo Aunós, dismissed to make way for ardent Falangist Fernandez Cuesta in the Ministry of Justice.

While the selection of this cabinet bore the old mark of General Franco's eclectic brand of politics, deferring and appealing to distinct and conflicting groups at the same time, on this occasion something new had been added: the allegiance of Catholic Action, personified in Martín Artajo. In the light of this appointment, General Franco's speech of July 17 a few days earlier assumed clearer significance. The inspiration for that address, it was apparent, came not from any sudden spontaneous concern over the matter of "succession," but from the immediate desire to appeal to the Monarchist and anti-Falangist convictions of a majority of Catholic Action. That speech was an essential oratorical prelude to winning Martín Artajo and to making him Spain's Foreign Minister.

The proposal to appoint Martín Artajo took Catholic Action leaders by complete surprise and precipitated a violent debate within its ranks. To a great many, thankful that thus far under the Franco regime their organization had been scrupulously cautious and inconspicuous politically, it seemed that Martín Artajo's acceptance would be the grossest political folly. Though he would formally have to resign as Director of the *Junta Técnica* before accepting a political post (according to the rules of Catholic Action), his acceptance could not fail to

identify the entire organization with the government of which
he would become a part—and precisely at a time, immediately
after the end of the European war, when Madrid fully expected a diplomatic attack from the United Nations.[2]

But the overture of General Franco held definite attractions
for those who thought, like the Cardinal Primate, that Communism's advance in Europe urgently demanded that Spain
maintain a "strong" anti-Communist regime. These advocates
of collaboration contended that the Generalissimo's July 17
speech clearly committed him to political retirement and Monarchic restoration. Moreover, General Franco had assured
Martín Artajo that the new cabinet would be purged of all
traces of Falange influence. And the Chief of State also hinted
plainly that he would very shortly appoint a transitory
"Council of the Realm" upon which his power would be con-
ferred to be passed on to a new King of Spain. The Primate
and Martín Artajo agreed to accept the appointment.

If they were surprised by the original offer of General
Franco, they were shocked when they saw the full cabinet
slate into which Martín Artajo's name had been written. No
less than four important ministries—Labor, Agriculture, Education, and Justice—were placed under leading Falangists, including the suddenly resurrected Fernandez Cuesta. This fact
was no less extraordinary than the fact that, in all probability,
the Generalissimo had been sincere in his original project to
eradicate Falangist influence in the cabinet by appointing such
conservative Monarchist sympathizers as the Catalonian financier Juan Ventosa. But for the first time he had struck an unexpected obstacle. Monarchist sympathizers had flatly refused
to enter his cabinet. Both his anger at this rebuff and the sheer
necessity of falling back upon the Party to find men willing

[2] Before hitting upon the choice of Martín Artajo, one of Franco's
thoughts had been to offer the Ministry of Foreign Affairs to one of the
most distinguished generals in the Spanish Army. The offer was never officially extended, but the rumor of its coming reached the general. To a
close friend, he stated his reaction tersely: "It's too late in my life to ruin
my career that way." Martín Artajo is a younger man by many years.

to accept the jobs compelled the Chief of State to revise drastically the program he had outlined to Catholic Action. He merely failed to advise Catholic Action of this fact. But what remained inexplicable was the apparent failure of Monarchist and Catholic Action leaders to agree on a common political stand, instead of confusing and defeating each other.

Out of the confusion the Generalissimo emerged happily. At a time when one political group found it possible to snub their Chief of State, he found it possible to harness the power and prestige of Catholic Action. Everyone in Madrid understood, moreover, that this had implications extending far beyond the domestic scene. The apparent identification of Catholic Action with his regime would carry enormous impact on Catholic opinion throughout the world—opinion which could exert strong influence on the decisions of foreign governments in their relations with the Spanish government.

Since that critical July of 1945, while the Spanish hierarchy has been fulsome in its public praise of the Franco regime, Catholic Action has been divided against itself (a fact which must be scored as another political victory for the Generalissimo). A large group delightedly accepted the opinion of Martín Artajo that his action meant nothing more nor less than the best way to battle the Communist forces winning ascendance in so much of the rest of Europe; and that moderate change in the Spanish regime (in the direction of Monarchic restoration) could be achieved with greater speed by working within the government than by trying to bully it from the outside. Despite their initial disillusionment with the cabinet slate as a whole, advocates of this position thought they found confirmation of their argument in January of the following year when the press and propaganda controls were taken from the Falange and intrusted to two new Catholic Action appointees in the Ministry of Education, Luis Ortiz Muñoz and Tomás Cerro Corrochano.

But it was not generally known that these two men accepted their official posts only after they had twice refused them and only after Martín Artajo had persuaded them to change their stand. Their first spontaneous refusal reflected the conviction of a large bloc of Catholic Action that Martín Artajo's entrance into the government had been a colossal blunder. For so long as the Generalissimo could successfully summon the support of so powerful a group as Catholic Action, he would be more than ever convinced of his own political infallibility. And if the issue resolved itself into a struggle within the government between Artajo, the advocate of reform and change, and Franco, the fanatic believer in his own indispensability, no *Madrileño* could doubt for an instant who would prove to be the superior political tactician.

The disinterested integrity of Martín Artajo's intentions could be questioned no more than his painful lack of political experience. Only in physique has he towered over his Chief of State. Broad-shouldered and tall, alert and youthful in his forties, his appearance and movements suggest a vigor and purposefulness that is rarely evident in his political activities. A lawyer by profession, his work in Catholic Action has virtually been his career. Educated by the Jesuits, he achieved a distinguished scholastic record. As a youth, he demonstrated his religious devotion by making the traditional pilgrimage on foot from Madrid to Santiago de Compostela. Active in Catholic university organizations, he joined the staff of Catholic Action's famous *El Debate* in his twenties, won some recognition for a strenuous anti-Communist editorial campaign. Shortly afterward he flirted intellectually with corporative theories of the state and wrote one undistinguished book on Catholic social doctrine. He displayed industry and administrative competence in a number of charitable and propagandistic activities connected with Catholic Action, and he was only in his middle thirties when he became Director of Catholic Action's *Junta Técnica*.

Not a single aspect of this career suggests the slightest acquaintance with raw politics, foreign affairs, or the methods of diplomacy. On the day when he took his oath of office, his cabinet issued to the Spanish people a communiqué describing its political purpose with a vague simplicity that was sincere and a political naïveté that was pathetic: "The new government, in beginning today its political life, affirms its faith in the future of Spain, confident that all Spaniards will continue to contribute to the great enterprise of erecting upon its traditional foundations the definitive structure of the Spanish State." Today that structure looks no more definitive, the "traditional" foundations no more in evidence, than at the moment when Martín Artajo swore his allegiance to the Chief of the Spanish State. Tomorrow, were those foundations suddenly to appear, they would be the result, not of Martín Artajo's labors, but of inexorable international circumstances.

The sad truth is that, since the day when Artajo became Foreign Minister, Spain's troubled international position has left him little time to study the delicate task of persuading General Franco to vacate the Pardo. He had been in office only ten days when the Potsdam Communiqué hurled a diplomatic grenade at Madrid with its firm statement barring Spain from membership in the United Nations because its government "does not, in view of its origin, its nature, its record, and its close association with the aggressor states, possess the qualifications necessary to justify such membership." Since that statement was issued, the series of stinging indictments of the Franco regime issuing from foreign chancelleries has compelled the youthful foreign minister to devote most of his attention to preparing denials and defenses for the government of which he is a member. .

The result has been plain to see. The man who entered General Franco's cabinet to accelerate change in the regime has emerged as the regime's most prominent public apologist. In little more than a month after he took office, Artajo's political role became clearly defined in his own declarations to the Spanish press (*Arriba,* August 23, 1945) proclaiming the legitimacy of General Franco's rule. He accepted the easy expedient of dismissing all foreign criticism of that rule as merely "the extraordinary international activity which atheistic Communism fosters, and its fundamental hostility to our country." He denied the Potsdam charge that the very origin of the Spanish regime branded it as a creature of the Fascist powers: "The Army, supported by the larger and better part of the people, rose against the tyranny of an unchecked multitude and, after a heroic struggle, succeeded in re-establishing order and installing a legal state." He defended the record of Spanish foreign policy during World War II with the preposterous assertion that "there never was any kind of concession, neither in the political nor the commercial nor the economic spheres, to the nations of the Axis."

What of Spain's future? Only a few weeks earlier had it not seemed to hold such regal promise?

Hopefully, the Foreign Minister believed that General Franco's Government "is heading toward new forms of popular representation and political liberty."

Cautiously, apologetically, he added: "It is absolutely necessary that Spain be able to carry out its political evolution at the pace and through the stages which are prescribed by our particular national character."

Weakly, almost wistfully, he concluded: "One day our political system will develop into the traditional Monarchy."

One day . . . some day . . . maybe not tomorrow.

But until the Prince would come, in this unromantic age not riding any gallant white charger but merely first-class on the Lusitania Express from Lisbon . . . until that day, the little textbooks in the little schools would continue to explain carefully to the little children of Spain:

"Spain is a totalitarian country and its Chief is His Excellency, the Caudillo."

El Caudillo. Commander in Chief of the Army, Navy, and Air Forces. Chief of the Movement. Defender of the Faith.

THE BATTLE FOR SPAIN

5 THE FALANGE PROPAGANDA MACHINE

BISHOPS of the Church, knights of the Army, castles in the air built of the Falange's promise of social revolution—all these have played their necessary roles in the complex game of political chess by which Francisco Franco has perpetuated his rule. But these alone could never have been enough. There have been, of course, the pawns as well. Their manipulation has been intrusted to a propaganda machine utterly typical of the totalitarian state, masterfully trained in the supple and sinuous strategy of deception and delusion, calculatedly conceived to excite and exploit the desired fears and hopes of the Spanish people—to cut and claw a nation's raw nerves laid bare by the ugly wounds of civil war.

I find it difficult to write about the propaganda machine of the Spanish State with any dispassionate objectivity. My official work in Madrid demanded such constant contact and conflict with it as to deprive me of that fine, broad perspective that can be enjoyed only at a certain distance from the object in view. But, for anyone with faith in democracy, another obstacle in the way of fair objectivity must be his profound fear and abhorrence of what such a propaganda machine attempts to do to the intellectual integrity of a people. Perhaps the atrocities of the Spanish State's security police are more melodramatic and shocking than the lies of its propagandists. Perhaps to crush a prisoner's skull with a club in a single murderous moment is a crime more reprehensible than to spend years striving to warp the mind inside. But I doubt it.

Even if all moral judgment is suspended, however, the political facts of the case should be recorded and known. For this is no mere academic matter of propaganda techniques which have only a kind of clinical interest. This is an issue involving the very mentality of a whole government and the enormous enterprise of endeavoring to impress that mentality upon a whole people.

2

The two extraordinary personalities who developed and, until 1946, directed the propaganda machine of the Spanish State were Gabriel Arias-Salgado and Juan Aparicio. The former held the office of Vice-Secretary of Popular Education, responsible not to any regular government ministry but only to the Secretary General of the Party. The Vice-Secretariat included four departments (or *delegaciones*) charged respectively with control of press, radio, motion pictures, and propaganda. Chief of the first of these departments, with the title of *Delegado de Prensa*, Juan Aparicio served as Arias-Salgado's first lieutenant.

(In January, 1946, Aparicio and Arias-Salgado were replaced by two men sponsored by Catholic Action, Luis Ortiz Muñoz and Tomás Cerro Corrochano. The previous July, by decree of Franco, the Vice-Secretariat had been abolished and the control of press and propaganda assigned to a new division created within the regular Ministry of Education, baptized the Sub-Secretariat of Popular Education. This action was supposed to signify the end of Falange control over the press and radio, but in fact the same Falangist officials—Aparicio and Arias-Salgado—continued to hold office. It was not until January 12, 1946, that General Franco found time to replace these men, though their positions officially had been abolished. Both the appointment of new officials and a subsequent official decree (March 26, 1946) granting "a greater freedom of movement" to the press were actions supposed to herald a new era of modified censorship. The amount of "freedom" involved could be judged by the warning in the March 26 decree: "The greater liberty which . . . is conceded to newspapers under no circumstances will be used to jeopardize the unity of the Fatherland, its foreign and domestic security, the fundamental institutions of the Spanish State, the persons who embody them, the rights proclaimed by the *Fuero de los Españoles,* principles of Catholic dogma and morals, ecclesiastical persons or institutions.")

Arias-Salgado and Aparicio worked together with greater harmony and mutual understanding than seemed possible in view of their contrasting characters and temperaments. The Vice-Secretary had been a pupil of the Jesuits. In his youth, he had studied for the priesthood, then gave it up to become an aspirin salesman. Born and raised in Galicia, he had maintained a lifelong acquaintance with the family of Franco, which was the only possible explanation for his appointment to the post of Civil Governor of Salamanca during the Civil War. In 1941, when he knew no more about the press or the radio than about nuclear science, he was chosen by Franco to head the propaganda machine of the State, for no apparent reason other than Franco's confidence in his personal loyalty.

In striking contrast, Aparicio ranks as one of the earliest revolutionary apostles of Spanish Fascism, belonging to the group around Ledesma Ramos which launched *The Conquest of the State* in 1931. Even in this extremist company, he had always distinguished himself by the radicalism and fervor of his social and economic beliefs. Indeed, he had been on the verge of joining the Communist Party at just the moment when the group around Ledesma had begun to form. He was equally conspicuous as a leader of the anticlerical wing of the Party. During the Civil War, he was named editor of the *Diario* of Salamanca, on the basis of a short and undistinguished journalistic career, and in 1941 accompanied Arias-Salgado to Madrid to become the dictator of Spain's press.

As personalities, neither of these two men was remarkable or distinguished. Arias-Salgado, while lacking practical knowledge of the most elementary problems of newspapers or radio or motion pictures, valiantly sought to conceal his ignorance with great urbanity of manner, effusiveness, vigorous gesticulation, and loud but vacuous rhetoric about the "Crusade" of 1936 and the new, beautiful Spanish Syndicalist State. Aparicio did not have to speak to make an impression. A round, swarthy face, propped by two flabby chins and always looking as if it had just been bathed in oil, swiveled nervously on top of a corpulent body, which he always steered with a solemn, determined dignity. His dark eyes invariably suggested either fright or anger. He was so much the caricature of the plump Fascist boss that one would have expected to find in a small provincial village in Fascist Italy that, on first meeting, it was difficult to believe that his office was not a theatrical stage. Of the two men, I believe Aparicio was the more intelligent, the more dangerous, the more fanatic.

It was the notorious Vice-Secretariat of Popular Education, under the direction of these men, which was directly responsible for the flagrant bias of the Spanish press throughout World War II: its shrill delight over every Nazi triumph, its cheap abuse of leaders of the United Nations, its shameful plagiarism of every axiom and cliché propounded by Dr. Goebbels. During the years 1943 and 1944 the Party press became so ludicrously and hysterically pro-Nazi that *Madrileños* half-jestingly, half-seriously jibed that yesterday's headline in such-and-such a paper read: CONDITIONS IN BERLIN MUCH BETTER THAN HITLER ADMITS. And I did know of several instances late in 1944 when frantically Germanophile editors in Madrid actually suppressed German military communiqués because, as one of them said, "their tone is too despondent!"

Our American Embassy press office was charged with the task of trying to force the responsible government officials, by protest and argument, to practice their protestations about "strict neutrality." As the Embassy's press attaché, I was authorized to wage these verbal battles directly with the Vice-Secretariat rather than leave protests to follow the frequently sluggish course of *Notes Verbales* through the tortuous channels of the Foreign Office. This procedure also was followed because the limitations of diplomatic language were such that it could never be expected to penetrate the idea-proof armor around the minds of the Vice-Secretary and his lieutenants. Simply as one example of my correspondence with the Vice-Secretariat, one which is typical both of the language used and the provocation provided, I will give the following letter of March 24, 1944, addressed to Sr. Arias-Salgado:

I have just received from the National Delegate of Propaganda his letter of March 21, which forbids the showing "in all Spanish territory" of the pictures *Casablanca* and *How a Soldier Is Trained.* . . . The basis for this prohibition, as stated in the letter to which I refer, is that the films "in their content do not respond to the concept of *strict neutrality* which is fundamental in the Spanish State."

Needless to state, I am always happy to see such reassuring statements of Spanish policy. I am surprised and disappointed to see, however, as I have in recent days, such striking concrete evidence that these assurances are not carried out in fact. It might even be said that these assurances seem rather to be a deliberate effort to disguise the facts. . . .

I have just been informed of the details of the grossly unneutral censorship imposed on the RKO film, *The Vatican of Pius XII.* Last October this film was submitted to censorship and wholly rejected. An appeal was made against this unjust ruling by the RKO company. The picture finally was approved—but, under order of a communication from the National Commission of Film Censorship dated December 24, the distributors were ordered to:

1st   Suppress all reference to persecution of the Catholic Church in Germany.
2nd   Suppress dialogue and scenes, referring to the presence of a representative of President Roosevelt at the Vatican.

3rd Suppress all dialogue and scenes referring to the existence of an American College in the Vatican.

Even with this astounding censorship, on January 11 your office suddenly reinstated the total prohibition on the showing of the film. It was appealed again. On March 11, the picture was again approved—but with the above censorship restrictions and with the additional injunction that the entire sequence referring to the visit of Pope Pius XII (as Cardinal Pacelli) to the United States must be deleted!

Is this the "strict neutrality" about which the National Delegate of Propaganda has just written me?

Is it true that the Falange Party—with all its talk of basing its doctrines upon supposedly Catholic foundations—is anxious to suppress the truth about the persecution of the Catholic Church?

Is it true that "strict neutrality" means that a film shown in Spain cannot admit the existence of an American College in the Vatican, or the presence of an American envoy, or the occurrence of the present Pope's visit to the United States?

In short, it seems necessary to inquire if the concept of "strict neutrality" does not truly mean only a veil of words behind which is patiently practiced a systematic discrimination against the United States and the United Nations.

Although our protests in this instance happened to produce the desired results, on other occasions, particularly in conferences with the Sres. Arias-Salgado and Aparicio, intelligible conversation was made impossible by an attitude of mind so tenaciously Fascist as to prohibit the most modest exchange of ideas. One of the Vice-Secretary's standard devices, when confronted with evidence of some slanderous attack on President Roosevelt in the Spanish press, was to exclaim excitedly that the American press said things just as harsh about General Franco, the head of a state with which America maintained normal diplomatic relations. To this, I would reply, of course, that his analogy was absurd because every American newspaper was free to speak its own opinions on any subject, whether it be Franco or the President of the United States; but in Spain every paper was an effective organ of the government, hence attacks upon the United States or its leaders obviously received official approval or they could not appear. And to this, in one exceptionally heated conversation, Arias-Salgado replied: "All American newspapers have to accept advertising and political contributions, so their freedom is a pure chimera. If President Roosevelt *wanted* to limit press freedom, he *could*. So the press is free only to the extent that the government *allows* it to be— and no more so. So you see the situation is the same as in Spain, except that here the State's power is exercised and in your country it is not. The power to censor exists in both places, so your press is no more free than ours."

This line of argument so appalled me, as a kind of Fascist dialectic bordering on madness, that when I returned to my office after this conference, I made detailed notes of the conversation. It took the following course:

EH—"It is in no sense a question of power but of principle. Freedom of the press is a basic principle of our life and is not of yours. President Roosevelt could neither create nor kill it. General Franco—or you—can do to the press what you like, whenever you like."

AS—"Well, then, do you mean that if I write a letter to *The New York Times* attacking the liberal ideas of your country, it will be published?"

EH—"If well enough written, almost certainly. What is certain is that it would not be censored because the editor did not agree with it."

AS—"But that is monstrous. . . . Worse, it's ridiculous! . . . What does freedom mean, anyway? Is everyone in the United States free to take opium and sell it without fear of punishment? Can you be free to write letters to your town newspapers urging your neighbor to murder his father?"

EH—"You're talking about morals or medicine, not politics or political rights. Perhaps the simplest definition of the freedom I mean is this: In the United States, no individual need fear—as millions do here—that any night, without warning, government police may come to their home, drag them from bed to jail without either explanation or trial or excuse."

AS—"What! Do you mean to say that trials are not framed in the
United States, that courts are not filled with unjust rulings?
What difference does it make to an arrested criminal if you put
him in jail or through a trial first, when he knows what his sentence will be anyway?"

EH—"My first answer would be that, if you do not think there is a
difference, ask a criminal. Secondly, the very fact you immediately label him a 'criminal' betrays the procedure you follow.
Who is his judge? You?"

AS—"*De Ninguna manera!* REASON IS THE JUDGE . . . etc. . . . etc.
. . . etc. . . ."

This conversation conveys in a way which mere allegation
cannot, the character of the Falangist mind. Men of this mentality had the authority to prescribe the character of the entire
press of the nation.

This authority was exercised in a variety of true totalitarian
ways. To every newspaper in the country the Falange (*i.e.*, the
Vice-Secretariat) appointed a director whose single job was to
be vigilant and firm in enforcing his newspaper's fidelity to
Falange instructions. The director's authority was unlimited
and was backed by the whole weight of the Party. Among the
nation's newspapers, the situations created by these arbitrary
appointments took different forms. In some instances, in which
the Falange-appointed director was also both the actual editor
and the proprietor of the paper, there was no internal conflict.
An example of this arrangement was the evening journal
Madrid under Juan Pujol, who, although known in his earlier
years as a Germanophile and identified with Franco's propaganda office during the Civil War, possessed at least more
journalistic experience and ability than most Falange appointees. But in countless other instances, the Party's appointments afflicted many of the oldest and most reputable journals
with men of little experience, less integrity and in violent conflict with either the proprietors or editors of the newspapers.
A typical case was *Ya*, the Madrid morning organ of *Editorial
Católica.* Throughout the war it strove to be the most impar-

tial and often pro-Allied journal in Spain. But its able employees, many inherited from pre-Civil War days, were constantly harassed by the incompetence and frankly pro-Fascist instructions of its director, Juan Pradera: a man of no journalistic qualifications who earned the contempt of all decent Spanish newspapermen for his stupidity, his vengeful attitude toward Allied sympathizers, his despicable tactics of currying favor with Falangist authorities by running to them with every scrap of gossip or conversation which might indict one of his colleagues for lack of enthusiasm for the Party. All efforts of *Editorial Católica* to get him removed were rebuffed by the Falange.

A similar situation developed with the traditional Monarchist daily *ABC,* owned by the Marqués Luca de Tena. To act as custodian of this paper, the Vice-Secretariat of Popular Education had appointed José Losada, who came to rank beside Pradera as an incompetent and unscrupulous tool of the Party, even worse than Pradera in his subservience to the Press Section of the German Embassy. As in the case of *Ya,* so the owners of *ABC* had to suffer either the control imposed by the Falange or confiscation of its property. In 1944, I did my best to force the removal of Losada on the basis of correspondence I discovered which had passed between him and the German press attaché, Hans Lazar. The letters were striking proof that Losada was little better than an employee of the German Embassy. I submitted photostatic copies to the Foreign Office, whose conservative career diplomats always welcomed material it could use in its battle to curb the Falange—and this was serious material. But the Vice-Secretariat stood firm in supporting Losada, and he continued to throttle *ABC* until March of 1946. Then he was removed and given the appropriate post of press attaché in the Spanish Embassy in Argentina.

Its authority to appoint directors to every newspaper in Spain was the Falange's first, most obvious method of control. A second, equally powerful instrument in the hands of the Party has been the allocation of newsprint. The Falange's

Paper Syndicate, controlling the importation and distribution of newsprint, has been under the direction of Guillén Salaya, an ex-Anarchist who joined the JONS movement at its outset and quickly became one of its most violent left-wing leaders: a burly, arrogant, uneducated man, who, to judge by his personal appearance, apparently views dentists and barbers with the same contempt he has for liberals or Americans.

This control of newsprint stocks has been a scandal, both journalistically and economically. No new newspaper, of course, could be founded in Spain without both the express permission of the Party and some assurance of receiving an equitable paper supply; as a consequence, no independent paper has been founded since the Civil War ended. At the same time, by its arbitrary allocation of paper to all newspapers, the Party has been able to enforce its prescribed ceilings on the circulation of non-Falange journals by citing the newsprint shortage as the justification. And on any occasions when a newspaper has not heeded Falange directives scrupulously, it has sufficed for the Party to reduce its allotment of newsprint to bring its editors into line.

At one and the same time, newsprint control has been a punitive power used against the non-Party press and a protective power for organs of the Falange. Preferential treatment for the latter has worked in more than one way. While it puts a brake on competition, it has saved many Falangist organs from bankruptcy. When a Party journal has been unable to sell more than a small percentage of its authorized editions, rather than suffer a reduction in newsprint supply (as would be inflicted on a non-Party journal), it has continued to receive its large allocations and thereby been enabled to sell its excess newsprint on the black market. Money thus gained not only goes into local Party war chests but is pumped back into a paper which otherwise would lose even too much for the Falange to support. A typical example among many papers in this class has been the *Solidaridad Nacional* of Barcelona, one of the most luridly Fascist papers in Spain, saved only by its black market manipulations.

A third decisive instrument in the hands of the Party has been complete control of the supply of news in Spain. The national news agency EFE enjoys an effective monopoly and a lavish government subsidy. In fact, EFE is not an official agency of the government but a privately-owned corporation whose board of directors has included a number of strongly anti-Falange figures. Despite this and also a number of minor conflicts with the Vice-Secretariat on matters of policy and administration, EFE has served the purposes of the Party or it would not have been allowed to exist. The news which EFE services to the nation's press is vigilantly censored in the nation's capital before release to the papers. (A "confidential" service of accurate world news is distributed to all important government officials, who are thus infinitely better informed than one would guess from reading the Spanish press.) Even when it reaches provincial cities, EFE's service is not immune from further censorship but is subject to the whims of local censors who, judging any item "imprudent," can forbid its publication.

While this ponderous and powerful machinery of the Falange has been at work, its labors have been prescribed by the system of government directives, emanating from the Vice-Secretariat of Popular Education. These directives from Madrid are in turn supplemented by directives from the *Jefaturas Provinciales,* which either elaborate on instructions received from Madrid or merely express the caprice of local authorities—backed by the full weight of the Party. The system of control by directives has been so rigid and all-encompassing that a few words cannot adequately suggest its character. For that reason, I am reproducing the exact texts of a few official directives issued over the last several years. All of these, of course, were classified as "confidential" or "secret" by the Falange authorities. The following selection is indicative of

their tone and of the infinite variety of news subjects over
which the Party's censors have watched with such care. . . .

November 9, 1939

It is absolutely prohibited to make any comment on the events in
Munich in connection with the attempt on the life of Chancellor
Hitler. Publication is authorized only of such news referring to the
event as is supplied by the EFE Agency, and this should be done
without undue prominence. Again we recall the total prohibition on
publishing a single news item received from foreign radios.

November 30, 1939

In the report on the ceremonies at El Escorial, it will be said that
the Caudillo wore the uniform of national chief of the Falange, but
no mention will be made of the fact that this was the first time he
did so.

January 17, 1940

The newspapers will refrain from publishing any news referring
to the automobile which Hitler has presented to the Generalissimo.

June 23, 1940

Although the confidential character of the directives emanating
from this office has been stressed repeatedly, again it is necessary to
insist upon it, because frequently there reach the Vice-Secretariat
versions of these, distorted by rumor, proving the existence of indis-
creetness in the handling of orders which must be attended with the
greatest reserve.

October 31, 1940

The newspapers will refrain from judging or prejudging the work
of the Government or the Administration, as well as from publishing
commentaries, over any signature whatsoever, which call for improv-
ing any function of the Government.

June 10, 1941

In commentaries on military developments in Syria, the newspapers will refrain from formulating or forecasting German-Italian
plans, while at all times paying careful attention to the official news
and communiqués from Berlin and Rome.

October 6, 1941

ATTENTION! ATTENTION! ATTENTION!

All newspapers will be obliged to publish three commentaries on the recent accords between Great Britain and the Soviet Union, with attention to the following instructions. . . .

The accords which recently have been received between the representatives of the democratic states and the Bolshevik leaders constitute a peril of the first magnitude for all Europe.

The democracies, in their frenzy to defend and maintain at all costs their existence in the face of the states of the New Order, have been blinded by their hatred. . . . Now Stalin has demanded and obtained from the democracies, as price for his collaboration, an open road for Bolshevik propaganda. Thus the men of London and Washington have placed themselves completely at the service of the Bolshevization of Europe and the annihilation of western culture. . . .

The unanimity and collaboration of all conscientious European nations in the battle against such dangers is in the interest of maintaining the cultural patrimony of Europe and signifies nothing less than the very life of the peoples of Europe.

January 29, 1942

Tomorrow the 30th is the celebration of the ninth anniversary of the rise to power of Hitler and National Socialism. The newspapers are reminded to make the opportune commentary.

February 5, 1942

All newspapers are forbidden to publish the law which is carried in today's Official Bulletin of the State on the regularization of the debt to Italy.

Instruction No. 29, 1942

The newspapers will take care that in the section devoted to feminine fashions there will appear no mention of the attractiveness of Paris fashions, since the survival of this old custom harms the attempts now being made to nationalize fashions in Spain.

September 23, 1944

It is absolutely forbidden by the National Press Delegation to use the word "Party" when referring to the organization of *Falange*

Española Tradicionalista y de las JONS, and instead there will be used only the word "Movement." . . . For God, Spain and its National Syndicalist Revolution.

3

In its desperate effort to withstand the shock of the decline and destruction of the Fascist powers, the propaganda machine of the Spanish State carried out an evolution in policy truly remarkable for its brazen dishonesty and appalling hypocrisy. Yet we would make no more foolish mistake than to allow our judgment of its integrity to confuse our judgment of its efficacy. We who have seen the whole panorama of Fascism unfold before us in the last two decades should have learned at least the bitter lesson that evil *can* prevail.

Under Falangist direction, the Spanish press and radio have followed the line of expediency in both the foreign and domestic spheres, simultaneously redefining its attitude toward World War II and drastically revising the characterization of the Spanish regime itself. In international policy, by the summer of 1943 the uncertainty of Axis victory became so obvious that the Vice-Secretariat decided to issue, in July of that year, a long political directive to the Spanish press completely revising all previous instructions. Starting from the principle that "We must consider world events with the necessary objectivity and realism," the Vice-Secretary asserted: "At no time have we said that the result of the Allied war effort would be to implant Communism in Europe." I cannot imagine what reaction the Vice-Secretary anticipated in his provincial lieutenants when they read this astonishing declaration, but there was no conscious humor in his tone as he continued:

The first, most important and decisive fact . . . is that SPAIN HAS NOT ENTERED THE WAR. . . . The vicissitudes of war, with its oscillations alternately favorable to one side or the other, may provoke satisfaction or regret among various sections of the population, but the Spanish State . . . has maintained its policy of

nonintervention. . . . Spain is subservient to no political interna-
tionalism. . . . Assistance received during the Civil War was directed
against Communism. . . .

A war always offers two possibilities: that of winning or losing.
Whoever enters a war knows this law. If he wins, he obtains advantages; if he loses, he suffers the consequences of defeat. What cannot
be is the chance of losing without the chance of winning—and for
that reason it would be ridiculous to link the fate of a country to the
result of a war in which it is not participating. By its own decision,
SPAIN IS NOT AT WAR.

This document meant more than the first official evidence of
the Falange's effort to rewrite three years of history. It was also
a supreme example of Falangist duplicity. The document from
which I have quoted was marked "confidential," but the Vice-
Secretariat made sure that it reached the hands of the American Embassy, which was supposed to applaud it as an eloquent
expression of Spanish neutrality. At the same time, the Falange
dispatched a *secret* directive to all newspapers instructing them
to disregard this "confidential" statement of policy and continue as before! The American Embassy, of course, was not supposed to see the secret directive.

It was not until one year later, in a directive dated August
23, 1944, that the national press received genuine orders to
adopt a policy accenting Spain's "neutrality." The Vice-Secretariat of Popular Education supplemented these orders with a
series of directives—all marked "confidential" and dated September 5, September 13, September 21, and September 28—
explaining with precision the new line of Falangist propaganda. Rather than cite lengthy quotations from the original
texts, which are in my possession, I shall summarize the important points:

1. The Spanish press was to hammer the theme that there were in
   reality two wars: in Europe, a war against Communism, and in
   the Far East, a war against Japan. While not actively intervening
   in either war, Spain extended her sympathies to those fighting
   both Russia and Japan.

2. The common denominator to be stressed, identifying Japan and Russia with one another, was the fact that both were "Asiatic" powers. In both wars, "Europe" and "western civilization" must be defended—by checking both the Russian and Japanese onrushes.

3. Spain's closest historic bonds were not with any European powers, even those who had aided her during the Civil War, but with the Latin American countries; and these were overwhelmingly on the side of the Allies.

4. The continuation of hostilities in Europe was to be deplored, both for the ruin it was bringing and the conditions it would produce favorable for Communist expansion.

Only a few months remained before the total collapse of Germany at the time when the Spanish press received these instructions. And yet, despite these directives from Madrid, supposedly "liberalizing" the official attitude toward news of and from the United Nations, whole areas of important information continued to be blacked-out by Falange censorship. To this day, no news worthy of the name has been published by the Spanish press on Nazi persecution of Jews and Christians in Germany. Men of the underground movements in German-occupied countries continued to be depicted always as Communist vandals, disorganized and ineffectual. Only after the war's end could any news—and little then—be published on Nazi atrocities. At the same time, every effort was made to wring tears from the people of Spain with gruesome stories of Allied bombings of German cities; and for the last six months of the war, the Allies were depicted as vengeful prolongers of a bloody conflict at a time when all the world wanted "peace."

Juventud, weekly publication of the Falange Youth Front, in its issue of April 18, 1944, cried out in typical Falangist anguish in a front-page editorial spread across the entire first page and headlined, THE WORLD DEMANDS PEACE: It argued:

The war has reached a point of such scope and confusion that it is absolutely impossible for it to end with the absolute victory of either one of the *bandos.* . . . Why, then, does the machinery of war continue running, with its swift rhythm? The Allies affirmed for months their fear of German imperialism; the German threat, according to their propaganda, was sufficient reason for all peoples of the world to unite in defense of peace and freedom. The United States dragged its masses to war waving the banner of a possible German invasion of American soil. These were the arguments of the United Nations to convince their peoples of the necessity of annihilating Hitler's Germany. Now, at the end of five years, can the Anglo-Saxon countries defend the same thesis? . . . The present reality is very different. . . . Germany has ceased all advances of an imperialist nature and is waging a defensive war. . . .

Peace is something more than a desire of Humanity, at the end of five unprecedented years of battle and effort. It is an imperative need demanded by the most elementary historic interests of the Christian States . . .

As the war entered its closing days, even the claims of political expediency could not suppress such nostalgic whimpering as *Arriba's* front-page editorial (May 5, 1945) entitled "Germany's Pathetic Symphony," exalting the "eternal values" of German life and happily concluding: "Germany cannot die."

On the day when the end of the European war was officially proclaimed, every newspaper in Spain was ordered to hail the event as a triumph—for General Franco! Thus *Arriba* on May 8 carried not a single picture of any Allied leader under its banner headline announcement of the great news. Instead there appeared a three-column photograph of General Franco, proclaimed as "The Caudillo of Neutrality." Like the rest of the Spanish press, *Arriba* editorially exulted: "For Spain, proclamation of peace in Europe marks the happy conclusion of a superb political feat"—the maintenance of Spain's neutrality. And *Juventud* told the youth of Franco Spain:

To celebrate the Day of Peace is to celebrate one of the most important victories of the Falange and of the Caudillo. Because without the presence of the Falange and of the Caudillo directing the policy of the country, we could not have arrived at this day, free from bloodshed and destruction. . . .

Only the presence of a Caudillo with his unalterable serenity and of a Falange totally independent and dedicated exclusively to the service of the Fatherland has been able to achieve this miracle of neutrality. . . .

Spain has been saved because she has had a Caudillo and a Falange; and History, which judges things without passion or intrigue, will proclaim the Day of Peace as the day of Falangist victory.

Obviously, the same urgent expediency which demanded successive changes in the Falangist theory of world politics also compelled the Party to make equally striking revisions in the Falangist theory of the Spanish State. The regime which for so many years had been happily saluted as a model totalitarian state, geared for enjoyment of all benefits of a New Order, suddenly was eulogized for its independence of all foreign influences, its "unitarian," as distinct from "totalitarian," character. When *Arriba* (May 23, 1943) featured a front-page editorial entitled "The Falange Is Not A Program" (but a "Movement"), *Madrileños* smiled and knew that they must prepare themselves to watch unsmilingly such a frenzied exercise in rationalization as only worried Falangists could produce. Since then, the amazing Falangist vocabulary has expanded to incorporate such terms as "organic democracy" and "Evangelical democracy." Church-hating and priest-baiting Falangists have busily thumbed the pages of the New Testament to find the raw material out of which their typewriters could mass-produce panegyrics of their Caudillo as the twentieth century apostle of Christ's social gospel. It has not been easy for many of these Falangist die-hards to let the Son of God usurp the place which they feel belongs rightfully to Ledesma Ramos—but they have realized that the chances of political salvation have depended upon discovering a redeemer more influential than the founder of the JONS.

Studied in the light of this newly discovered gospel, General Franco, the Chief of the Spanish State, has now emerged as "the democratic expression of Spain." In the Falange's own honeyed words (*Arriba,* September 30, 1945):

In this world's hour, Spain, free from the consequences of a cruel war, in process of healing the wounds which our inevitable internal war opened, is grouped around Franco with the same splendid determination as in 1936. Under his command, we find still alive and permanent the reasons which led us formerly to battle; the same hopes are fresh, the heart ready for the same sacrifices. Never has a political figure enjoyed such popular acclaim as the Caudillo. Because all of us, all we Spaniards, are with him. For that reason, Franco is today the essence of national life, the highest democratic expression of Spain.

4

Since the end of World War II, the propaganda machine of the Spanish government has found itself viewing the United States in a light very different from that which seemed to cast such dark shadows two or three years ago. In those years when the gods of war smiled so seductively upon the Axis powers, all the resources of the Falange were mobilized to translate into Spanish, the directives of Dr. Goebbels—with special emphasis on the theme of the "decadent democracies" of the West. But since the wave of the future has become the backwash of yesterday, the propaganda appeal of the Spanish regime to the people of Spain has anxiously sought to demonstrate that deep mutual friendship links Spain with the United States and Great Britain. This has been merely a corollary of the argument that all of Spain's international woe has been the wicked work of Communists, and that only because of the exigencies of international politics have other nations allowed Russians to menace the peace of Spain.

In its various changing characterizations of the United States the Falange propaganda machine has, of course, seized upon a variety of news, comment and opinion from the United States to suit its particular political need of the moment. Its selection of material at all times has been revealing and instructive.

Three years ago, the material gathered and exploited by both the German Embassy and the Falange came almost ex-

clusively from one source: the left-wing and "liberal" American press—its attacks upon the Franco regime, upon the State
Department, and the American Ambassador for their policy
of "appeasing" General Franco. These fervent denunciations
admirably served the ends of both German and Falangist
propaganda. They were amassed to demonstrate to the Spanish
government's non-Falange and anti-Falange elements the
alleged futility of making any concessions to American diplomacy, so irreconcilable was the hostility of American opinion.
Moreover, much of this editorial material contained such flagrant misstatements of fact that it tended to fit neatly into the
Falangist argument that criticism of the Spanish regime abroad
merely transcribed Communist handouts.

One striking example was the persistence with which badly
informed liberal journals in the United States for a long time
wrote of the Spanish underground organization, the *Junta
Suprema de Unión Nacional,* as if it were an alliance of all
democratic elements waging clandestine war on Franco and
his minions. Every informed source in Spain knew that the
Junta was the exclusive product of the Communist Party and,
in the judgment of many Spanish Republicans and Socialists,
it was a dangerous foe of democracy. The fact that so many
liberal journals in America saluted the *Junta,* as the vanguard
of what they called "Spanish democracy," furnished excellent
evidence in support of the Falangist argument that Americans,
at a distance of three thousand miles, could not distinguish
between a Communist and a democrat, so that their eager
advocacy of Spanish "democracy" really signified a Communist
threat.

It was natural that German propagandists and Falangist
leaders should take great pleasure in placing such articles from
the American press before General Franco to refute the contention of some Foreign Office officials that Spain should be
genuinely neutral in its foreign relations. Thus many of the
most shrill American editorial indictments of the Franco regime—apparently written in the belief that newspaper attacks

on German influence in Spain would impair that influence—
actually played directly into the hands of the very forces which
they denounced most vociferously. And ignorance of the facts
brought these journals to make precisely the same confusion
of "democracy" and "Communism" which was the constant
purpose of Falangist propaganda in Spain.

Since the end of the European war, the propaganda machine
of the Spanish State has faced a different problem. Far from
seeking evidences of a hostile American press with which to
badger pro-American factions within the government, it has
sought and exploited every expression of American opinion
which can be construed as sympathetic or even tolerant toward
the Spanish regime. This has been done, of course, at precisely the time when American policy has been endeavoring
to express hostility toward the Spanish regime—and with the
precise purpose of concealing that hostility from the Spanish
people.

The verbal ammunition which Falange propaganda has im-
ported from the United States since the end of World War II
has come, with scarcely a single exception, from the archconservative press as a whole and from Catholic journals in particular. These "useful" expressions of American opinion often
have not referred to Spain directly but have nonetheless fitted
neatly into the official Spanish theory of world relations. Thus
any of the cynical criticisms of the United Nations or any of
the most fiery philippics against Russia are grist for the
propaganda mill in Madrid, working overtime to convince
the Spanish people that war between Russia and the Western
powers is a matter of a short time, at which happy moment
new Spanish Blue Divisions will spring up to fight alongside
the British and Americans. What applies to the American
press, of course, applies also to American politicians and their
pronouncements. During November of 1945, for example, the
Falangist evening paper in Madrid, *Pueblo,* in a series of "Man
of the Day" articles, paid its tribute to such figures as Kessel-
ring, Raeder, Yamamoto, Victor Emmanuel, Keitel; and the

only American public figure to win such recognition was Senator Burton K. Wheeler.

But all such instances have been trivial when compared with the frenetic enthusiasm, the ecstatic editorial joy, with which the controlled press of Spain has received many of the utterances of Catholic leaders and organizations in the United States. Among those thus honored, first place probably belongs to the writer, William Thomas Walsh, whose exorbitant enthusiasm for General Franco's regime has kept alive the oratorical tradition of the most eloquent members of the Nazi Party. Thus (*Arriba,* September 4, 1945):

FRANCO HAS MADE SPAIN THE BULWARK OF
THE CATHOLIC FAITH IN THE WEST

Without his valor and his wisdom,
almost all Europe would today be
Sovietized

Only a few weeks after this declaration received lavish publicity, *Arriba* returned to the fond labor of carrying Mr. Walsh's voice to the Spanish people. This time he completely dominated the front page, with these warning words in headlines:

EXPULSION OF FRANCO WOULD MEAN THAT
THE SOVIETS HAD TAKEN OVER EASTERN
AND WESTERN EUROPE

THE FRANCO REGIME IS NOT FASCIST SINCE
IN SPAIN THE STATE IS SUBORDINATE TO GOD
AND SECONDARY TO THE INDIVIDUAL

This startling statement (by a man who has never spent a day in Spain) was attributed by *Arriba* to an address by Mr. Walsh before the *Instituto Católico de la Prensa* in New York; and the value which the Falange placed upon Mr. Walsh's services can be judged by the fact that the headlines alone ran six inches deep across the entire page.

While Mr. Walsh's pronouncements (of the many of which I have selected only two typical illustrations) receive this fine reception from the Falangist press, it is well worth observing that neither he nor the Party press ever has mentioned the fact that all the writings of the foremost contemporary Catholic philosopher and French Ambassador to the Vatican, Jacques Maritain, are absolutely banned in General Franco's Catholic Spain. Jacques Maritain has stubbornly refused to subscribe to the argument that his Church is in need of the kind of "defense" offered by Franco and the Falange.

But Mr. Walsh has not been alone. He has had to share the affection of the Falange with others. Among these, the Brooklyn *Tablet* has been perhaps best beloved. At regular intervals, the Falangist press of Spain has become delirious over such tributes as this from Brooklyn (*Arriba,* August 14, 1945):

THE CRIME OF SPAIN IS NOT HAVING SUB-
MITTED TO STALIN'S DICTATORSHIP

THE GREAT AMERICAN WEEKLY "THE TABLET" DE-
NOUNCES THE "RANCOROUS AND UNMERITED ATTACK"
ON SPAIN IN THE POTSDAM COMMUNIQUÉ .

On other occasions, editorial rejoicing has been provoked by such good tidings as these (*Arriba,* March 26, 1946):

"THE CATHOLIC NEWS" CONDEMNS THE AMERICAN
CAMPAIGN AGAINST SPAIN

THE HONOR OF THE UNITED STATES IS
BEING IMPERILED BY AN INSOLENT
LEFTIST MINORITY

What is tragic in all this systematic exploitation of Catholic journalism in the United States is the fact that the average Spanish citizen lacks sufficient knowledge of either the American press or of American Catholicism to assess, for example, an editorial in the Brooklyn *Tablet* at its true value. A great many

Spaniards know that there are almost 25,000,000 Catholics in the United States; but when their own press refers to "the great weekly" published in Brooklyn, few Spaniards are certain that this is not a mouthpiece of the united Catholic ranks of America. Consequently, the government-controlled press has enjoyed rather uniform success in convincing its people that the full power of the Catholic Church in the United States stands ready to defend the Franco regime in Spain against the malevolence of what *The Catholic News* (according to *Arriba*) so glibly called "an insolent leftist minority." And I should emphasize that, beyond angering leftist opposition groups within Spain, this victory for Falange propaganda has profoundly dismayed and shocked liberal Catholic groups in Madrid, who are in a position to know a great deal more about life in Spain than their sister organizations in the United States. In fact, I doubt if there has been anyone more amazed and aggrieved by the editorializing of the Brooklyn *Tablet* than the Papal Nuncio in Madrid: wise Msgr. Cicognani, who has labored, quietly but earnestly, to persuade some of the Spanish hierarchy's more voluble bishops, that there is more than a little danger in their argument that the fate of their Church turns on the fate of the Franco government.

I have referred thus far only to isolated cases—though their pattern has been fairly clear—in which American voices have been transcribed and rebroadcast to suit the needs of Falangist propaganda. But there remains to be considered the point at which this pattern becomes a system. This point is reached with the activities in Madrid of an American news agency which places its world-wide service at the disposition of a government-subsidized, government-controlled, and government-censored news monopoly.

Until April 1, 1945, the two largest American news agencies, the Associated Press and the United Press, had confined the activities of their Madrid offices to outgoing news files, while the Spanish news monopoly, EFE, was satisfied with whatever American news its own correspondents could gather and what-

ever it received through its exchange agreement with Britain's
Reuters Agency. By the end of 1944, however, it had become
apparent to the men in charge of the Vice-Secretariat of Popular Education that political advantage could be gained from
securing a contract with one of the American agencies. The
United Press entered the competition for the Spanish contract
by sending one of its Vice-Presidents, Mr. A. L. Bradford, to
Madrid. The United Press won the EFE contract and on April
1, 1945, began its world service of news to the Spanish news
monopoly. Perhaps it is pertinent, in this connection, to recall
the exclusive interview which Mr. Bradford had with General
Franco before leaving for the United States. In addition to
giving the Chief of the Spanish State another splendid opportunity to reiterate his affection for the democracies of the
world, Mr. Bradford gratuitously added his own satisfaction
with the state of the Spanish nation: "Regardless of whether
or not one is opposed to the government of General Franco,
Spain is today, without a shadow of a doubt, a notable example
of tranquillity and progress in Europe." With this generous
tribute to the regime of General Franco, Mr. Bradford concluded his business mission in Spain.

What has followed has been the logical result of the political
circumstances in which the United Press must operate. Those
circumstances can be summarized briefly: when a free press
and a controlled press meet on the same ground, the former
inevitably and inescapably becomes the servant of the latter.

The United Press Service has placed at the disposal of the
Spanish government a world news service from which the
Spanish press authorities can select and exploit those items
fortifying their own official position—*while publicly attribut-
ing those items to an American source*. The propagandistic
effect has been devastating. Through clever manipulation and
frequent distortion, through a judicious mixture of exaggeration and suppression, the government propaganda machine
frequently has been able to state its case on world affairs in
words spoken by the United Press.

The task has been a simple one for the Spanish government. Let an individual United Press correspondent, in any capital of the world, write a dispatch reporting criticism of American foreign policy, or deploring the plight of ill-fed Germans, or emphasizing conflicts between the United States and Russia, or focusing on disagreements in the Security Council of the United Nations. Any of these will be carried in the Spanish press with such clear, emphatic attribution to the United Press that the Spanish reader is led to believe that an organization called the United Press, rising as a single body to speak with a single voice, had issued a definitive pronouncement on a major world problem. If the desired effect cannot be completely achieved in this way, it can be done with headlines deftly twisted in true Falangist fashion.

Examples of the use of this device in the Spanish press have been too numerous to allow any selection of cases that could presume to be fully representative. But a few instances must be cited for the full flavor of this situation to be appreciated:

May 16, 1945. . . . Arriba carries this three-column headline across the top of its front page: UNITED PRESS SAYS THAT RUSSIA AT EVERY INSTANT IS FAILING TO FULFILL YALTA AGREEMENT. The text of the story reveals it to be the commentary of a Paris correspondent of the U.P. discussing the question of repatriation of war prisoners.

November 19, 1945. . . . Informaciones gives a three-column headline across its back page to this story: PHILIPPINES NOMINALLY SOVEREIGN BUT IN FACT WILL BE A PROTECTORATE "LIKE CUBA AND PANAMA," SAYS THE UNITED PRESS. In this instance, the headlines are accurate reflections of the text of the U.P. story: superlative material for Falangist propaganda's thesis about American tyranny in Latin America!

December 21, 1945. . . . Arriba feeds the fires of anti-Russian hatred with another U.P. story, again given the familiar recipe of three-column headlines on the front page: "MAC-ARTHUR WILL RESIGN HIS POST IF RUSSIANS PARTICIPATE IN OCCU-

PATION OF JAPAN"——"HE HAS SO INFORMED UNITED STATES GOV-
ERNMENT," SAYS UNITED PRESS. . . . How vastly more impressive
to publish such a story as the pronouncement of an important
American news agency, rather than as a mere allegation of
the EFE Agency in Madrid!

February 6, 1946. . . . *Arriba,* reporting the deliberations
of the United Nations Security Council in London, happily
recounts the disagreement among the United Nations which
it likes to see: NO ACCORD ACHIEVED YESTERDAY IN THE UNO—
UNITED PRESS SAYS AN ATMOSPHERE OF PESSIMISM EXISTS WHICH
CANNOT BE DISGUISED. . . . As usual, the story gets three-column
headlines across the top of the front page.

April 14, 1946. . . . *Arriba* is reporting the news of Poland's
charges against Spain made before the Security Council of the
United Nations meeting in New York. This time (for it is an
issue so critical for Spain) four columns are needed for the
headline: UNITED PRESS BELIEVES THAT POLISH ACCUSATION WILL
NOT BE SUFFICIENT TO ACHIEVE SANCTIONS AGAINST SPAIN.

All these examples speak for themselves, and the total political impact of this constant and systematic exploitation of
an American news service cannot be exaggerated. For the
propaganda machine of the Spanish government, it has been
a superb double-edged weapon. At one and the same time, they
have been able righteously to boast that the Spanish press is
carrying more "American" news than ever before, and to exploit that news in a manner carefully calculated to serve the
political purposes of the government of Francisco Franco. It
is easy to understand why one of the basic axioms inspiring the
strategy of Falangist propaganda has become this: "If we can
get the United Press to say it, we do not have to say it ourselves."

5

The preceding pages are informative principally on the devices, the tricks, and mechanics of the propaganda machine of

the Spanish State. But, however important these things are, it is no less important to understand the more esoteric political gospel inspiring this propaganda. This gospel does not necessarily appear in the official directives which government authorities issue to the nation's press. It takes form from certain beliefs which the men around General Franco hold firmly if not passionately. These beliefs constitute the justification which these men make to themselves for the power they wield, but they also are the axioms which they strive most earnestly to force the Spanish people to accept. In the final political analysis, it does not matter a great deal if the majority of the people ridicule and reject most of the pretentious boasts and puerile rationalizations of Falangist propaganda—provided that these basic tenets of the government's gospel are made to sound plausible enough to win general acceptance.

I believe that the key axioms in the Spanish State's political argument in its own defense are the following:

First: Any attempt to challenge openly the rule of General Franco could result only in unlimited civil war, with the eventual triumph of Communism in Spain.

Secondly: While the economic situation of Spain is critical, with inflation and scarcity running their mad race toward financial disaster, the rest of the European continent is not in a state of such political or economic security as to give it the right to suggest new formulas for the cure of Spain's ills.

Thirdly: Although the record of the foreign relations of the Spanish regime betrays at least moral and verbal compromise with the Axis powers, General Franco nonetheless spared Spain full participation in World War II, and for that all Spaniards should be grateful.

Fourthly: The future pattern of world relations is clear. The Western democracies and Soviet Russia are speeding toward open armed conflict which, while provoked by the aggressive tactics of Russian imperialism, will quickly translate itself into an ideological crusade against Communism. As this history unfolds, the United States and Great Britain, recognizing the strategic importance of Spain as an Atlantic and Mediterranean power, will also embrace Spain in their world-wide courtship of any and all anti-Communist governments.

These are not frivolous propositions. They are serious arguments which have been expounded, elaborated, and insinuated into the thoughts of a considerable part of the Spanish population through the persistent labor of a virtually omnipotent propaganda machine.

Spaniards of all social classes and political affiliations openly express contempt for their press and radio—but they read the one and listen to the other. And whatever they see or hear is, to the best of the government's ability, carefully measured as the most persuasive variation on its basic political propositions for each social or political group. Thus the costly social-security program of the Falange (which in the typical year of 1943 dispensed 365,000,000 pesetas, according to official figures) receives lavish publicity and is contrasted with a dire picture of nineteenth century autocratic privileges which would allegedly result from a Monarchic restoration. (This theme is for proletarian audiences.) Simultaneously, other government propaganda exalts the benefits of "order" which accrue to the middle class and wealthy landed aristocracy—and this is contrasted with a vivid characterization of the excesses and disorders which occurred under the Republic. (This theme is for rightist and Monarchist audiences.)

Even less complicated and more blunt appeals are marked and addressed to other groups. Catholics are told that only Franco has the ingenuity to outwit all Communist intriguers working to make Spain "a Soviet colony." The military are ominously reminded of how the last Spanish Republic undercut their privileged position and of how anxious the political left is to avenge itself for what the Army did in 1936. The politically-disinterested professional man—the doctor and architect, chemist and lawyer, merchant and professor—is insistently asked: Are these days not better than another civil war? Are you not at least free (provided you remain politically-disinterested) to carry on your profession in peace? Is not your life more "normal" than during most of the last fifteen years? And as for the student in the schools and universities of Spain, he has only officially approved texts in which to study the evils of "liberalism," the beauty of "the Crusade of 1936," the articles of the Catholic faith, the supreme "patriotism" of Franco.

But the effectiveness of the Spanish State's propaganda upon the Spanish mind cannot be fairly measured only by the variety of its many appeals to special groups of opinion. For the spontaneous thoughts and emotions of the Spanish people, their fears, their longings, their habits, all these affect the efficacy of propaganda directed at them from any source. And in that mental and emotional character of a whole people there are certain important qualities which have made them susceptible to the kind of appeal addressed to them by their government since 1939. These qualities can be stated briefly: The Spanish people have been war weary since the grim end of their Civil War. They have been profoundly Catholic in faith for centuries. And they have been intensely nationalistic and resentful of foreign dictation for all time.

Since the end of the Civil War in 1939, to amend Marx's dictum slightly, a specter has been haunting the people of Spain—not the specter of Communism but of renewed civil war. War fatigue means war fear. But it has been a state of mind not describable merely in terms of exhaustion or lethargy. It has been an active, fervent conviction that almost any political price was worth paying to escape the disaster of renewed civil strife. Only the most superficial observer could dismiss this fear as the artificial product of Falangist propaganda; instead, the very fact that that propaganda has relentlessly played upon that fear merely testifies to the government's own recognition of it as one of the crucial keys to the mind of the people. Nor has this fear obsessed only the privileged who would dread disorder as much for the loss of property as the loss of life which it would bring. The underground opposition of the left has felt and recognized the compelling power of this fear. These men, hopeful of some day building a democratic Spain, have appreciated fully the political necessity of escaping the stigma which Falangist propaganda seeks to attach to all opposition as the precursor of civil strife. They have understood, too, the plain truth that the Army which was largely responsible for their defeat in 1936-39 has been made even stronger and more confident than it was then. And they have had the common sense to realize that, were they to triumph in a grand clash of arms, they might inherit from that strife a legacy of such bitterness, of such tragic economic and social problems, that it might jeopardize the very enterprise for which they had fought.

As for the Catholic faith of the people of Spain, it is a thing so profound, so subtle, and so enduring as almost to defy description. I have already spoken of the churches of Spain in these years—not empty or half-filled museums, but overflowing places of worship and devotion. Among the women praying, the predominant color is black, which most of them have worn scrupulously since some tragic day in the years of the Civil War. For those who died on either side, the prayers for their souls are the same, and the black speaks of the same mourning for all those who in life suffered and fought under banners of different and conflicting colors until they shared the awful unanimity of death. To these women and their men, from the ornately carved pulpit a man speaks who too often is weak, misguided or ignorant, but they know that it was not he who propounded the faith and the doctrines which they have inherited from their fathers. And to leave these churches of Spain is not to leave behind this faith, in chaste seclusion from one Sunday to the next. I remember vividly the first musical show I attended in a Madrid theater: my attention constantly left the throaty flamenco singers on the stage to study in amazed fascination the backdrop curtain on which was painted no scene of lush romance but of a priest upon the altar, elevating the Host! It was an extreme but, as I was to learn, not so extraordinary evidence of the degree to which the daily life of the Spanish Catholic is surrounded with the symbols and gestures, suggestions and demonstrations of his intensely personal and magnificently un-self-conscious faith. Because, with almost equal intensity, he is so often anti-clerical, the Spaniard easily deceives the foreigner who cannot share his facility for distinguishing between a priest and a religion. This foreigner, unable to understand the profound faith of the Spanish people, finds himself as far from the tantalizing truth as another who assumes that the clergy of Spain speaks for those people. More penetrating than most epigrams is that which says that, in Spain, even most atheists are Catholic.

And beside this religious faith, in the Spanish character, rises the towering national pride of the people of Spain. Conscious (even the least literate) of a history and racial composition stamping their peninsula as an area peculiarly distinct from the general European pattern, remarkably sensitive to the special natural and artistic beauties of their land, the moving magnificence of their country's triumphant moments in history—the people of Spain are proud of their pride. Their rebellion has been instinctive, at times seeming almost willful and capricious, in the face of any attempt by a foreign people to seize their soil, to compromise their independence, to exploit their misery or divisions. Accustomed by history to finding itself at the busy crossroads of conflicting international forces and influences, the Spanish people, divided and tormented as they have been in the years since 1939, have not changed these instincts so deeply rooted in their being. Thus, for example, it has been common occurrence for the most ardent Falangists to scorn and deride the right of Italy or Germany to claim a debt of Spanish gratitude for their contributions in the Civil War, while being among the most eager to assure the prompt withdrawal of the Italian "volunteers" from Spanish soil immediately after the Civil War's end. With equal fervor have the most liberal partisans of the cause of the

United Nations denounced British possession of Gibraltar and such British economic penetration in Spain as the Río Tinto mines. With unfailing repetition throughout Spanish history, the spirit of patriotic pride has surged contemptuously over the steepest barriers of political difference to sweep into national unity men of the most contradictory persuasions.

All these elementary aspects of Spanish national psychology are certainly facts less susceptible to precise analysis than the national budget or the troop dispositions of the national army. But they are of incomparably greater importance—throughout Spanish history and today.

I have said that the propagandists of the regime of General Franco have played upon these historic and temperamental qualities of the people with instrumental skill and persuasiveness. That is true. But I am sure that it is equally true that the tiring exercise of their wits has led these men to calculate on oversimplifications of these qualities, forgetting their complexity and infinite subtlety.

For war fatigue, which cannot last indefinitely, can arouse the fiercest detestation of a regime which perpetuates itself by evoking every bitter memory of civil strife, by systematically opening and rubbing the scars and sores which have never been allowed to heal.

And a religious faith that is deep and enduring cannot long confess to the necessity of being supported by political benefits and weapons, whose use can only be an acknowledgment of a lack of faith.

And a national pride, righteous and intense, also can compel a people, not merely to defend courageously its soil against foreign invasion, but also to create, at whatever cost, a state and society which will command the respect of the free nations of the world, among whom a seat of dignity and honor has been empty for too long.

From these, the deepest sources of Spanish life, can come, with devastating speed, the will and the power to destroy the sceptered myth, to let shine again the golden heresy of truth.

6 THE SECURITY SYSTEM OF THE SPANISH STATE

FEAR fortifies the Spanish State. The most practiced strategy of the regime of General Franco is to propagate fear in its myriad monstrous shapes: fear of civil war, fear of Communism, fear of church burnings, fear of Russia, fear of property damage. To stimulate terror in these forms is the transcendent purpose of the government's propaganda machine.

But inevitably there are those who cannot be terrorized by words alone, who remain resolutely unmoved by the officially sponsored chamber of horrors which, according to the national press and radio, is the future of Spain if the security of the Franco regime is challenged. For these stubborn citizens of Spain, the Spanish State has devised instruments of fear more effective than newspaper editorials: the characteristic instruments of a police state. Hence it is the prescribed function of prisons and labor camps to carry on, in the Falangist scheme of things, at the point where the mere propaganda of fear fails to achieve its full purpose.

2

I remember vividly an evening in late October of 1942. A driving rain was hitting the pavement outside and the windows of our office on the Calle Don Ramón de la Cruz. I was working after hours; all our Spanish employees had left for their homes.

A little before 9 o'clock, our watchman came in to tell me that a woman was in the hall asking urgently to speak with some Embassy officer. A bit disgruntled by an interruption at such an hour, I went out to the hall and saw my visitor. She was a stooped but still robust figure, a woman probably in her late fifties. Her darkly bronzed face bore those clean, sharp lines which so much misfortune and so grand a resilience have stamped on the countenances of the old women of Spain. Her cheap clothes were soaked with rain, and under her arm she carried a sloppy bundle wrapped in paper.

Her story was simple. Her husband, a carpenter, had come seven days ago to our office to get his copy of our weekly news bulletin. When he left, he soon realized that he was being followed by plain-clothes police of the Falange. After a few blocks, at a safe distance from American Embassy property, they had pushed him into the doorway of an apartment building, searched him for the bulletin, cuffed and slapped his face, dragged him to the cells below ground of the *Dirección General de Seguridad* ("General Direction of Security") in the Puerta del Sol. There he had remained incommunicado.

His wife had succeeded finally in tracing him through the local district police office. When she had called at *Seguridad* to try to help him, officials brusquely told her that he was being held in solitary confinement. She could not communicate with him because the offense with which he was charged was political. He was a "Communist." This was known because he had been reading the American Embassy news bulletin, a thing which only "Communists" did.

For three days following her first rebuff, she had returned to the *Seguridad* offices, vainly begging permission at least to leave food for her husband and a change of clothes. Until this afternoon, she had been refused. This afternoon, she was told that her husband needed fresh clothes, that she could take his old ones with her immediately because he could no longer wear them.

That was her whole story. She untied the paper bundle under her arm. She neither whimpered nor trembled nor spoke. She merely showed me some ragged underclothes. They were liberally spotted with blood, were solidly soaked in some places, especially in the crotch of the shorts.

She wanted to know what the Embassy could do, not only to get her husband freed but—how was she to support and feed her children, since his unexplained absence had already cost her husband his job? I gave her money, promised weakly that we would do what was possible, and told her to come back in two days if her husband were still confined. She came back the second day to tell me he had been released. He had been submitted to ten days of steady torment without a single charge having been formally made against him, without his appearance before any sort of magistrate. He was warned on his release to stop reading American propaganda.

This was simply one of what then seemed like an endless series of episodes. They constituted a systematic campaign on the part of the Spanish police and Falange to smash the American information program in Spain with tactics as cunning as they were ruthless. The Party and police believed they could win their objective by either of two methods: by frightening Spaniards away from our offices, or by forcing on us the realization that we were providing the effective cause for the torture of countless innocent people and therefore must voluntarily abandon our work. For the better part of the autumn these attacks continued methodically without frightening the *Madrileños,* who kept coming by the hundreds to our offices. But the incidents of arrests and beating reached such a number and intensity that they almost achieved their purpose by the second method on which the Falange had counted. At one time I did discuss with the ambassador the possible need to suspend temporarily our publications rather than continue knowingly to provide the occasion for tragedy for so many families.

The problem would have been different if the Embassy could have intervened effectively to help those arrested and tortured. But Embassy action was worse than useless in most cases. While the Foreign Office would blame *Seguridad* for the outrages, *Seguridad* would blame the Falange, the Falange would blame "irresponsible" persons whose identity was undiscoverable. But even if responsibility were satisfactorily established, the government would defend its action on the grounds that the detentions were made because the victims were old, known "enemies of the State." The fact that they had been found reading the American bulletin was merely "an unfortunate coincidence"! To give a convincing answer to this line of argument, the Embassy would have had to undertake the impossible task of reviewing the personal antecedents of every prisoner to show that he was not "an enemy of the State" (which he probably was, at least at heart). Moreover, a diplomatic protest from the American Embassy which reached the offices of the feverishly pro-Nazi officials of *Seguridad* was like a kiss of death for the prisoner, who would suffer added torment on the grounds of being a friend of the hated *yanquis*.

Despite this tragic cost, we did not discontinue our publications, partly because we knew it was precisely what the Falange wanted us to do, partly because we decided that, since it was to the people of Madrid that our publications were addressed, then they had the right to be the judges of our policy. They continued to come: that was their verdict. Finally, the campaign of attacks slackened off. Though isolated incidents continued, the concerted plan of assaults was obviously abandoned as futile.

These attacks of official Spanish agencies "maintaining order" exemplified the conviction of the Spanish State that compulsion and ruthless suppression of opposition must be considered normal and essential functions of government.

That conviction was uncompromisingly stated in the fundamental Law of Political Responsibilities (February 9, 1939). Following a preamble devoted to huge praise of its own moderation, this Law explains in Chapter I: "Offenses are all acts contributing to subversion between October 1, 1934, and July 18, 1936, and all those acts opposed to the Nationalist Government after the latter date, whether they were acts of commission or serious acts of omission." The definition of offenses sweeps through no less than seventeen distinct categories of "criminal" acts, from deliberate action against the Movement to the wide realm of "acts contributing to the anarchy prevailing before the Nationalist Movement." All these are punishable by death, imprisonment, fine, exile, or loss of citizenship, as determined by prevailing military law applied by the National Court of Political Responsibilities.

Ruthless punishment of the politically disaffected has not been merely a capricious sort of warfare waged by the Spanish State upon little nests of opposition when and as they have been discovered. On the contrary, this has been a deliberately calculated over-all strategy of the Spanish regime, designed to keep burning throughout the nation the fires of hatred which raged in the conflagration of 1936-39. As a political weapon, it has served in its own sphere in the same way that the regime has exploited, as a propaganda weapon, the contention that only civil war could result from any attempt to challenge the rule of Franco. For in every sphere, *it has been the consistent policy of the Spanish regime to extol itself as the victor of 1939, to summon the support of those who were its allies in 1939, to evoke all the loyalties and passions and fears which the Civil War aroused.*

Proclaiming itself to be the unique alternative to future civil war, the regime of General Franco works for its own survival by systematically exploiting the heritage of past civil war.

3

While it is not possible to make an exact count of the number of political prisoners in the jails of Spain today, it is easy to calculate the resources of the various government agencies whose function it is to catch and keep these prisoners. This function is called maintaining "tranquillity."

It has already been noted that the nation's armed forces and various security-police agencies receive more than forty per cent of the regular government budget, virtually all the "extraordinary" budget, and a grand total of approximately 6,500,000,000 pesetas, amounting to fifty per cent of the entire government budget. Yet, in addition to this rough estimate, the detailed government budget reveals additional allocations for related law-enforcing agencies. Thus, out of the budget for the Ministry of Justice, the amount assigned to the prisons of Spain (personnel and maintenance) comes to 121,230,748 pesetas. Under the innocuous general heading of "the Presidency of the Government," a sum of 800,000 pesetas is earmarked for penal colonies in Africa. Another sum of more than 650,000 pesetas comes from the same appropriation for the maintenance of the Special Tribunal for the Repression of Masonry and Communism. From these sources come the funds to equip the various punitive agencies of the Spanish regime: the regular forces of the *Dirección General de Seguridad,* its secret police, the *Guardia Civil,* the Falange militia whose dissolution in provincial areas is purely theoretical, the secret police of the Falange. In any decisive test of strength, therefore, the forces of underground opposition confront the massed ranks of a regular army of over 700,000 men, the great bulk of the *Guardia Civil* (over 50,000 men), the *Policía Armada* (about 20,000), the half-suppressed Falange militia (about 5,000) and the allied University Militia (close to 10,000).

The number of political victims which these security forces have claimed cannot possibly be judged from any of the official estimates made by the Spanish Ministry of Justice. These are worthless, of course, if for no other reason than because the vocabulary employed by the government in defining a "political prisoner" is so elastic and elusive as to be virtually incomprehensible.

A remarkable example of the use of this official penal vocabulary occurred in May of 1945. The Associated Press office in Madrid had sent to the outside world a detailed report on the shocking living conditions of prisoners in the Nanclares de Oca concentration camp in northern Spain. After the Falangist press (which, of course, never printed a line of the original A.P. story) exhausted itself with vituperative editorials denouncing the Associated Press for its "slanders against Spain," the Spanish Foreign Office decided to sponsor a visit of all American and British correspondents to inspect the camp. Although sufficient time had elapsed for some quick and obviously new improvements in the camp's sanitary facilities, the correspondents discovered conditions to be different in only one or two minor details from the description related by the A.P. But a critical point of dispute between the Associated Press and the Foreign Office was whether or not the camp contained *political* prisoners. Spokesmen of the Spanish government heatedly contended that the admittedly inferior housing and sanitary facilities at Nanclares had to be endured only by the most vicious common criminals.[1] The correspondents were allowed to talk with some of the prisoners and one of them dared to risk future punishment by vigorously insisting that he had been charged only with a political offense.

Upon their return to Madrid, the correspondents were called to the office of the General Director of Security. He greeted them with great affability and assurance that they had found no "political" prisoners at the camp. Had they? . . . The cor-

[1] The original firsthand information on which the Associated Press had based its story came from a former *political* prisoner in Nanclares. But obviously, it could not bring this man forward to substantiate its story without inflicting him with another prison sentence.

respondents lost little time in raising the issue of one prisoner, whose name they had noted carefully. The Director of Security, after a certain amount of evasiveness, ordered the file on this prisoner brought to him for examination. When he had glanced through it, he exclaimed triumphantly that, of course, this man had not been charged with a political offense. The director replied, "He denounced the Spanish regime in a public place, a café I believe. . . ." The correspondent who first recovered from the shock of this statement asked, "And that is not a political offense? . . ." The reply: "Of course not. It has nothing to do with politics. It is simply a common offense against public order."

While this kind of argument has made an empty mockery of the Spanish government's official statistics on its political prisoners, it has not made any easier the task of accurately estimating their numbers. Consequently, guesses in the press of the world outside Spain have included figures as high as 500,000. This is undoubtedly a vast exaggeration.

To start from a few reasonably certain facts, at the beginning of 1946, from every personal and official source known to me, I made the most careful and detailed study of the numbers of political prisoners in the jails of Madrid (both city and province). The results were the following: about 5,000 in the Carabanchel Prison, which is the provincial jail; 1,000 in Yeserías; 2,000 in the women's prison of Ventas; about 500 in Santa Rita; an equal number in the underground cells of the *Dirección General de Seguridad;* a total of approximately 4,000 in the two prisons in Alcalá de Henares which are used exclusively for political prisoners; and between 4,000 and 5,000 in small-town prisons scattered around Madrid and in the penal labor battalions working along the Sierra Mountains. This total figure of 17,500 represented the number of political prisoners in the area around Madrid alone. Among other major centers having comparable prison colonies are Barcelona, Valencia, Sevilla, and Burgos. But it is not easy to deduce from these facts any precise national total of political prisoners. I do not believe it possible to make any more exact statement than this: the total for the nation is probably not less than 150,000, nor does it in all likelihood exceed 225,000. Depending upon which Spanish government statement of the last two years is consulted for comparison, this estimated total is from 5 to 10 times larger than any official of the Spanish government has publicly admitted.

To the total of political offenders behind prison walls, there must be added the thousands of Spanish citizens who enjoy what is known as "conditional liberty" or *libertad vigilada*. These are the men and women who have been released after sentences lasting a few months or a few years (frequently without ever having appeared before a court of any description). Their probationary status restricts their movements, compels them to report regularly to local police authorities, effectively excludes them from employment in government offices, in trades controlled by the syndicates, or in any organization which would fear official reprisals for "harboring" employees of such political background. An official circular of instruction addressed to all business enterprises in Spain instructs them to report all employees who are on *libertad vigilada:* their names, parentage, age, civil status, and the police jurisdiction to which they are responsible.

It is difficult to capture a full and clear picture of the swiftness and capriciousness with which police power is exercised against political "undesirables." The records of *Seguridad,* modeled along Nazi lines, are thorough and well-organized, ensuring systematic vigilance over all suspected "enemies of the State" not behind prison walls. But the restless energies of the security police must also seek expression in bars and cafés of the slum sections of important cities; there police agents enter suddenly, demand to see the documents of everyone in the place, take off to jail anyone whose antecedents seem unsatisfactory or who merely does not seem "reliable" in demeanor or appearance. The purpose of such tactics is not so much to catch an occasional "dangerous" individual, as to impress the general population with the fact that the police forces of the State are active and vigilant, may strike anywhere at any time.

Once arrested, the individual victim finds himself confronted with a legal and penal procedure which, while depriving him of the most elementary decencies and frequently inflicting the cruelest tortures, possesses the further torment of completely bewildering him by its infinite complexity, its long, laborious labyrinthine ways, from which escape seems impossible.

In a typical case, the victim's trials (this word should not be construed in its legal sense) begin with a "denunciation" by an official or by any simple acquaintance who either suspects his political inclinations or bears a personal grudge. Until recently, a denunciation could be made, the accused be arrested, tortured, and sentenced without the accuser ever having to appear personally to substantiate his charges. The police would "investigate" in their own fashion and with their own hardy techniques. Although today it is technically necessary for anyone making a denunciation to appear personally in suppport of his accusation, no effective change is made in the system, since in practice the police will investigate thoroughly any charges of political conspiracy against any individual, even if the charges come from an anonymous or disreputable source.

All cases of a political nature fall in the jurisdiction of the *Brigada Politico-Social,* who act on the basis of an order for arrest issued by the *Jefe Superior de Policia.* Arrest is made by plain-clothes men armed with revolvers. If the arrest takes place in an outlying area in the provinces, the agents of the *Brigada* usually like to enjoy a few extra days of leisure away from Madrid, while the victim passes the time in the local jail. The latter always tries to get transferred to Madrid as rapidly as possible. This is not only because of the indescribable filth of provincial prisons, but also because local police authorities are never familiar enough with the law even to know what steps can be taken to bring about a trial: the prisoner may languish for months in confinement, without hope of hearing a specific charge or perhaps even of having his name taken for the prison records. So the person arrested in a provincial town usually makes it his first job to find enough money to pay the transportation of himself and his keepers to the national capital.

The prisoner's first stop in Madrid is a cell in the basement of the building on the Puerta del Sol occupied by the *Dirección General de Seguridad*. If he should be so fortunate as to have some social prominence or to be a person for whom some favored foreign embassy has expressed concern, he will be placed in one of three rooms on the first or second floors of the building, where living conditions are sufferable. In all other cases, the prisoner disappears to the ordinary cells below ground. The exact size of this network of underground cells is not known outside the *Seguridad* offices, but it is extensive and may cover the equivalent of several city blocks. An average cell measures about six feet square and "accommodates" four prisoners, but other cells are specifically designed to prevent the prisoner from finding an area long enough in which to lie flat upon the floor. The food is calculatedly intolerable, the usual diet consisting of no breakfast, a bowl of watery soup for lunch and the same for dinner.

Interrogation of the prisoner begins within twenty-four hours of his arrival at his new home and, whenever necessary, involves the use of a select number of vicious devices to induce statements subsequently labeled "confessions." The extraction of fingernails and toenails is usually the first of these devices used, since it is regarded as one of the less convincing means of persuasion at the disposition of the authorities. Favorite targets in the next stage are the eyes and genitals, submitted to a variety of punishments. Female prisoners receive treatment, in the best medieval tradition, expressly designed for their more sensitive organs. In important enough cases, a punishing but rather costly gas treatment is administered to the prisoner. When this does not suffice, it is followed by the passage of electric current at a moderate voltage through the prisoner's body. These refinements do not exclude, of course, the use of leather belts in floggings or of heavy boots ground into the stomach of the prisoner strapped to the floor. Two of the officials who most frequently preside over these sessions are known familiarly to their victims as David and Arias. They are names which will not soon be forgotten.

According to Spanish law, detention at the *Seguridad* should not exceed a period of forty-eight hours, at which time the prisoner should be released or brought before a magistrate. Not occasionally but systematically this law is violated in cases dealing with political prisoners. Six weeks' detention in the cellars below the Puerta del Sol is considered a short time. In countless cases, several months elapse before formal charges are presented, and if there were space to accommodate more prisoners at one time, these cases would be the general rule.

Not the least lamentable aspect of the police system is the fact that the officials of the General Direction of Security receive such little pay that they cannot resist the temptation to improve their living standards by corrupting the laws they are supposed to defend. A regular agent of the Political-Social Brigade receives about 400 pesetas a month; even an inspector, with the responsibility of assuming charge of cases, gets only 800 pesetas. Moreover, while official economy holds down these basic wages, lavish bonuses are provided for the discovery and successful prosecution of an important political offense. This encourages petty officials to use the most violent forms of torture and to prolong as much as possible the solitary confinement of prisoners in the hope that they may "confess" some fact which can be converted into pesetas at the *Seguridad's* rate of exchange.

The prisoner's stay in the cells of the Puerta del Sol ends when his dossier has been completed, based upon his written and signed "confessions." He is now transferred to a regular state prison (in Madrid, this would generally be the prison of Carabanchel) and his case passes under the jurisdiction of a military judge. In Carabanchel, the prisoner finds conditions only slightly improved over the cells in the Puerta del Sol. Although the prison was built along rather modern lines, divided into a series of galleries each of which is supposed to accommodate 120 prisoners, each gallery is made to serve for between 500 and 600 prisoners, bringing the total to an overflowing 5,000. The water supply is consistently defective, lighting is irregular, food is inferior. The menial work in the prison is done by the prisoners themselves, called *destinos* when they are assigned some regular duty by the prison authorities. These *destinos* constitute a gallery by themselves (Number 1) and enjoy certain privileges denied the other prisoners—although the price for such privileges is the presence of numerous police spies scattered among them. The prisoners in Gallery Number 3 are kept separated from all others: they are those who already have received their death sentences. Its average population is about 400. The turnover averages between 10 and 20 per week. Gallery Number 2 belongs to those prisoners whose death sentences have been commuted to sentences of 30 years' imprisonment. Gallery Number 6 is reserved for persons charged with Masonic activities. Since this charge is a convenient catch-all for prisoners against whom no real evidence exists, the gallery's population usually averages a congested 600.

Now (the prisoner may have just arrived from the cells of the Puerta del Sol or he may have been waiting since his arrival two or three months ago), the prisoner's case becomes subject to virtually an entire review under military authority. The investigation is carried out by a group of military officers under an Inspector General, who is himself an army general. Not infrequently the investigators in this instance make an earnest inquiry into the facts, particularly as to whether the "confession" signed in the offices of the General Direction of Security was extracted under duress. This more scrupulous attitude toward the prisoner is explained by two facts: these investigators get no bonus for uncovering "information," and most military authorities like to discredit the Security officials, whom they regard (correctly) as effective agents of the Falange. The results of this military investigation are passed on to the *Auditoría General,* a body of some twenty military-legal counselors under the Captain General of the Province.

Without further procedure, it is possible at this point to direct the release of the prisoner on the grounds of insufficient evidence and without any formal trial and acquittal. Such release, however, can authorize only provisional liberty until the Captain General himself (the chief military authority in each province) has signed the order, for he alone can sign definitive acquittals or convictions. Thus it frequently happens that the prisoner's routine is the following: he spends a few months in the cells of the Puerta del Sol, another two or three months in the provincial prison while the overworked and understaffed military investigators reach their conclusions. He is then released but only on conditional liberty, which demands that he report to a designated court twice a month and forbids him to leave Spain. This can last for a year or two before his dossier actually reaches the Captain General for a signature confirming his release. In other words, he can have spent 6 months in jail and another 18 months on conditional liberty—without ever having being formally charged, tried or acquitted by any court! And, at any time, at the discretion of the Captain General or the whim of the *Seguridad,* this process can begin all over again!

If one could add up the number of persons who have been executed or sentenced to jail only through error or the inefficiency of the Spanish judicial system, the total would be imposing. One such case was the execution in February of 1946 of Cristino García Granda and other former fighters with the FFI in France—the execution which raised such a storm of protest in France and led to the immediate closing of the French frontier with Spain. The sentences were passed in Barcelona. Under normal procedure, such sentences have to be sent to Madrid for confirmation, a matter which usually takes

many weeks. The case of Cristino García was still under study
in Madrid when the authorities in Barcelona took matters into
their own hands. Actually, officials in Madrid had intended to
authorize delay in carrying out the sentence, or commute it
to a prison term (not from any motives of charity but because
they foresaw the international repercussions). But once the
sentence had been executed and the protest in France had
reached full volume, the Madrid government had to defend
the action taken in Barcelona.

In the event that a prisoner's case is brought to trial before
a formal plenary session of the Tribunal of Military Justice,
the defendant is allowed to choose his counsel from a list of
military officers submitted to him. He is not permitted to hire
private legal counsel. Even if he were, he probably could not
afford the expense; or, if he could afford it, he would find it
difficult to get a lawyer who would risk his standing in the
defense of an "enemy of the State." The Tribunal is composed
of a president, two judges, and the prosecutor himself. They
pass a sentence which is never surprising in its close approxi-
mation of the penalty which the *fiscal* or prosecutor has already
recommended in writing. With few exceptions, trials are completely secret. Appeal is virtually impossible. Executions are
generally carried out swiftly after the pronouncement of sentence and in secluded areas, where the sound of firing squads
will not disturb the populace of a country whose "tranquillity"
is so vigilantly safeguarded.

Of those who pass through this judicial procedure and somehow escape imprisonment or execution, one large class suffers
a punishment known as *inhabilitación civil:* the deprivation
of all civil rights. This punishment is frequently applied to
persons charged with Masonic activities, of whom the security
police have been able to uncover some 15,000. The penalty
imposed in all these cases is described in the same remorseless
words: "absolute and perpetual disqualification from the exercise of any function in State, public, or official corporations,
in subsidized concerns or enterprises under government fran-

chise, from management or membership on the board of directors of private enterprises, as well as any position of trust, authority, or management in the same. . . ." [2] This is a sentence of economic exile from society.

I have not yet mentioned a special annex to the main structure of the Spanish security system: the labor battalions of political prisoners. It is unnecessary to explain that their existence is not one of the achievements of the "New State" publicized by the Spanish press. In truth, no complete picture of them can be drawn, so heavily are they screened from public view, nor can even the total number of men in these battalions be counted with any precision. I believe that 10,000 would be a conservative estimate. Some of the known facts about them are the following:

There have been seven of these battalions. Each bears its identifying number, and the numbers run from 91 through 97. They have been divided between European Spain and Spanish Morocco. Numbers 91, 93, and 97 have been working in Africa; Numbers 92, 94, 95, and 96 are in continental Spain.

Organized in the weeks immediately after the "Glorious Victory" of 1939, these battalions were formed from the ragged ranks of prisoners of war or political prisoners who were young and strong enough to work on some of the nation's urgent reconstruction projects—roads, bridges, railroad lines. The majority of these workers were recruited from the thousands of youths who had been called up under regular government conscription in 1936 or later, and consequently had served in the Republican army. Against only a small percentage of them was there even a charge of political crimes. But they nonetheless constituted a useful reservoir of manpower for the tasks confronting the new regime in 1939. Although their exploita-

---

[2] I have translated this, from the text of an official sentence before me, reading in Spanish: "inhabilitación absoluta perpetua para el ejercicio de cualquier cargo del Estado, Corporaciones Públicas u Oficiales, Entidades subvencionadas, Empresas concesionarias, Gerencias y Consejos de Administración de empresas privadas, asi como cargos de confianza, mando y dirección de los mismos. . . .

tion in 1939 had been advertised as a temporary emergency measure, the battalions have continued to exist.

In Africa, Spanish Army headquarters at Ceuta have directed the battalions' work. In the summer of 1945 (the most recent date on which I have exact information), the three African battalions were located at La Nasa, some thirty kilometers from Ceuta, at Targuis, near Villa Sanjurjo, and at Corta de Río Martin, about eight kilometers from Tetuan. They were at that time under the command of Lieutenant Colonel José Díaz Hernandez.

Conditions of work and life in these battalions have been even worse than in the prisons, although in 1945 a modest effort was made to improve them. Bridge, canal, and road construction has been their chief task. Generally, work has been assigned in terms of specific projects, to be completed within a specified time, rather than on the basis of a workday of a fixed number of hours. Accordingly, labor from seven in the morning until eleven at night, with a half hour allowed for midday meals, has been a common schedule. Food has been indescribably bad. Beatings, of course, have been the common form of discipline. Attempts to escape such conditions have been frequent, because the guards are generally light. But the only safe avenue of escape has been across the border into French territory, where Moroccan frontier guards count upon a reward of 250 pesetas for every escaping laborer they seize. Punishment following capture is well designed to discourage future attempts to escape. The labor camps are usually located anywhere from two to five kilometers from the scene of work; this distance must be marched every night when the day's work is through. Clothes are scanty. Flimsy tents offer no comfort from winter nights. Tuberculosis, jaundice, and malaria are the common diseases.

In continental Spain, the main centers of activity of the labor battalions have been in Andalucía, in the coal mines of Asturias, and certain areas of the Sierra Guadarrama. One of the battalions spent months on the reconstruction work on the railroad line between Madrid and Burgos.

Out of the labor of these men, many officials of the Spanish government have developed a lucrative business. All battalions work under the management of private contractors. In addition to what is euphemistically called their maintenance, the men receive a theoretical wage averaging around 8 pesetas a day—which is excellent business from the contracting company's viewpoint, since this is about one-half the prevailing wage for such labor. But this theoretical wage is not paid directly to the workers but to the government *patronato* which controls and "rents" them. Out of the 8 pesetas received, the *patronato* pays 50 centimos to the laborer; if he is married, 2 pesetas go to his wife, and 1 peseta for each child under 15 years of age—to a limit of 3 children. Thus the maximum payment to any laborer and his family amounts to 6 pesetas per day, while the average payment is estimated at 3 pesetas. On the basis of this average, the *patronato* is left with a profit of 5 pesetas per day per laborer.

The wretched victims of this system, as I have noted, are not heavily guarded. One of the reasons for this may be that the expenses of such guards would raise the overhead of the *patronato* considerably. But security is not too difficult to maintain, simply because escape from the labor camp brings with it no opportunity for fruitful work in a legitimate enterprise. The "ex-convict" has no ration card, no legal residence, no identifying papers, r.o syndical membership card. His only refuge is with the guerrilla bands of the mountains. Escapes from camps to the mountains have become increasingly frequent. Thus are the ranks of the exiled *within* Spain steadily swelled.

4

All the forces mobilized by the police agencies of the Spanish State have not been sufficient to satisfy the Falange. Vigilance and vengeance are labors in which Falangists, too, must share.

Consequently, while the Party has been stripped of many of its most coveted functions, it still can serve, as it always has served, as a "security" force of punishing power.

The special activities of the Falange in this sphere assume various forms, united in their common oppressive purpose. There has been, of course, simple and direct use of thugs and gunmen to inflict their own brand of extra-official punishment upon persons of suspect political inclinations. A list of even the known incidents of this kind would fill a volume of encyclopedic proportions. Provocation for such assaults ranges over a wide variety of offenses: reading American or British information bulletins; listening to a foreign radio; celebrating too demonstratively Allied V-Day in Europe; displaying copies of a biography of Roosevelt in book-store windows; murmuring against the high cost of living; reading a clandestine Republican or Monarchist letter or pamphlet. Little is required to qualify one as an "enemy of the State."

A different type of Falangist control relies not upon rubber hoses, clubs or pistols, but upon the authority to grant work cards in the labor syndicates. Issuance of these permits, of course, depends upon the individual having a "clean" political record. The slightest doubt of the worker's fidelity to the principles of the Movement suffices to bring about withdrawal of his right to work in his trade or craft.

A third typical police function discharged by the Party is the maintenance of complete records on the life, background, habits, and political character of all Spanish citizens. In every major city, the Party hierarchy forms a neat and elaborate pyramid. Under the municipal *Jefatura* are ranged "District Chiefs," "Sub-District Chiefs," "Block Chiefs" and "House Chiefs." The latter are charged with full responsibility for individual buildings and the actions of all its residents. By regular submission of standard printed forms, the House Chief must keep his superiors informed on every detail of the lives of the citizens under his vigilance. The typical official form requires names, date of birth, profession, place of work for each person; the monthly rent paid, the number of rooms in each apartment, the former residence of each individual, the number of his ration card. The House Chief must note if any persons under his jurisdiction belong to any branch of the Party. He must also provide detailed information on the building which he guards: whether it has a cellar, running water, unlighted rooms without windows, gas, central heating, elevator, and so forth. All this data, of course, is of vital importance in the event of street rioting or civil disorder of any kind.

While this information is systematically gathered, the Party also conducts periodic surveys designed to uncover "undesirables" who may constitute a potential nucleus of discontent within any district. A typical instance of this kind of inquisitive vigilance was an official and confidential circular instruction issued in August of 1944 by the *Jefatura* of the Falange in Madrid. It was addressed to all District Chiefs. It read as follows:

It being necessary to prepare with the greatest urgency a file of REDS and UNDESIRABLES, including the affiliation and greatest possible amount of data on each individual; and it being recognized that it is vital that the work be done with the greatest prudence, discretion and care to avoid regrettable mistakes, so that this data will be the most exact and detailed possible;

Therefore, you are directed to record the following in an effective manner:

First: REDS WHO HAVE BEEN MILITANT, with the fullest pertinent data on their background and present circumstances (whether free, in prison, on conditional liberty, etc.).

Second: UNDESIRABLES. Those people who, without a definite political character, take advantage of disturbances for their inadmissible purposes.

Third: FOREIGNERS, residing in our country since our Glorious Liberation, with indications as to their occupation and means of livelihood.

Fourth: RED SYMPATHIZERS, that is, those who today, without being dangerous because of their actions, are enemies of our Movement and spend their time disparaging it by passing about rumors and complaints. . . .

It is trusted that you will appreciate the importance of this matter, IT BEING A POLITICAL MISSION OF THE HIGHEST ORDER, and that you will execute it in the shortest possible time.

You will be responsible for any flaws or errors in the work of your District.

This, like all official Party documents, concluded with the favorite Falangist salutation: "For God, for Spain, and for her National-Syndicalist Revolution."

5

A large number of officials of the Spanish government have never sanctioned the manners and methods of the State's security police. This is true for the simple reason that they have remained ignorant of the facts. I doubt if Francisco Franco himself has any precise knowledge of the price exacted for the "peace" which, in his moments of oratorical fervor, he professes to see all around him. And I believe that there is more than a little sincere indignation in the Spanish government's angry denials when critics from the outside world condemn the criminality of Spain's penal system.

Nor is it difficult to understand why awareness of the facts has not always penetrated to the upper levels of Spanish officialdom. Agents and officers of the *Seguridad,* of the convict-labor *patronato,* or of the Falange police are not in the habit of publicizing their tactics outside of their own vicious circles—certainly not to cabinet ministers, who receive reports which say, in effect, little more than that "order is being maintained."

But can it be contended that this ignorance is less shameful than would be active complicity in the crimes committed? On the contrary, I doubt if any more savage commentary can be made upon the functioning of the totalitarian state in Spain than that its very designers and directors have failed to see its grossest cruelties. For this is an instance in which they cannot be forgiven because they know not what they do.

Again it must be emphasized that the persecutions, the arrests, the tortures, and the executions are not accidental or incidental vices in the character of the regime. They *are* the character of the regime: innate, inherent, ineradicable. They are not even the systematic work of men whose malice breeds madness. They are the way of life by which the regime must live. As it could be born only from civil war, so it must live by the perpetual, unrelenting waging of civil war.

Nor has world history allowed the momentum of that perpetual war to slacken. A year or two years after the democratic nations destroyed Naziism and, with it, all dear dreams of a Fascist Europe, more urgent than ever has become the Spanish State's need to depend upon defense by force. The pace of perpetual war must be accelerated, without pause, without respite, without remorse. It is an inexorable law of motion governing all tyrannies: as the gospel of fear and hate, propagated by words spoken and words written, becomes less convincing and harrowing, more shrill and more vacuous, then must the sanctions invoked in the name of that gospel become more pitiless and more punishing.

Yet, even at its grimmest moments, the history of Spain is fond of quixotic footnotes. And in peculiarly perverse fashion, life in a Spanish prison has its momentary compensations:

When V-Day came in Europe, the only mass celebration in the Spanish capital took place behind the walls of Yeserías Prison. Its warden—moved by kindness, by political foresight, or by a sense of irony—had let it be known to his convicts that they might, as he knew they wished, celebrate the victory of the United Nations.

It was a festive occasion. Dirty, tired, tormented men ate

and drank precious little hoards of wine and bread. Hundreds of carefully snuffed-out cigarette butts were lighted, and in Yeserías there was such a luxurious smoke-filled atmosphere as never before. Glasses clinked in sly political toasts. And in the corners, little groups gathered around a man who would mount upon a chair, lean discreetly forward, and give a swift political speech, full of wonderful words like *libertad* or *tierra* or *democracia,* uttered with delicate emphases and inflections but made to sound almost eerie by the judiciously hushed tone of his voice. The men were happy.

Beyond the walls of Yeserías, the free citizens of Madrid did not celebrate. They retired quietly to their homes to read their evening papers, which told them that this day was a moment of triumph for the Caudillo, who had preserved the peace of Spain.

7 THE FORCES OF OPPOSITION . . . THE RIGHT

A GOVERNMENT whose essential armament consists of police and propaganda defines its own character with unmistakable clarity. Its leaders, after a long process of self-indoctrination, may have convinced themselves that they are the stern and righteous custodians of the "best interests" of the people, whose ignorance, weakness or passions must not be allowed to maim or cripple the body politic. But it remains nonetheless a government without the people, above the people, and against the people.

A government whose practiced strategy is to sow dissension, to play off one political or social group against another in an endless cycle of conflict-breeding-conflict, cannot for long hold fast the trust or allegiance of any single group. The wearying war of mutual destruction approaches an inevitable end, when the embattled forces awake to the futility of their struggle and seek out its first cause. The heat generated in the perpetual circle of conflict becomes so intense that whatever or whoever had been standing safely and smilingly in its center suddenly is surrounded by a ring of flames. And they will burn inward.

Consequently, there is nothing surprising in the fact that an overwhelming majority of the people of Spain oppose the regime of Francisco Franco. Reasonable estimates of that majority may range from as little as seventy to as much as ninety per cent. The precise statistics within those limits matter little. Anyone who has lived any length of time in Madrid, during any period since 1939, knows how difficult it is to find people, officially unconnected with the regime, who express satisfaction with it.

These are incontestable facts. They are also, however, facts from which the most unreasoned and preposterous conclusions can be deduced, because "oppose" is a soft and flabby word. It slides smoothly over the surface of political realities but it never grips them firmly. These realities provoke concrete questions, such as: Against what aspects of the Spanish regime is opposition directed? What are the various motives and purposes of this opposition? With what is it equipped? Who are its leaders? How does it express itself? And, above all, why has it not prevailed?

To ignore these questions and be content with the observation that eighty per cent of the Spanish people "oppose" their government reflects an insight about as penetrating as it would be to summarize the political conditions of the United States in the single observation that the American people overwhelmingly favor "democracy." It is scarcely necessary to point out that, when the word "democracy" is used by Thomas E. Dewey, Henry Wallace, the National Association of Manufacturers, the *Daily Worker,* and the *Catholic News,* they are not all speaking in the same idiom.

In Spain, the question of whether or not the great masses of the people are united in their longing for freedom (which they are) is less crucial than the question of whether or not they are united in their definition of freedom (which they are not). The variety of definitions which an itinerant student of semantics could gather in Spain must include what he hears from a textile capitalist in Barcelona, outraged by the social security program of the Falange; a Communist leader, envisioning a dictatorship of the proletariat; a Sevillian aristocrat, fretful over the expense of the government's public works program; a petty bourgeois who owns a perfumery in Madrid, whose ideological dreams of a Republic are beset by frightening nightmares about another civil war; a factory worker in Bilbao, who has always been a Socialist and hates the Communists as fiercely as he hates the Falangists; a doctor or lawyer who is firmly convinced that liberty without order is a mockery and that only a liberal Monarchy can hold the perilous balance between the two; an Anarchist who has just finished seven years in jail and torment, who just wants a gun and a chance. . . . Freedom, yes—but *whose* freedom?

Furthermore it is not only a matter of definitions. It is also a matter of immediate decisions and choices. All the men and women of Spain who fear and despise the government of General Franco constitute a formidable majority. Each one of them knows and seeks a better alternative to this regime—*but many fear a worse one*. To every political group, this fear brings specific, haunting questions. Should a Socialist accept a course of action entailing risk of civil war, when that war would give Communists their best chance to exploit their superior organization? Would a Communist find greater or less freedom to operate under a restored Monarchy? If an Anarchist found himself in a Republic dominated by Marxists, would that not force an end to his hopes for a syndical paradise? If a restored Monarchy brought with it enough liberality and humanity, could not the progressive forces of the left thrive and grow faster? Or would it not be wiser for the left now to fight resolutely on the issue of the Spanish regime of General Franco, rather than take chances on a Monarchic regime whose superficial liberal façade would protect the most autocratic privileges, whose small, sly concessions to the workers and petty bourgeoisie would only dull the edge of proletarian wrath and blunt its power?

All these sharp issues lie beneath the slick surface of the generalization that the Spanish people "oppose" the Spanish government. That opposition—overwhelming but divided, resolute but disunited—assumes meaning and importance only in terms of its specific targets, its weapons and resources, and its ultimate political aim.

2

In January of 1941, almost an exact decade had passed since King Alfonso XIII had fled from Spain. Both the Republic and the Civil War had followed and had gone, and a strange new order of things was emerging in the land from which he had been exiled. And it was but a few weeks before his own death when, on the fifth of the month, Alfonso declared in a manifesto to his people:

"I offer to my Fatherland the renunciation of my rights, so that by the historic law of Succession to the Throne, my son, Prince Don Juan, is automatically designated, who will incarnate in his person the Monarchic institution and who will on the morrow, when Spain judges it opportune, become the King of all the Spaniards."

Since that day, the aristocracy and all Monarchists of Spain have affirmed their allegiance to his royal highness Don Juan de Borbón y Battenberg, Count of Barcelona, "who is to reign in Spain with the name of Juan III."

The Monarchists, of all political groups opposed in one sense or another to the regime of General Franco, are the easiest to characterize and comprehend. For they constitute the only political aggregation which deplores the two most crucial events in the last quarter of a century of Spanish history: the electoral victory of the Republican forces in 1931 and the establishment of the "New State" in 1939. Consequently, they must advocate a reversion in Spain's political evolution to a set of conditions which cannot be found at a more recent date than 1923, before General Primo de Rivera established his dictatorship.

Since 1936, when the assault upon the Republic seemed so full of promise for Monarchist hopes, the history of those hopes has been an almost unbroken record of disillusion and frustration. In the early stages of the Civil War, almost all habitual adherents of the Monarchic institution dared believe that the road was opening—albeit paved at a grisly cost—for the restoration of "traditional, legitimate authority." The landed nobility envisaged quick relief from the ominous threat of the Republic's agrarian laws. Most Catholics anticipated a glorious resurrection of the Cross and the Crown. The wealthy bourgeoisie looked forward to the kind of prosperity and order guaranteed by those symbols. And Carlist Requetes, with their rifles and red berets, raced from their well-stocked Navarrese arsenals to offer themselves, bold infantry and gallant cavalry, as the fanatically courageous shock-troops of General Franco's armies. For them, this was a war in which the secret enemy was the whole four hundred years of world history that had unleashed the satanic forces of democracy, liberalism, industrialism, Protestantism, Marxism, atheist France, imperialist Britain, and materialist America.[1]

But all the king's horses and all the king's men did not suffice. General Franco gave the first plain and dismaying indication of his position when the Act of Unification (April 19, 1937) forcibly merged the entire Carlist movement with the

[1] The Carlist movement dates from 1833, when Ferdinand VII died and left his throne to his daughter Isabel. Reactionary groups denied the validity of this succession of a woman to the throne. Their real motive was the fear (shortly proved to be groundless) that the group of advisers around Isabel, who would act as regents until she reached her majority, were too liberally inclined. Those who denied her right of succession advanced the candidacy of Carlos, brother of Ferdinand, and waged civil war in support of their claim for six years, until they were finally defeated. In 1870 another great Carlist revolt took place and again, despite the famous warrior courage of the Navarrese Requetes, as the Carlist soldiers were called, they were crushed. In September of 1936, the last legitimate Carlist pretender (*i.e.*, male descendant of the original Carlos) died and the line of succession had to pass to a woman, thereby invalidating its original pretense of legitimacy. Despite this, the Carlists (or, as they are also labeled, the Traditionalists) continued to persist as a group forged by a century's history and warfare, and distinguished within the broad ranks of Monarchists as the archreactionary element.

Falange (an action which caught many Carlist leaders so un-
awares that, like Count Rodezno, they endorsed it with almost
incredible lack of comprehension or foresight). And the composition of the Generalissimo's first post-Civil War cabinet
(August 10, 1939) was enough to turn dismay into despair—
with its inclusion of only one apparently authentic Monarchist
figure in Esteban Bilbao as Minister of Justice. The Glorious
Victory was of the Movement, not the Monarchy.

World history was as heedless of Monarchist aspirations as
was Francisco Franco. Only five months elapsed after the end
of the Civil War before World War II began. This fact profoundly affected Monarchist chances because it decisively crystallized Nazi Germany's policy in Spain—and in 1939 there was
nothing more decisive in all of Spain than the wishes of that
policy. Berlin had every reason to be pleased with its handi-
work in Iberia. It was true, indeed, that the signing of the
Nazi-Soviet Pact in August had made Falangists in Madrid
appear as pathetically bewildered as Communists in New
York. But the Nazi Foreign Office knew perfectly well that the
new Spanish regime had too few friends in the world to start
any carping or quibbling over what looked like shaking hands
with the devil. Hence, while preparing and executing the
assault on France, Berlin had every reason to insist upon maintenance of the precise status quo in Spain. It was not a moment of sufficient leisure for the German Embassy in Madrid
to study seriously the sentimental illusions of Spanish grandees.

Confronted with such unyielding circumstances not of their
own making, the Monarchists of Spain have been persistently
plagued within their own ranks by a stubborn political dilemma not unlike that confronting the Western powers in the
question of their diplomatic relations with the Franco regime.
To the great majority of Monarchists, that regime made itself
steadily more repugnant, not merely by its obstruction of the
cause of restoration of the throne, but also by all its Fascist
attributes and tactics within Spain. It had established, moreover, a foreign policy plainly if not crudely hostile to that Eng-

land so revered by most of the Spanish aristocracy—for its own
Monarchic majesty, for its lucrative trade relations with Spain,
for the polished education which its schools gave to so many
children of the aristocracy. But while these sentiments might
swell spontaneously in Monarchist hearts, the plain political
truth was that there existed but one man who, if he wished,
could effect a swift restoration of the Crown: General Franco.
Just as Allied diplomats in Madrid had to be accredited to a
distasteful government for the very good reason that no other
government existed, in similar fashion many Monarchists believed that their cause could be advanced only by courting a
man whom they would prefer to banish. Yet, to this line of
argument, other Monarchists retorted that such a policy not
only compromised their political integrity but also defeated its
own ends by fortifying General Franco's own self-assurance.

The division thus produced within Monarchist ranks has
been, of course, precisely the kind of discord which the Generalissimo has exploited all around him. The conciliatory, com-
promising Monarchist faction has found its leader in Estebán
Bilbao: a weak, uninspiring politician who in his youth studied
for the priesthood and in his maturity has become President
of the Cortes, presiding with pathetic solemnity over its mock
deliberations. The earnest, intransigeant Monarchists have included in their ranks such distinguished figures as the brilliant
former president of the Royal Academy of Medicine, Dr. Greg-
orio Marañon, and famed Spanish philosopher José Ortega y
Gasset. But the line between these two groups has never been
either a clear or impassable one. It has wavered with the Monarchists' constantly changing speculations on General Franco's
intentions, and it has been crossed and recrossed by men who
one day acknowledge the Generalissimo as a sincere friend of
the Monarchy, the next day denounce him as its most hypocritical foe.

While the political tactics of General Franco have stimulated
this fretful agitation, the ranks of the Monarchists, over the
last decade, have suffered also from a number of outright de-

fections. When the first skirmishes of the Civil War began, a not insignificant number of Monarchist sympathizers shortly thereafter deserted to the Falange and became devoted apostles of the gospel of the New State. Striking evidence of the loss suffered by the Monarchists can be found merely by consulting the list of signatories to a widely circulated Monarchist petition which appeared during Republican days, in December of 1934. Virtually every prominent Monarchist of that date signed this petition—and yet the list includes names whose former Monarchist association has been completely erased by their subsequent roles as Falangist leaders. There were the Basque industrialist who became one of the most fervent Falangist advocates of a new Spanish imperialism, José María Areilza; the ubiquitous Eduardo Aunós, who has served the Spanish government in innumerable offices including that of Minister of Justice; the shrill Catalan historian of the Falange, Bertrán Guell; the faithful Falangist playwright, Tomás Borras; two diplomatic figures who subsequently moved in and out of the Party embrace, José Felix Lequerica and José Yanguas; the pseudo-Fascist intellectual credited with coining the word *Hispanidad,* Ramiro de Maeztu; and the ardent exponent of Falangist political theory, José María Pemán. The fact that these and a good many other Spanish citizens shifted so easily from Monarchist to Falangist ranks was not only a suggestion of weakness in Monarchist ranks: it was also an illuminating commentary on the political character of many of the people attracted to the Monarchist cause.

In the four years in which I watched the political tragedy unfold in Madrid, the most earnest Monarchist attempt to display prestige and power came in July of 1943; and its result, significantly, turned out to be the most damning measure of the weakness of the Monarchists. With the United Nations on their offensive march, the course of World War II seemed to mark the moment as a favorable one to apply some firm pressure on the Caudillo, while the memory was still fresh of his effusive endorsements of the Axis powers. Pressure took the form of a petition addressed to Franco and sponsored particularly by the Duke of Alba, Spanish Ambassador to the Court of St. James's.

The petition's plea for immediate restoration of "the Traditional Catholic Monarchy" relied heavily on the argument that, before the world conflict ended, Spain must find herself governed, not by any dictatorial improvisation, but by "a definitive regime, consistent with Spanish tradition," such as to "offer an unbreachable defense against the onslaughts of forces of disintegration and revolt both within and without Spain," that is, the political forces of the left. The petition also argued that, while the Franco regime had already compromised itself with the Axis powers, a Monarchy would be "free from all foreign pressure and influence."

In a political sense, the number of signatories to such a document was more important than the sternness of its language. Its sponsors had professed confidence of at least fifty important endorsements. They ended with twenty-six. These included but one military figure (the politically insignificant Lieutenant General Miguel Ponte), one admiral, two mayors (of Cuenca and San Sebastian), three prominent old-time Monarchists (the Duke of Alba, financier Juan Ventosa, and Antonio Goicoechea of the Bank of Spain), one of the founders of the Falange (Alfonso Valdecasas), and four deserting members of the Falange's National Council (Pedro Gamero del Castillo, Manuel Halcón, Jaime de Foxa, and Juan Fanjul). It was an aggregation so unprepossessing as to provoke more pity than scorn.

As the supreme effort of Monarchists to seize the political initiative from General Franco, its failure and consequences deserve some explanation. From its start, the plan struck a simple and formidable obstacle: the fear of Monarchists to accept the personal consequences of any action. More than a score of convinced and ardent Monarchists refused to give their signatures to the petition. Others, while refusing to sign, agreed, with a touch of boldness that could scarcely be called devastating, to address "respectful" personal letters to their

Chief of State. All who sponsored the petition had shown their ingenuousness in counting upon the signature of Estebán Bilbao, but he easily evaded on the grounds that, as President of the Cortes, official propriety would be violated. The Blue Bishop of Madrid, in private conversation, said that he agreed in principle with the petition but that he could not tarnish his personal loyalty to the Generalissimo. Having met all these rebuffs, the petition died not with a bang but a whimper. News of its existence reached the Pardo prematurely and Franco quickly had the wretched document withdrawn from circulation and brought to him. This unhappy end at least afforded some apologetic Monarchists the opportunity to claim that they could have mustered a more prestigious list of signatures if only . . .

The aftermath was a varied political revelation. General Franco had a tempestuous meeting with the military who had dared to sympathize with the plan. As for the four members of the Falange *Consejo Nacional,* they escaped with nothing more drastic than expulsion—but only after a wild session of the Council during which ardent Falangists like José Luis Arrese and Sancho Dávila vied with each other in furious debate on the most appropriate punishment for the "traitors," not excluding summary execution.

The case of the Duke of Alba was different. Of all those associated with the petition, his signature had carried the most prestige, and his demeanor had been the most aggressive. But without the slightest disturbance on the political surface, he continued his ambassadorial duties as General Franco's emissary near His Britannic Majesty's Government. Why? From Franco's viewpoint, Alba was too skilled a diplomat and too popular in certain London circles to allow his dismissal. From the Duke's viewpoint, he concluded that he could win more important converts to the cause of the Spanish Monarchy in London than on his Sevillian estate. From such curious combinations of conflicting interests has the regime of General

Franco been able so often to maintain its political poise at moments of greatest nervous stress.

But the most bizarre touch of all was of another variety. From the Pardo, through official channels, and to the public at large (but with special attention to Monarchists) came a cleverly rumored "explanation" of the Generalissimo's harsh attitude toward those who had signed the petition. It was an explanation that could have been produced by only the most inventive imagination and the most resourceful political cunning. This officially sponsored version of the events that had just occurred advanced a remarkable theory: the Generalissimo had wished to sponsor a Monarchic restoration only after the Falange Party had been completely demobilized and liquidated. Restoration at the present moment would have served only to pile the political machinery of a Monarchy upon the existing Falangist machinery of government, which would produce confusion bordering on chaos. Moreover (the theory explained) the signature of certain Falangists had proved that the petition had been secretly sponsored by leaders of the Party seeking to escape from their unpopular roles by treacherously infiltrating into the Monarchist ranks—and the wise and farseeing Caudillo was determined that the detested Falangists would not thus evade the consequences of their wicked deeds!

The startling audacity of the men who invented this tale did not halt at spreading it merely by word of mouth. There was carefully printed a circular letter, typical of the vast number of such political documents drifting constantly from hand to hand and café to café in Madrid. The letter was entitled and addressed: "TO THE AUTHENTIC MONARCHISTS." In the most righteous and indignant "Monarchist" tones, it vilified all signatories to the recent petition as unscrupulous political opportunists seeking to exploit the "true" Monarchist cause as their own political refuge. Fervently exclaiming that Monarchist ranks must solidly exclude all the hated and frightened Falangists who were using these despicable tactics, this document was written, printed, and distributed *by the Falange itself!* [2]

It was not difficult to understand the purposes which inspired this exercise of duplicity on the grand scale. General Franco, of course, had seen that there was no political advantage in emerging from the whole episode in the role either of a dictator infatuated with his own power or of an overardent protector of the Falange. It was preferable that all sufficiently credulous opinion, whether Spanish or foreign, believe that the Generalissimo was pursuing a strategy so subtle and prescient that its sly secret could be imparted only to the politically uninitiated. From the Generalissimo's viewpoint, all this could be achieved by the propagation of a political fantasy that also would bewilder the more ingenuous Monarchists beyond all hope of bringing into focus a political scene already blurred beyond their powers of recognition. [3] No one knew better than General Franco the lingering hope in so many Monarchist minds that he yet would emerge as the sponsor of the Crown . . . the tantalizing hope which bred such vacillation, which would not die because its fulfillment would be a cheap solution for so many problems. . . . Maybe the Caudillo was right . . . maybe he would. . . .

For the would-be restorers of the Spanish throne, all this was disaster.

What mattered was not the mere failure to move the Chief

[2] The plan to issue the document was conceived jointly by Party Chief Arrese and one of his chief aides, Manuel Valdes, *Vice-Secretario de Servicios* of the Falange. The letter was written by employees of the Vice-Secretariat of Popular Education, possibly by Juan Aparicio. It was printed at a shop (on the Calle Nuncio, Number 7) which regularly handled official work for the Vice-Secretariat.

[3] I knew of several Monarchist leaders who fully accepted the *franquista* interpretation of the Caudillo's performance. One in particular argued with me at length and protested that only obtuseness could prevent my seeing the shrewd, long-range purposes of Franco. This attitude is not quite so difficult to understand as it may seem, since these people did not have the unmistakable proof of the Falangist authorship of the "authentic Monarchist" letter which came to me only by the sheerest chance.

of the Spanish State, to wring from him even the slightest concession, the slenderest promise. What mattered so much was
that, when confronted with that failure, these men found
themselves utterly without resources, without appeal to political reinforcements of any kind, without some alternative
course of action, without even a political martyr who might
lend dignity to defeat. In this boldest public affirmation of
Monarchist faith, not a single important army general had
stirred. No bishop had spoken from his pulpit. No Falangist
had betrayed the least fear.

With the tumbling leaves of the autumn of 1943, the prestige
of the men whose faith was fixed upon the Cross and the
Crown fell to cold and barren political ground. It has stirred
since, but it has never risen.

3

At the age of thirty-three, Don Juan de Borbón y Battenberg, Count of Barcelona, has spent the longest time in exile
of any prominent Spanish political refugee. He has been awaiting the moment to ascend the throne of Spain for sixteen
years. During the years of World War II, until his arrival in
Lisbon in January in 1946, his political headquarters were
established in Lausanne, Switzerland.

During the war years, communication between Madrid and
Lausanne was often difficult, sometimes impossible. This contributed to the confusion of Monarchist leaders within Spain,
who were constant victims of the most contradictory gossip
and rumors purporting to be authentic indications of Juan's
political strategy.

To my certain knowledge, however, Monarchists were able
frequently enough to use the Spanish diplomatic pouch between the Foreign Office in Madrid and the Spanish Embassy
in Berne for transmission of their messages—thanks to the prevailing Monarchist sentiment of career officials in Spain's diplomatic service. It was one of the innumerable oddities of

Spanish politics that, often at the times when Franco and the
Falange were most incensed over Monarchist agitation, the
facilities of Franco's own Foreign Office were exploited in this
fashion.

Between the pretender's Swiss villa and General Franco's
Pardo outside Madrid there passed a steady political correspondence. The letters by diplomatic pouch and the ciphered
cables which have made up this correspondence are a much
more revealing indication of the character and purposes of the
Monarchist movement than the fretful and futile agitation of
Monarchist politicians in Madrid. Some of these letters and
telegrams became "public" documents in the form of repro-
ductions printed and widely distributed by Monarchists in
Madrid; others have remained confidential.

The first document of any significance in this wartime correspondence came with a letter to the Generalissimo from the
pretender in March of 1943. Don Juan sought, earnestly and
a bit ingenuously, to call a halt to the Chief of State's obvious
temporizing and evasion on the restoration issue: "Your Excellency has set forth, in effect, as a period of transition, a space
of time sufficient to carry out the revolutionary work which
has been projected but whose program can be described either
as very vague in its definitions or as susceptible to interminable
development." More important, the pretender firmly rejected
any suggestion that his restoration be predicated upon his endorsement of the Falange Party or its program: "My acquies-
cence in this would imply a patent denial of the very essence
of the Monarchic virtue, profoundly averse to the fostering
of party divisions." Concluding with some acidulous references
to General Franco's foreign policy, Don Juan drily described
"your present neutrality" as one which "displays a quality of
partiality . . . systematically proclaimed in the press and even
in official declarations."

In the months that followed, the pretender continued to
express, to Franco and to all who visited him in Lausanne, a
policy of this tone and purpose: firm in certain basic prin-

ciples, yet suggesting dissatisfaction rather than hostility toward the Franco regime. But the intransigeance of the Generalissimo was expressed not only in curt replies to the pretender but even more plainly in his stern retaliation upon all Monarchist agitators in Madrid. Expulsion from public office, arrests, occasional exile to provincial towns or the Canary Islands became frequent. These "outrages" compelled the pretender to adopt new language and new tactics. On January 25, 1944, addressing Franco not as Chief of State but as "my respected general," Don Juan dispatched a letter carrying his first unequivocal denunciation of the Spanish regime:

I shall soon have completed 13 years of exile during which I have come to know the situation of Spain and the Spanish way of thinking with a clarity and independence which I should have found it difficult to achieve in the Royal Palace, in that atmosphere of adulation which always surrounds the powerful. . . .

Your Excellency is one of the very few Spaniards who believe in the stability of the National Syndicalist regime. You are one of the few who believe that our nation, still irreconcilably divided, will have sufficient strength at the end of the World War to resist the attacks of extremists. You are one of the few who believe that you can succeed, through mollification and concession, in gaining the respect of those foreign nations which have noted with disgust your policies toward them. . . .

I am convinced that Your Excellency and the regime which you direct cannot survive the end of the war. . . .

I always have refused to accede to Your Excellency's written requests to me to identify myself with the Falangist State, because I have believed it to be incompatible with the very essence of the character of the Monarchy. . . . But I am now firmly convinced that this attitude of mine is not plain enough to assist the future interests of the Fatherland, since many persons might interpret my silence as meaning association with the present regime. This obliges me to make known, in Spain and throughout the world, the total lack of compatibility between that regime and the Monarchy.[4]

[4] Three days later, the pretender made public this letter by handing a copy of it to the Berne correspondent of *La Prensa* of Buenos Aires.

But this resolute declaration of policy was but a few days old when all the political calculations of the young prince were suddenly violated by an event which apparently took him by complete surprise. The governments of Great Britain and the United States, their patience destroyed by the slippery evasiveness of Madrid's Foreign Office, employed their most feared economic weapon against the Spanish government: they announced immediate imposition of an embargo on all petroleum shipments to Spain. This drastic action might have seemed, at first glance, to harmonize advantageously with the prince's own sudden declaration less than a week before. But it appeared in no such light to the pretender. He immediately feared that conservative elements in Spain, angered by the hardships which the oil embargo would bring to the entire Spanish economy, would turn their wrath upon him, in the strong suspicion that he had deliberately timed his statement to benefit by the "anti-Spanish" blow struck by the Western powers. And to accompany this fear, there undoubtedly stirred in the pretender's mind a sudden new hope: perhaps General Franco, facing this unexpected crisis in his foreign relations, might be receptive to another amicable review of the possibility of immediate restoration. Accordingly, on February 3, in his urgent anxiety both to escape the criticism he feared and to test the hope he cherished, the pretender telegraphed the following remarkable message to the Generalissimo:

IN A LETTER ADDRESSED TO YOUR EXCELLENCY ON THE 25TH LAST AND IN RECENT STATEMENTS TO PRESS ANTICIPATING INTERNATIONAL COMPLICATIONS WHICH I HAD PREDICTED FOR SOME TIME, I HAVE ADOPTED THIS ATTITUDE SOLELY FOR PATRIOTIC PURPOSE OF PREVENTING SITUATION DEVELOPING IN WHICH ONLY TWO POLITICAL SOLUTIONS OPEN TO SPAIN WOULD BE MAINTENANCE AT ALL COST OF YOUR EXCELLENCY'S REGIME OR THAT WHICH THOSE VANQUISHED IN OUR CIVIL WAR ARE TRYING AND WILL TRY TO IMPOSE WITH FOREIGN AID.

I AM CONFIDENT THAT YOUR EXCELLENCY INTERPRETED MY AT-

TITUDE IN THIS WAY. I APPEAL WITH ALL MY HEART TO YOUR WELL-
PROVED PATRIOTISM THAT, FORGETTING DIVERGENCES OF OPINION,
WE MAY REACH AGREEMENT PERMITTING RESTORATION OF THE
MONARCHY WITHIN BRIEF TIME THUS ESCAPING PRESENT DIFFI-
CULTIES AND SAVING SPAIN FROM DANGER OF NEW CIVIL WAR.

BY ACTING IN THIS MANNER WE WOULD STILL BE IN POSITION TO
DEFEND THE PRINCIPLES WHICH LED US TO RISE UP AGAINST THE
POPULAR FRONT. TOMORROW PERHAPS IT WILL BE TOO LATE. I AM
SURE THAT YOUR EXCELLENCY, CONSCIOUS OF THE GRAVE DANGERS
WHICH THREATEN SPAIN AND ANXIOUS TO OVERCOME PRESENT DIF-
FICULTIES, WILL NOT REFUSE TO CONSIDER THIS ONE SOLUTION
WHICH THE INTEREST OF OUR COUNTRY SO URGENTLY DEMANDS.
LONG LIVE SPAIN.

(Signed) JUAN, COUNT OF BARCELONA

The vanity of the hope which inspired this message was
equalled only by the lack of political integrity which it displayed. All reasoned political judgment obviously had been
swept aside by the overpowering temptation to gamble on a
quick chance to regain the coveted throne. Only the most un-
informed estimate of General Franco's character could have
induced Juan to believe that his message would be received as
anything more than a crude attempt to exploit the Caudillo's
political predicament. Only the most unstable and vacillating
political principles would have allowed the pretender to issue
this clumsy, conspiratorial plea to thwart all Republican aspirations—with even greater determination than he had expressed (only a week earlier) in his denial of the Falangist
state.

The telegraphic reply from General Franco might have
frozen the wires that carried it:

I REPLY TO YOUR TELEGRAM OF THE 3RD.

YOUR STATEMENTS, MADE WITH AN EYE TO APPEALING TO FOR-
EIGNERS, HAVE CREATED A VERY BAD IMPRESSION IN SPAIN EVEN
AMONG PERSONS MOST CLOSELY ATTACHED TO THE MONARCHY.

THEY STRIKE A DISCORDANT NOTE IN THE FACE OF THE UNITY
WHICH ALL SPANIARDS WHO ARE NOT REDS, BOTH WITHIN AND OUT-
SIDE THE COUNTRY, HAVE RESPECTED.

RECENT DEVELOPMENTS IN SPAIN'S FOREIGN RELATIONS ARE DUE
ONLY TO OUR ACTIVE DEFENSE OF OUR RIGHTS AND OUR SOVER-
EIGNTY. SPAIN IS NOT WILLING TO LOSE THE FRUITS OF OUR VIC-
TORIOUS CRUSADE BECAUSE OF THE WORLD WAR NOW BEING
FOUGHT, AND IT WILL DEFEND ITS SOVEREIGNTY WITH ALL MEANS,
NOT COUNTING DAYS OR YEARS, TO THE LAST MAN AND THE LAST
CATHOLIC.

THE RESTORATION OF THE MONARCHY TOWARD WHICH WE ARE
HEADING FIRMLY IS NOT ASSISTED BY THE DISSIDENCE AND CON-
FLICTS PROVOKED BY MONARCHIST GROUPS NOR BY PUBLIC EXPRES-
SIONS OF DISUNITY AND HOSTILITY TOWARD THE REGIME BORN OF
OUR CRUSADE AND FREELY RECOGNIZED BY ALL NATIONS.

I HAVE TRIED AT ALL TIMES IN MY LETTERS TO OVERCOME YOUR
OBSTINACY AND I TRULY REGRET THE DISAGREEMENTS CAUSED BY
OBVIOUS ERRORS WHICH YOU ARE UNWILLING TO DISAVOW.

WHAT I CANNOT AND NEVER WILL DO IS TO BETRAY THE SPIRIT
OF THOSE WHO FOUGHT BESIDE ME, CONVERT SPAIN INTO A LOWLY
AND UNCHIVALROUS NATION, OR ANYTHING BUT WHAT MY CON-
SCIENCE AND DUTY DEMAND I SHOULD DO IN THE BEST INTERESTS
OF SPAIN.

This stinging rebuff was the pretender's only reward for his
abject appeal to Franco to enter a new alliance against the
political forces of the Spanish left.

Another year of world events and of sober reflection impressed upon Don Juan de Borbón and his counselors certain
important facts. By the beginning of 1945, it was apparent to
them, first, that General Franco did not have the least intention of sponsoring a restoration of the throne before the end
of World War II; secondly, that the end of the war was imminent; thirdly, that despite the nearness of peace and the
Monarchists' own expectations, the Western powers showed
little if any inclination to apply serious political pressure on

the Franco regime. Finally, it was apparent that no nation in Europe was going to revert to a social or economic order resembling that of prewar years; and no political movement could expect to prosper if it failed to heed that fact.

With these considerations in mind, on March 19, 1945, the royal pretender issued to the Spanish people a manifesto which seemed to signify the resolution of many of the paralyzing political doubts of the past years, and which stated Monarchist purposes with fair clarity and precision. The manifesto declared:

Today, six years having passed since the Civil War ended, the regime implanted by General Franco, inspired from the beginning by the totalitarian systems of the Axis powers, so contradictory to the character and the tradition of our people, is fundamentally incompatible with the circumstances which the present war is producing in the world. The foreign policy followed by the present regime also compromises the future of the nation.

Spain runs the risk of finding herself dragged into another fratricidal conflict and of seeing herself totally isolated from the world. The present regime, whatever may be its efforts to adapt itself to the new situation, provokes this double peril; and a new Republic, however moderate it be in its beginnings and intentions, would not be long in drifting toward one of two political extremes, inducing the other extreme again to take recourse in another civil war.

Only the Traditional Monarchy can be an instrument of peace and of concord to reconcile Spaniards; only it can command respect in the foreign field, through an effective state of law and achieving a harmonious synthesis of order and freedom based upon the Christian concept of the State.

For these reasons . . . I raise my voice and solemnly ask of General Franco that, recognizing the failure of his totalitarian concept of the State, he abandon power and open the way for the restoration of the traditional regime of Spain, the only one capable of guaranteeing Religion, Order, and Liberty.

Under the Monarchy—just, tolerant, and healing—there must enter a number of reforms vital to the interest of the nation. The primary task will be: immediate approval by popular vote of a political constitution, recognition of all international rights, of the rights inherent in the human person, and guarantee of the corresponding political liberties; establishment of a legislative assembly elected by the nation; recognition of the diversity of the regions of Spain; full political amnesty; a more just distribution of wealth and the suppression of unjust social differences. . . .

Strong in my faith in God and in my imprescriptible rights and duties, I wait for the moment when my greatest longing may be realized: the peace and concord of all Spaniards. Long live Spain!

This moment for which the Bourbon pretender longed was not brought appreciably closer by the speech of General Franco on the following July 18, though he did indeed promise restoration of the traditional Monarchy. This declaration of purpose, viewed in the context of the Generalissimo's correspondence with the Count of Barcelona, merely confessed in public a vague intention privately expressed innumerable times before. Beyond that intention, the Caudillo did not even hint at any of the crucial questions implicit in the issue of a new throne. What was to be the fate of the Falange? What constitutional provisions would be guaranteed? What political price would General Franco exact, either for himself or for the men or principles with which he had been identified for so long?

Nor did the rather artificial drama of the pretender's transfer of headquarters from Lausanne to the Portuguese capital of Lisbon, in January of 1946, materially affect the political situation. It did, indeed, bring Don Juan to Iberian soil, at least geographically closer to his ultimate goal. But his political chances could not be measured in mileage, and even the trip itself had brought its own disillusionment when the British Foreign Office hesitated and stalled for days before granting the pretender a transit visa in his flight to Lisbon.

Foreign Minister Martín Artajo's usually even temperament gave way to vehement expressions of anger to the British Ambassador in Madrid when this delay occurred. He heatedly charged that the London Foreign Office, after all its indications of anxiety to see quick and peaceful political change in Spain, was stupidly and stubbornly impeding that change by putting obstacles in the way of the pretender's flight to Lisbon. Actually, the British Foreign Office had no serious reason or justification for refusing Don Juan a transit visa, but it was nervously afraid that issuance of the visa and Juan's departure from London for Lisbon would be construed as British sponsorship of his political mission. What was illuminating in Martín Artajo's conversations with the British Ambassador was his plain, unabashed confidence that Juan's arrival in Lisbon would materially accelerate political change in Madrid. This was a revealing measure of the Foreign Minister's own ingenuousness, as well as his ignorance of General Franco's political plans.

The pretender's passport contained all the evidence needed to judge his political strength. For the Portuguese visa which it carried would never have been issued by the Lisbon government without previous consultation with General Franco. On all former occasions the Generalissimo had been anxious to keep Don Juan in Switzerland. One of the valued services which Berlin had rendered Franco during the war years had been to frustrate any attempts by Don Juan to escape through the Nazi-occupied territory which ringed Switzerland.

Neither caprice nor weakness had induced Madrid to permit now a journey which it had prevented for so long. The decision was based upon a shrewd estimate of both international and domestic politics. At the moment when the issue of the pretender's trip arose, the General Assembly of the United Nations was meeting in London. There seemed to be ominous rumblings of an impending storm that might hurl some diplomatic thunderbolts at the Spanish regime. Spurred by rumor to prepare for the worst, men in and around the Pardo saw the possible wisdom in having the pretender to the Spanish throne near at hand, if the need arose for some dramatic countermove to meet a United Nations challenge. The General Assembly, however, allayed any such fears by merely repeating the verbal formula of the San Francisco Conference for snubbing Franco, albeit with a little more rhetoric.

Even apart from such speculations on the international scene, the presence of Don Juan in Lisbon could still be exploited to the political advantage of the regime of General Franco. For the pretender's journey to Lisbon entailed a grave political risk for his cause: should he establish residence at a distance of a mere two hours' flight from the Spanish capital without being able to progress further, his personal prestige would suffer enormously. In a political sense, he could afford not to be King of Spain when in Switzerland; he could not afford it when on Iberian soil. The Caudillo had anticipated that the typical Spanish citizen's reaction to the pretender's arrival in Lisbon would be to conceive of him as rapping imperiously at the gates of Spain demanding immediate admission. Supremely confident that he could keep those gates closed as long as he wished (or open them only on his own terms), General Franco could bring bitter frustration to his royal adversary. By these tactics, his regime was able to convert what should have been a happy and politically significant moment for the Monarchist cause into a moment heavy with the humiliation of its enemies' indifference.

4

What makes a Spanish Monarchist?

To answer that question, it is not quite sufficient to speak only of the selfish protection of landed or capital wealth, or the desire of titled families to share in the conspicuous luxury and conspicuous waste of a royal court. For of all the distinctions that divide Monarchist ranks, none is more profound than that which separates two groups who may be labeled respectively the "professional" Monarchists and the "opportunist" Monarchists.

The latter group has been recruited from among those Spanish citizens who, while individually professing many different political doctrines including even a moderate Socialism or a temperate bourgeois republicanism, have believed in the immediate (but temporary) wisdom of a Monarchic restoration. This belief has sprung from three sources. First, they have known that no history (not even perverse Spanish history) records any example of such self-abnegation on the part of victors in a civil war as compels them, after years of power, to exchange positions with those they vanquished. Secondly, they have feared the immeasurable tragedy that another civil war would bring. Finally, they have hoped that a Monarchic restoration could bring an end to a regime which clearly does not intend to commit political suicide, offer escape from the alternative of civil war, and establish sufficient guarantees of basic human liberties as would allow the people of Spain, slowly but freely, to develop a political and economic order of their own choice.

For the men who advance this hope, men of humane disposition and liberal determination, the Monarchy is not a revered institution but a useful expedient. Reduced to its simplest and crudest terms, their argument becomes the practical contention that peaceful evolution in Spain (not evolution within the Franco regime, but evolution away from the Franco regime) can come only with the support of the Spanish Army; and the only alternative to the Franco regime which could win the active support of the Spanish Army (or the Spanish Church) would be a Monarchic restoration. As for the aftermath of restoration, even if it should fail to fulfill its promise of greater freedom for the Spanish people, the open struggle that would have to follow would be no worse than that which would be precipitated by any attempt to overthrow the Franco regime by force. Such is the argument of the "opportunist Monarchists."

The position of the "professional Monarchists"—the great mass of the landed aristocracy, the wealthy capitalist class, the chronic Spanish conservative whose reactionary credo suggests a psychopathic case—is crude in its simplicity. These men have denounced the regime of General Franco with no motive more elevating than the typical bourgeois fear that a totalitarian state, if hard-pressed politically, might try to transmute itself into a kind of proletarian dictatorship. For these men, Monarchy means Safety—from social legislation, from expensive public works, from independent labor unions, from division of huge Andalucian or Extremaduran estates, from political parties, from state education of the people, from freedom itself. For them, restoration promises more than a new king. It promises a whole new nineteenth century.

The poison of this thinking has infected most of the Monarchist movement. It explains much of the moral weakness of the men and of their principles. It reflects itself in a pretender who, despite the speed with which he subsequently cultivated a new political vocabulary, as late as 1944 was still offering himself to General Franco as an ally "to defend the principles which led us to rise up against the Popular Front." It betrays itself in the fact that, despite the relative lightness of the official persecution which the Monarchist movement has suffered, it has failed completely to produce a leader with any evidence of political vision or the most elementary requisites of statesmanship.

And it is this virus which has produced the all too realistic caricature of the typical Monarchist in the minds of the Spanish people. He is a man of much education and little learning, of material wealth and intellectual poverty; a man whose spirit would wither if deprived of the essentials of sleek clothes to wear, appetizing meals to eat, immaculately clean sheets to sleep between; a man whose self-control in political debate shows in his never pounding a table with the risk of breaking a well-manicured fingernail; a man who never uses sharp words, thinks with clear ideas, or splits an infinitive; a man whose most moving expression of indignation is a hand that shakes so tremulously as he talks that the tea spills sloppily into the saucer.

8 THE FORCES OF OPPOSITION . . . THE LEFT

HE LAST of the four years of my official mission in Madrid, while I continued to edit the output of informational and propaganda material, was primarily dedicated to work of another sort: political intelligence. Gathering and sifting political facts and rumors of such great volume and varying merit as could be found only in a Latin country in unseen turmoil, I found the major part of my time occupied with the preparation of confidential and secret political reports, many to the Military Intelligence Service of the War Department but most to the Department of State.

In October of 1945, this political work, which had covered an unlimited field, was narrowed to focus upon a special aspect of Spain's political life. It happened at this time that Washington reassigned to another diplomatic post an officer of the Embassy whose particular task for several years had been liaison with the underground leaders of the opposition forces, the leaders of the left. The Embassy's Counselor (W. Walton Butterworth, adroit career diplomat, who a month later became Chargé d'Affaires) directed me to devote the maximum possible time to association with the underground leaders, to report upon them, their achievements, weaknesses, and strength. This I continued to do until I left both Madrid and diplomatic service in the following May of 1946.

What followed was an experience that reached beyond the conventional pattern of diplomatic relations (although that pattern is never so quietly conventional as it appears from a distance). The characters who came upon the scene were scarcely the conventional type. A mild-mannered bank clerk in Madrid: he was an active and ardent leader of the Socialists. A fairly prosperous contractor in the building trade in the Spanish capital: he represented a circle of moderate, middle-class Republicans who met weekly at a friend's house in the tradition, but scarcely the atmosphere, of the eighteenth century French salon. A brilliant, dynamic former editor of an important provincial newspaper under the Republic: he got out of jail late in 1945, after seven years' imprisonment, to renew immediately his powerful influence within left Republican groups. A handsome blond, blue-eyed boy of nineteen, soft in speech, cultivated in manner, easy and affable in disposition and demeanor: he frequently made his perilous journey from the Asturian mountains to Madrid, to report on guerrilla activities and secret labor-union organization in the tense, explosive mining country.

There were innumerable others, but among them a certain few of different and less heroic strain deserve mention. I remember two of them in particular. They made their appearance, calling to see me at my office, not many weeks before I left Madrid. Modestly dressed, quietly earnest in manner, they introduced themselves as members and "official representatives" of what they described as "the newly founded *Partido Español Secreto*." They explained that they were the humble spokesmen for the youth of Spain—the young men of the universities and schools who were outraged by the intellectual slavery which the Franco regime imposed upon them. These men (explained their delegates) had dedicated themselves to bringing the Four Freedoms to Spain—but they needed American encouragement and, above all, American arms. The two young men spoke with emotion of "the glorious memory of your illustrious President Roosevelt," who surely had understood the cause of Spanish freedom. All "liberal" Spaniards had counted upon Allied victory in the World War to bring an inglorious end to the Franco regime—and these men could not be disappointed now, could they?

For quickly rehearsed rhetoric, the words of the two young men were not as unconvincing as they should have sounded. But they had not rehearsed long enough to invent a name for their organization more impressive than the absurd "Secret Spanish Party." Nor, in changing to their costumes of fairly cheap suits and coarse shirts without ties, had they remembered to remove their black silk socks and shoes of the costliest leather. As briefly as I could, I explained to the Falange agents that my only official concern was with cultural and informational activities bringing closer together the Spanish and American peoples.

Various as the characters and professions of the men with whom I met, so too were the scenes of our meetings. For many it was easy and safe enough to come openly to my office in the Press Section. They carried cards of membership in our circulating library, on the same floor as my office, and on their visits browsed leisurely for some minutes. After checking out a book, they gave my secretary a prearranged assumed name. After they left, following our meeting, if questioned by police as to their movements, they had their library cards and their books to demonstrate the innocence of their visit to our offices.

In other cases, especially of men almost certain to be under police surveillance, it was best to meet at a not too crowded hour in any of the cafés along the nearby Calle Serrano. Over *café expreso* we could talk leisurely (despite the occasional presence of an obvious *Seguridad* agent assigned to most cafés in the transparent role of an habitual customer) of many things —of the latest political maneuvers within the National Alliance of Democratic Forces, the attitude of the British Embassy, the effect of the closing of the French frontier, or some recent guerrilla raid upon a *guardia civil* outpost.

Again, at other times, an excellent meeting place was the

rostro, Madrid's sprawling secondhand market. Here, mingled in grand disorder, were diplomats' wives seeking bargains in lace or silver; slick jewel thieves slyly showing stolen diamond rings or emerald pendants; the shabbiest peddlers of everything from frayed towels to pieces of tin. Here it was easy to meet with my friends, to wander from shop to shop pricing Spanish tables or Portuguese chairs, fingering pieces of Dresden china, studying Goya etchings—and talking as we went.

In these various places and circumstances, I came to know intimately a great number of these men, not as lifeless symbols of impersonal political forces, but as human beings and as friends. For the present, they remain anonymous friends. But they need no names to identify their characters or their principles, for theirs is a spiritual lineage and heritage that has found expression in every age, among all peoples. They are the cursed, courageous believers in freedom's credo:

> They call us aliens, we are told,
> Because our wayward visions stray
> From that dim banner they unfold,
> The dreams of worn-out yesterday. . . .
>
> We fling our answer back in scorn:
> "We are less children of this clime
> Than of some nation yet unborn
> Or empire in the womb of time."

These could well be their words, for this is their spirit. This they taught me.

But they taught me something else, not less important. The facile eulogy of poetry or prose is, for them, neither the greatest tribute nor the greatest service. Men of whom the poet wrote could take no easy delight in the poet's praise, precisely because their spirit is as he described it. The ecstatic tributes of their friends (they know) come all too often from hearts that love not wisely but too well. Better for them than smooth phrases of adulation is careful comprehension, better than reverence is understanding. To cheer their vagrant vision is

no service. But to understand why *their* nation remains yet un-
born is the greatest service of the wisest friend.

Men of good faith, in a land of ill will, on an earth of little
peace, they need, above all else, that the people of the world
know and appreciate the reasons why their faith has not prevailed.

2

Spain's political problems can neither be defined in epigrams, governed by axioms, nor solved by syllogisms. The people's clamoring, compelling spirit of fierce individualism is
only one source of the complexities that defy brisk, easy definition. Throughout the Spanish nation, now and throughout
modern Spanish history, political lines intersect economic lines
and both cut ruthlessly across regional lines. Poverty-stricken
peasants of Extremadura are reactionary; prosperous mer-
chants in Bilbao are Socialists. Communists hate the Falange's
brutal tyranny; tyrannous landholders and factory owners hate
the Falange's social program; the Falange detests both, and
each fears the other. The most devoutly Catholic sector of
Spain is also one of the most passionately anti-Franco, occasionally the most anticlerical. Basque separatism tends to be
politically conservative, Catalan separatism is radical, Galician
separatism is sheer cussedness. Both Anarchists and Communists distrust each other as profoundly as either distrusts the
Falange, and both arouse the fear and suspicion of all Socialists. Yet, were a conservative Monarchy to be restored in
Madrid, undoubtedly ex-Falangists (who have been so largely
recruited from ex-Communists and ex-Anarchists) would join
both these parties on the extreme left-wing benches of the
Cortes in an alliance to battle the return of feudal privileges.
To reduce this political scene, or any part of it, to the shallow
banalities of a "liberal" vs. "reactionary" debate, with an
Anglo-Saxon political vocabulary, only sacrifices the substance
of political truth for the convenience of literary labels.

In describing or evaluating the forces of Spanish democracy, the matter of vocabulary entails one of the most stubborn difficulties. Of the scores of consular reports or hundreds of newspaper articles which I have read about Spain, I do not recall one which was not, in at least some respect, misleading merely in its use of words. This is usually unintentional and probably unavoidable, since political reporting demands an arbitrary choice of descriptive political adjectives. These adjectives seem to apply to clearly defined organizations but in reality refer only to shades of opinion, each merging into the next and none possessing plainly marked limitations.

To refer to "parties" within the political opposition can be accurate enough but dangerously deceptive. This is apparent if a moment's thought is given to the conditions under which these "parties" live. Their existence is illegal and clandestine. Their lives, collectively and individually, are subjected to the most vicious, systematic persecution. Their leadership may have to change several times in the course of a single month as the result of sudden arrests and executions. Their ability to maintain communications between one province and another is tenuous in the extreme. In these circumstances, "parties" really mean what properly could be described only as "units of resistance" (or "groups" or "movements"). Yet, various of these "units of resistance" profess loyalty to certain political principles which are distinguishable from all others and which have been inherited, in fact, from genuine political parties as they once existed in a free political environment. Hence, they function as "units of resistance" while they also represent political "parties." This distinction is fundamental to any true understanding of the forces of Spanish democracy mobilized against the totalitarian regime of General Franco.[1]

[1] The alternate use of the words "Spanish democracy" and "the left," in describing the same political forces, is another instance of the difficulty of precise political reporting about Spain. I am using these words to describe simply all those groups, outside the Monarchist movement, who are struggling or hoping for an end to the Franco regime and the establishment of

These forces have been brought together in a political union under the name of the *Alianza Nacional de Fuerzas Democráticas* (National Alliance of Democratic Forces). Since its founding in October of 1944, the National Alliance has been composed of representative leadership from Socialist, Republican, left Republican, and Anarchist underground movements. Not until February of 1946 did the Communists abandon and dissolve their own separate organization, the *Junta Suprema de Unión Nacional* (Supreme Council of National Union).

The inaugural manifesto which the National Alliance distributed clandestinely throughout Spain in the autumn of 1944 specified lucidly and succinctly, a set of principles to which the Alliance has consistently adhered. Plainly identifying its own cause with the world-wide struggle of the United Nations, the Alliance expressed its main hope in the preamble of its manifesto:

Spanish democracy, the first to spill its blood in war against the Nazi menace, and standing, in spirit and in truth, on the side of the United Nations, is absolutely certain that the triumph of Allied arms is the victory of Democracy, of all Democracy, of all national Democracies.

The political program of the National Alliance contained a set of "bases of accord" indorsed by all underground movements. These principles were: (1) "re-establishment of the Republican order"; (2) "creation of a democratic government to assume all power until the will of the people is consulted through universal suffrage"; (3) "maintenance of social and public discipline with all firmness and decision"; (4) "repair

a government based upon the will of the Spanish people freely expressed. In a parliamentary regime, of course, some of these same political forces would properly be labeled "conservative" or "rightist," in the light of their social or economic philosophy. But in the political relationships of the present, they can be described as forces of "the left" in their wide agreement that the Falangist State must be destroyed, that the Monarchy is an uncertain alternative, that a free, parliamentary government must be restored.

of the confused judicial system," *i.e.*, revision and recodification of the national laws, review of criminal responsibilities of Falangists, compensation for damages suffered under the Falangist State; and (5) "gradual extension of public liberties." The National Alliance further pledged that, with the establishment of these liberties, "the government, following an electoral census, will call general elections and will submit its own policy to the Cortes for approval; and the Cortes, expressing the will of the nation, shall decide the political future of the country." In the field of world affairs, the manifesto declared: "The international policy of the government will be inspired by these principles: adherence to the Atlantic Charter, the Good Neighbor policy, collective organization for peace, recognition of the stature of Spain as a Western and Mediterranean power, and special concern for our relations with the Americas."

Issuance of this declaration, despite the very general terms in which its principles were stated, did signify two noteworthy achievements. It set forth a series of objectives which received the endorsement of not some but *all* underground movements in Spain. Moreover, it demonstrated that the leaders of the left no longer cherished the frail illusion of some sudden political change automatically and immediately restoring a completely democratic order. On the contrary, they accepted the probable necessity for a transitional regime, bringing a "gradual" restoration of personal freedoms and maintaining public order "with firmness."

Two years after its creation, the National Alliance's greatest, if not unique, achievement has been the fact that its members, despite their various and distinct ideological tendencies, have remained loyal to this statement of basic principles. Beyond this important accomplishment, the National Alliance has not been able to make any serious, direct contribution to the overthrow of the Falangist State. It does not exercise command over any nationally organized army battling the police guardians of that State. It has not sought to increase the amount or improve the quality of clandestine propaganda within Spain—which has remained the work of the individual underground organizations within the alliance. It has been unable to impress its views upon public opinion in the world outside Spain—partly because of the patent difficulty of communications, partly because of the huge propaganda resources of the Franco regime, partly because the superior international organization of Communist propaganda attracted more foreign attention to the Spanish Communists' *Junta Suprema* before its dissolution in 1946. The National Alliance, in short, has served less as a political force than as a political forum.

Among the distinct political forces whose voices have been heard in this forum of the National Alliance, there can be no doubt that the most effective underground organizations belong to the Communists and the Anarchists. One revealing index to the amount of activity of these movements has been the quality and volume of their clandestine propaganda. In this the Communist Party has produced a quantity more than double that of all other groups combined. Its editorial merit is conspicuously superior to the average of all other parties: more newsworthy, more persuasive, and generally neatly printed and illustrated. The Anarchist output equals the quantity of all other parties except the Communist, and, next to Communist production, it is the most articulate and presentable.

It is not surprising, of course, that the two groups who practice the strategy of violence and would welcome revolutionary action have displayed the most effective organizations in the underground battle against the Franco regime. But this is less significant than the fact that, since the end of World War II, the strength and prestige of Communism have grown swiftly and at the expense of all other parties of the left.

The sources of Communist strength are not difficult to discover. Of all opposition forces and factions, Communists alone have been able to count upon valuable material aid from outside Spain, with international Communism regularly furnishing arms, money, propaganda, and men. These supplies have supported a typically compact and efficient cellular organization which is admirably geared to underground activity (while other political groups that might perform brilliantly in a "parliamentary" atmosphere stumble and falter in their attempts at revolutionary work). And in its popular appeal throughout Spain, competing with all other parties of the left, Communist propaganda has become enormously persuasive in its argument that Soviet Russia is the only international champion of Spanish democracy, while the Western powers are either so timid or so inarticulate as to make their equivocal position, if not unintelligent, at least unintelligible.

The Communist *Junta Suprema de Unión Nacional* was founded earlier than the National Alliance, in September of 1943, and for more than a year it remained the only underground organization in Spain presuming to speak for more than a single political party. It was, to be sure, a baseless presumption. Despite its exorbitant claims of Socialist, Republican, and even Catholic support, the *Junta* never became more than a typical and exclusive organ of the Communist Party. But the fact that Communists were the first to attempt such an organization was characteristic evidence of the energy and initiative of the Party's leaders, many of them trained abroad and dispatched to Spain for this precise mission.

Perhaps because its leadership has been better trained and politically more mature than that of other Spanish underground groups, the Communist Party in Spain has often seemed to think more clearly and to act with surer purpose. Hesitancy and internal disunion have been apparent only once in the long battle under the Falangist State—for a few months after the dissolution of the Third Internationale. Communists had maintained at all previous times their rigid Party unity by reference of all doubtful questions to the Third Internationale; and when this unchallengeable authority apparently was dissolved, "deviationists" began to appear within Communist ranks in Spain—questioning some of the more devious tactics of international Communism in recent years, suffering qualms over the danger of violence in Spain, drifting toward a pacific kind of Socialism. But it was a short-lived disturbance, and Communist ranks shortly closed as solidly as ever before.

Since then, the direction of Communist leaders has been firm and precise. The Communist Party of Spain is (for the present) strictly a political organization, dedicated to the single purpose of overthrowing the regime of General Franco and unconcerned with eventual social objectives or the subtleties of Marxian dialectic. It advocates the widest possible alliance of all forces opposing the Falangist State regardless of their particular social or economic philosophies. Pursuing this policy scrupulously, Spanish Communists have carefully avoided issues which could easily divide the opposition. In their appeal to the peasants and the petty bourgeoisie, they have taken pains to suggest no assault upon the sanctity of private property. Among the clandestine labor unions of the underground, they have made no effort to revive strictly Communist unions, the cause of so much conflict with Socialists in the past; instead, they have worked in "loyal" co-operation with the secret growing units of the Socialist UGT. On religious questions, Communist propaganda has systematically avoided public indictment of the Spanish Church and has even suppressed mention of the issue of Church-State separation.

But in one important objective, Communist leadership has failed. It has not succeeded in allaying the suspicion and hostility of all other movements of the left. This fear and distrust have arisen not only from the usual Socialist wariness of Communist tactics but also from the specific experience of the Spanish Civil War. Socialists and the moderate left have never forgiven the Communists for the attempt to convert the Republican into a Communist cause, for Communist exploitation of Russian assistance to further their own political advancement. This inherited distrust flamed into angry indignation in 1943 when Communists organized the *Junta Suprema*

and attempted to force Spain and the world to accept it as a
coalition of all "democratic" forces. A year later, when true
representatives of these forces joined to constitute the *Alianza
Nacional,* perhaps the most striking passage in its inaugural
manifesto was the sharp denunciation of "the false position
taken by the Communist sector, determined to maintain a
so-called Supreme Council of National Union and to usurp
the names of other parties and organizations." Socialists, Republicans, and Anarchists seemed almost to be shouting in
outraged protest: "We deplore their obstinacy, and we categorically declare that the forces subscribing to this manifesto
have no relationship whatsoever with the so-called *Junta Suprema* nor do they recognize it. The National Alliance refuses
any collaboration with the enemy and the dangerous kind of
friendship arising from such collusion."

This caustic reference of the National Alliance to "collaboration with the enemy" was inspired by the deep suspicion
that Communist ranks in Spain had been deeply penetrated
by Gestapo agents. Socialists and Republicans, like most Spaniards, knew that scores if not hundreds of German agents had
been assigned the mission of provoking enough disorder within
Spain to open the way for entry of German armies in an
"order-restoring" capacity. They also knew that these agents
were acting, wherever possible, as *agents provocateurs* in
leftist underground organizations, and they firmly believed
that the Communist Party was serving as cover for a great
number of them. Since the time when this suspicion was
keenest, in 1943 and 1944, Socialists and Republicans have
been disturbed by another similar fear: that frightened Falangists were fleeing in large numbers for political refuge to the
Communist Party, from which hundreds of them had emerged
fifteen years before. Against this background, the entrance of
the Communists into the National Alliance in February of
1946 was marked by a conspicuous absence of fraternity or cor-
diality. Even on this occasion, spokesmen for the Socialist Party
rose to speak caustically of Communist tactics in the past

(especially during the Civil War and at the time of the Russo-German Pact) and warned sharply against their future use. Only a few days later, in their clandestine publication *CNT,* the Anarchists echoed the same cry and curtly warned the Communists not to attempt to seize control of the National Alliance from within. Declared the Anarchists: "Maneuvers of no shape or form will ever be permitted to succeed."

While it has been the consistent and not too difficult policy of all non-Communist elements of the Left to make plain their attitude toward the "Reds" (*rojos*), less easy has it been for them to maintain their own clear-cut political identity. This difficulty, precisely like the difficulty of finding an exact political vocabulary to describe these "parties," arises from the constraining circumstances of their existence. The immediate issues confronting all underground forces are exacting in their stark simplicity: we vs. the Falange, freedom vs. Franco, lives (ours) vs. deaths (ours). To accept and to fight these issues leaves little time for the leisurely propagation of precise social or economic programs distinguishing one "unit of resistance" from another and transforming these "units" into "parties" in a political sense. Editorial indictments of the Falange differ little in a Socialist or Republican leaflet, just as bombs thrown by an Anarchist explode in a way no different from those tossed by a Communist. As a result, the marks distinguishing one underground organization from another principally consist of general tendencies inherited from a time when political issues could be openly debated.

Of all elements of the left, the Anarchist underground organization is most painfully lacking in any political program or promise. The movement is even unsure of its own name: most Anarchists have abandoned that title in favor of "Libertarians." Orthodox Anarchism—propagated so successfully in Spain more than fifty years ago by Bakunin's disciples that it won a proletarian strength greater than in any other country of Europe—has virtually disappeared, along with George Sorel's syndicalism. Except for an ardent emphasis on the need

to aid the peasantry and to end the shameful oppression of
Spain's land-glutted absentee owners, little that is concrete remains of the old Anarchist gospel. What does persist is the
fanatical energy and courage of Anarchist leaders. They are
as passionately anticlerical and anti-Communist as ever. But it
has become more than ever difficult to know to what end that
energy is dedicated beyond the destruction of the Falangist
State. As a result, this numerically large, compactly organized,
and fiercely militant movement finds itself susceptible to the
most unpredictable political changes and impulses. Many Socialists have long suspected that it will offer kinder haven to
frightened Falangists than have the Communists.

Between Anarchists and Communists on the one side and
Socialists on the other, there are plain differences and conflicts
of opinion, some arising from traditional policies, others from
political peculiarities of the moment. Whereas both the former
parties are emphatically proletarian parties, the Socialist movement has an essentially bourgeois center of gravity. Although
its powerful UGT union (*Unión General de Trabajadores,*
"General Union of Workers") had a fairly successful record of
competing both with Communist unions and the Anarchist
CNT (*Confederación Nacional de Trabajadores*), nonetheless
the intellectual inspiration and leadership of the Socialist
Party has almost always been middle-class. In general, Socialists battling the Franco government have had less confidence
than Communists and Anarchists in the efficacy of violent
revolutionary action.

Socialist prestige and policy have been seriously influenced
by factors beyond their control, particularly the policy of the
British government toward Spain. Like all the non-Communist left, of course, Socialists have looked to the Western democracies for encouragement and help comparable to what
Russia has systematically furnished the Communists. But this
reliance on, and association with, the British government
naturally became even greater when the latter became a Socialist regime. Since the triumph of Britain's Labor Party,

British policy in Spain has affected the character of Spanish Socialism in two crucial ways. First, the London Socialist government's determination not to disturb relations with General Franco, while a crushing disappointment to all democratic forces opposing the Generalissimo, impaired Socialist prestige especially and immeasurably weakened the hopes of moderates that there could be any escape from the violence advocated by the extreme left. At the same time (and perhaps partly to offset this result of British policy), the British Embassy in Madrid, anxious for a pacific evolution in Spain, has endeavored to strengthen the chances for such evolution by urging Socialist leaders to consider a Monarchist restoration at least as an interim transitional regime. But the immediate consequence of this pressure has not been to repair the badly damaged Socialist prestige but rather to deepen lines of conflict within Socialist ranks.

When the major political lines separating one underground movement from another are often so blurred and obscure, internal divisions within any of these movements cannot be expected to be more clear or categorical. Nonetheless, within the broad limits of Socialist opinion, there have persisted the same divergent tendencies that frequently proved so disturbing before and during the Civil War. These tendencies were three, each personified in an outstanding public leader. Julian Besteiro, the professor of logic, a man of the highest intellect and integrity, had led the intellectuals: temperate, middleclass and anti-revolutionary, they had sought to translate into Spanish politics the language of British Fabianism. At the opposite extreme had stood burly, aggressive Largo Caballero: the "Spanish Lenin," the fiery political opportunist who preached violent revolution and friendly alliance with the Communists but never had time to read Marx till late in life. Between these two antithetical and antipathetic figures had stood sturdy, astute Indalecio Prieto: the Basque newsboy who grew up to become both a wealthy industrialist and an ardent Socialist, who was unmatched by any of his political contem-

poraries as an orator, a parliamentarian, or a political or-
ganizer. It was his particular and difficult role to struggle resolutely against the centrifugal forces within Spanish Socialism.
But these have persisted, ramified, and multiplied the problems of his followers battling against the Franco regime—striving to chart and follow a road to democracy that can safely
skirt the chasm of Communism, yet not wind aimlessly into
the gloomy valley of middle-class reaction.

To pass from Socialists to "Republicans," another question
of vocabulary arises. The whole Spanish underground is, of
course, "Republican" in the simple sense that it hopes for the
eventual establishment of a republican form of government,
but in this sense the word lacks precise political meaning. Nor
can a Republican "unit of resistance" be confused with the
great inactive mass of the Spanish citizenry who hold a passive
predilection for this form of government but no real role in
the underground itself.

Within the underground, an active, clearly defined Republican group possesses distinguishing political marks. Like the
Socialists, though more thoroughly, it is a middle-class party;
unlike them, it does not hold Marxist doctrine. In their attitude toward revolutionary violence, Republicans waver hesi-
tantly: they are more skeptical of its effectiveness than Anarchists or Communists, yet not so fearful of it as most Socialists, who, of all groups, are most sensitive and alert to any
chance of Communist ascendancy through protracted civil
strife.

Beyond these broad generalities of belief, Republican
opinion breaks off into two traditionally opposed factions.
The weaker, less influential of the two is moderate, its position
marked out by advocacy of a republican form of government,
minimum social legislation, a temperate attitude toward the
Spanish Church: in general, a political position that would
correspond roughly to slightly right of center in a Spanish parliament. Much stronger is the left Republican faction, in all
their philosophy bearing the stamp of the French Encyclo-

pedists. They are vehemently anticlerical, insistent on the dis-establishment of the Church and the advancement of secular education. Their social program is closer to that of the Social-ists than that of the moderate Republicans: sweeping agrarian reform directed toward peasant ownership of big estates (though not as socialized co-operatives), break-up of industrial monopolies, heavy state appropriations for schools and univer-sities, and a continuing program of public works including road and railroad construction, reforestation and irrigation projects.

Republicans (moderate and leftist), Socialists (of three diver-gent tendencies), Anarchists ("Libertarians" without a pro-gram) and Communists—all these forces battling for the re-birth of a Spanish republic offer what is perhaps the most striking, yet most easily explainable, paradox in Spain's po-litical life. They unquestionably represent that hatred of the Falangist State and that longing for freedom shared by the overwhelming majority of the Spanish people—and yet they are, in fact, all minority factions. Why? Again, by the very nature of clandestine political activity, challenged and circumscribed everywhere by the armed, massed might of a police state. This does more than prohibit the enlistment of great numbers of the people in secret, compact "units of resistance." The utter impossibility of open political discussion denies the people the chance to define and formulate their own theoretical political allegiance, just as it prevents underground "units" from emerg-ing as political parties. Political thought, like political organi-zation, cannot progress far beyond the simple, sweeping issue of Franco vs. Freedom. Without the popular development and expression of such thought, all underground forces serve essen-tially as simple custodians of the enduring but unspoken prin-ciples of Spanish democracy.

Judged against this background, the question of the relative "strength" of the various underground forces breaks down into two separate issues. The first is their strength as effective un-derground organizations at the present moment. The second is their probable relative strength in a free political environment.

Today, in their common struggle against General Franco's totalitarian state, the relative effectiveness of the underground movements unmistakably places them in a definite order. This order is the following: Communist, Anarchist, left Republican, Socialist, and moderate Republican.

Tomorrow, were the hopes of these forces to be fulfilled and each "resistance unit" to emerge with the popular allegiance that would transform it into a "party," this hierarchy would be drastically revised. All leaders of the left, regardless of their personal political predilections, agree that the almost certain preponderance of strength would rest with two parties, Socialists and left Republicans. In third and fourth positions would emerge either Communists or moderate Republicans, both distinctly minority parties. Only the "Libertarian" movement defies possible prediction. Confronted with a popular election, it might abstain completely, participate with its own candidates (on an unforeseeable platform), or indiscriminately support miscellaneous anti-Communist candidates.

I believe that these forecasts, almost unanimously held by all leaders of Spain's democratic forces, are supported by certain firm truths emphatically conveyed by the history of the Spanish Republic, the experience of the Civil War, and the temper of the Spanish people after the years of Falangist tyranny. One sure truth is that the possibility of Communism emerging as more than a vocal, strong minority party is sharply limited both by the people's anxiety to avoid the path of violence and by that stubborn, rebellious individualism of the Spanish spirit so alien to the dogmatic discipline of Marxist dialectic or proletarian dictatorship. A second and equally plain truth is that political freedom in Spain inevitably would provoke an immediate, eager expression of popular determination to carry through social and economic reform on a scale no less sweeping than that promised by Socialists and left Republicans. Finally, there can be no doubt that, once granted

that freedom of action and expression, the great majority of
the Spanish people will seek to destroy for all time any such
political authority of the Spanish clergy as would allow it ever
again to become the apologist and defender of another totalitarian state.

Between this generally predictable future and the grimly
apparent facts of the present, there lies an indefinite number
of tomorrows, and across that plain of time momentous events
may well move at more than a creeping pace. Out of the tragic
present has already come one dynamic development of incalculable consequences: the growth of the strength and prestige
of Communism. So long as today's tragedy continues to be the
drama of an endless chain of tomorrows, that growth will continue, for the forces of Communism are operating in the environment with which they are best equipped to deal and in
which their steady expansion can only be at the expense of all
other forces of the left. Of the full, frightful price which the
Spanish people are paying for the perpetuation of General
Franco's regime, this may perhaps be the most grievous cost
of all.

3

In the big caves of the Guadarrama or the Sierra Morena,
or among the Asturian mountains dark with coal and over-
hanging night, almost every evening, as twilight comes, hundreds of men clean the bores of their rifles, strap their feet
with tight-roped sandals, stuff cartridges into shabby pockets
and pouches. Down precipices, through forests chilled with
night air, across shallow streams or along green rolling slopes,
they move silently and unhurriedly. They sense no urgency of
time, for they have had all the hours of sun in which to make
ready, and the hours of the night ahead are long and safe.
They move, unharassed by fear and ignorant of despair, toward the target of the night. This time it may be a civil-guard
detachment at its regular station on the highways. If so, they
have probably already found a way of warning in advance one

or two of its recruits who are known to be "friends." Or it may be a barn or storehouse where there is bread or potatoes. Or perhaps it is the home of a doctor whose surgical instruments, which have not been sterilized in years, can nonetheless extract a bullet from an arm or pick out bone fragments. To kill enemies, to fill stomachs, to heal wounds—these are the needs of this life and of these men.

Others work with less lethal instruments. They have ink, a few reams of not too clean paper, a chattering mimeograph machine, and, very rarely, perhaps an offset press. They work in damp cellars in the cities, or just outside in drab, harmless-looking huts. These men talk and write and print, often incoherently or too hysterically or just illegibly. But they probably know their own faults because they know their own clamoring faith and angry emotions which make them almost inarticulate in their eloquence. These men hope to explain and to extol what the men in the mountains are doing. They hope also that they themselves understand what the others are doing.

It is not always easy to understand—not even if they had access to the secret files of the *Dirección General de Seguridad*. These files would reveal, for example, that in a typical month (March of 1946) the government's civil guards in Andalucía alone had to battle off an average of two and a half guerrilla attacks every day. But not even these records could tell the exact motives of these attacks, the real purpose of the men who came down from the dark mountains. Were they a vanguard battling in a political cause? Were they only men carrying into the twentieth century the gaudy, often heroic tradition of Spanish banditry? Were they refugees from penal-labor battalions, living and fighting as they did for the simple, necessary reason that there was no other way to gain their daily bread? Or were they men who had fled to the hills from cities where they could find no jobs, no money, no home or food?

Neither those desperately concerned with these questions (because their lives may be involved) nor those academically curious (because their political opinions are involved) can find clear answers. Only a negative truth can be stated with certainty: there is *no* convincing evidence that the warfare of Spain's guerrilla fighters has been organized on anything more than a small local scale or that it has been dedicated to any purposes beyond the winning of specific objectives, fought for in each locale, on each night, by each group of men.

Nor is it possible to state a precise estimate of the total number of active guerrilla fighters in all the Spanish mountains. Various circular bulletins of the underground have claimed that the total has been 30,000 or even higher. Foreign political observers in Madrid (who may be more impartial but certainly cannot cite any more authoritative sources) generally agree on a little more than half that figure.

Although both the motives and the numbers of these forces defy precise analysis, it is possible to see and to gauge the eventual impact of their activities. In a strictly military sense, they have been able to achieve little. Much as they have harassed civil guards, such scattered forces cannot create any serious shift in the balance of armed power within Spain.

In terms of public opinion, both within Spain and in the outside world, the consequences have been mixed and of doubtful advantage. News of attacks upon the guardians of General Franco's "order," especially when colored by extravagant rumor, has had its heartening effect on many groups and has provided underground publications with a certain amount of dramatic material to enliven their earnest editorializing. Many of these widely circulated clandestine sheets (particularly those of Communist origin) have developed the practice of publishing "communiqués" from the "headquarters" of various guerrilla forces: a neat but unconvincing editorial device.

But all serious leaders of the left realize that the warfare of Spain's guerrillas (and the publicity it has received) has other consequences. Within Spain, exaggerated reports undoubtedly have frightened a great number of citizens of moderate opinion. While never having had any association with the Franco regime, such people have tended to shudder and huddle closer to the Generalissimo when driven by the fear that banditry and republicanism may become so confused as to be indistinguishable in any political crisis. Outside Spain, many elements of world opinion, grievously misled by lurid published accounts of guerrilla fighting, have become victims of the false illusion that this kind of struggle might topple the government of General Franco. The irresponsible enthusiasm of certain sectors, for example, of the American press has produced extraordinary periodic reports of "civil war" supposedly "flaring" throughout Spain; other accounts, little short of hysterical, of the incursion of a few score Spanish *maquis* across the French Pyrenees in 1944; and such fanciful tales as that carried in 1943 by one of the most popular American weekly magazines, "informing" its readers of the seizure by Spanish guerrillas of the entire town of Malaga on the southern Mediterranean coast. All such reports as these have conspired to distort, beyond recognition, the true problems and hazards of the forces battling the regime of General Franco. This very distortion has disarmed much of world opinion in its own struggle to understand Spain and the needs of its people.

Distortion and misunderstanding of facts have inevitably prevailed among Spaniards themselves struggling under and against the Falangist State. Their insatiable appetite for political news forces them to rebel against the dull diet of their controlled press and to feed upon the spicy fare of rumor. The frequent result has been enormous popularity for the most romantic and unfounded stories.

In February of 1946, a typically pathetic instance of this kind occurred. A youthful Spaniard from the town of Guadalajara one day brought to my office a strange mechanical contrivance. He explained that it had "fallen" in the fields behind his house and that he and his friends, upon examining it, had seen on one side of it a steel plate which bore English lettering identifying it as United States Army equipment. A phone call to the military attaché's office resulted in a simple explanation. It was a weather-testing apparatus sent up on a balloon by the Air Transport Command base at Barajas airport just outside Madrid; blown by the winds, it had been given up as lost. A week later, the following story began to circulate in the Spanish capital: a few days ago, a mysterious unidentified plane had flown over Guadalajara and had dropped by parachute a radio transmitting set, shortly discovered and seized by the police; but the plane had returned again, dropping another set which had escaped the clutches of the police. This "air mission" was plain proof that the underground forces were growing in strength and were now receiving supplies flown in from France!

About a month earlier, there had occurred another episode demonstrating again the often illusory and deceptive nature of "reports" from "the underground." The episode was the following:

Citizens of several small villages outside Madrid—Cenicientos, Arenas de San Pedro, Cadalso de los Vidrios—had been harassed by a curious but not unique kind of "guerrilla warfare." The wealthier families were receiving extortion notes which threatened kidnaping of some member of the family unless certain sums of money (as much as 10,000 and 15,000 pesetas) were paid to the "guerrillas." Several families had given in. The climax came when one of the richest citizens of Cenicientos received a demand for 50,000 pesetas. His instructions were to put the money in a box of specified dimensions and give it to the driver of the bus on the Madrid run, who would be asked to surrender it when he reached Madrid. The threatened citizen filled the prescribed box with blank paper and notified the police to prepare to arrest the man who claimed it at the bus terminal in Madrid. The arrest was made. The prisoner turned out to be a messenger in the employ of the bus company who had acted on instructions from the company's manager. The police arrested the manager and got a quick confession that he had been responsible for the series of extortion notes which had been plaguing the vicinity. Far from being a "guerrilla leader," he was the chief Falange official in Cadalso de los Vidrios, a son of wealthy and socially prominent parents who had lost one of his legs fighting for Franco in the Civil War.

A final incident of a very different character was even more revealing:

At ten-thirty on the night of February 15, 1943, all the buildings on the Calle Genova near the Plaza de Colon, in the heart of Madrid, were shaken violently by the blasts of two time-bombs. The bombs exploded in the office building of the Vice-Secretariat of Popular Education. Intended to blow Gabriel Arias-Salgado and his desk into the dark blue sky above, the bombs succeeded only in opening a gaping hole in the outside wall of the building. With no hesitation but with undisguised enthusiasm, the Communist clandestine organ *Reconquista del Estado* rushed to print with a "communiqué" from no lesser source than the "High Command of the Guerrillas of Spain." In terse military language, it read:

> Center Front. Thursday, February 15, at 10:30 at night, the 22nd Group of the *Agrupación Guerrillera* of Madrid attacked with bombs the Delegation of Press and Propaganda of the Hitlerite Falange. The central window of the main salon was smashed, causing among the Falangist personnel 2 dead and 7 wounded, 3 of them seriously.

While the impulse to invent a casualty list was not surprising, it was indeed amazing to see this Communist baptism, with the name of the "22nd Group" of the Madrid guerrillas, of a squad of Falangist secret police! For the truth soon developed that the episode had marked the violent outbreak of an internal feud within the Falange and within the Vice-Secretariat itself. The purpose of the effort had been to frighten Arias-Salgado and other Falangist officials suspected (with so little justification!) of becoming too conciliatory toward the Allies. But while Falangist officials knew this to be the cause of the whole incident, they availed themselves of the opportunity to arrest a score of underground leaders and to unleash an hysterical editorial campaign against the "Communist" perpe-

trators of the outrage. And, since Communists were eager to
accept credit for the performance while Falangists were
equally anxious to conceal their own internal struggle, the
public protestations of each perfectly suited the political
purposes of the other.

All these and innumerable similar occurrences have not led
even the most cynical or timid of Spanish leaders of the left
to any absurd conclusion that the greater part of guerrilla
activities resembles a compound of thievery and the devious
work of *agents provocateurs*. But they do realize, more clearly
than most of the outside world, that neither the justice nor
the success of their own cause can be made to depend upon
the battles waged by these guerrilla forces. And they recognize
the simple but easily forgotten truth that neither every bomb
thrown nor every shot fired at the police of the Spanish State
is necessarily the sound of democracy on the march.

Meanwhile, the men in the dark mountains continue their
relentless struggle, whether inspired by some grand distant
political vision or by the more humble but no less urgent
necessity to keep food and life in their bodies. Their purposes
often elusive of definition, their deeds often murkily confused
with simple banditry, their objectives often lost in defeat and
death, they nonetheless seem to carry with themselves that
quality of reckless resilience, that spiritual stamina with
which the people of Spain always arise from the depths of
tragedy. . . .

> . . . For I have known the lightning's hour,
> The poet's inward pride,
> The certainty of power.
>
> Bayonets are closing round.
> I shrink; yet I must wring
> A living from despair
> And out of steel a song.

4

One plain political truth about contemporary Spain is beyond serious doubt: the National Alliance of Democratic Forces does not possess the armed strength to smash its way to power. A second fact, no less certain and no less important, is this: the National Alliance has not yet found a specific political formula for winning power in any other way.

For the democratic forces in Spain, all study of the present and speculation on the future ultimately depends upon their relationship to political forces beyond the borders of Spain. Only secondarily are these forces the chancelleries of foreign nations where diplomatic policy toward Franco Spain is determined. Primarily they are two widely separated groups of Spanish exiles: the Giral group of Republican exiles in Paris, and the Monarchist headquarters in Lisbon.

The attitude of the Spanish left toward either of these groups is subject to sharp variations, both from one political moment to another and from one underground organization to another. But despite this, certain considerations have dictated a fairly clear and consistent attitude of mind, if not an expressed policy, on the part of the National Alliance as a whole.

Not a single important leader of the Spanish underground whom I knew advocated the Giral group as the permanent future government of Spain. This in no way has prevented many leaders of the left from applauding the Giral "government" as a highly useful asset on the international scene. These men have recognized the service performed by the Republican exiles in persistently reminding the opinion and conscience of the democratic world of Spanish democracy's desperate battle for existence. There are also a few of democracy's champions within Spain who (despite serious misgivings) consider the Giral group the logical contender for the role of a transitional Spanish government. But there are others whose misgivings are so profound that they view the Giral group, despite its activity on the international scene, as a serious political liability.

Reasons for this attitude are neither obscure nor quixotic. The onetime leaders of the Spanish Republic have been longer in exile than the years which their Republic lasted. As exiles, they have suffered the same fate as befell exile regimes from other European countries during World War II, whether the particular political cast of those regimes was liberal or conservative. Most men in Spain believe that their former leaders have lost touch with local realities, and that those who have lived and suffered these many years beyond the Pyrenees are better equipped to direct Spain's political future than the men in Mexico City or Paris.

Nor has the judgment of the years been always kind on the role of these men in 1936 and after. Indictment of them occasionally is specific, in a given faction's denunciation of an individual for his particular political role, his unsavory reputation, or a vacillating record in his exile years. A more frequent indictment is general, mercilessly sweeping and unqualified: when all the debate is over, these men, after all, were identified with a political failure. It is reasonable that underground leaders in Spain ask: Why must we revert to this leadership ten years later? Can we not now offer Spain something better, a government more durable with leaders more mature and more skillful? In April, 1946, in Madrid, a left Republican stated the case in these words:

"We have had a good many years, many of us in prison, in which to think and reflect, if nothing else. Naturally we have thought about what happened in 1936. Almost all of us have come to this conclusion: the Republic did not fail in 1936, but the Republicans did. Believing as we do, we cannot accept the old reactionary arguments that Spain is unable to develop a stable Republican government, that the people are incapable of making it work, or that any Republic would be at the mercy of wild public passions or the guns of a Fascist-minded army.

We must believe, as we do, that a Republic can succeed in Spain. But that does not force us to accept all the mistakes that were made the last time a Republic was tried. Instead, we must admit the frequent failure of our particular leadership in the thirties. Suppose that a big American enterprise like Ford went bankrupt and had to be completely reorganized, would the stockholders re-elect the same executives and managers? In a case like that, people would not say that the Ford car or the Ford company was a total failure; they would simply look for new and better leadership. That is what we must do."

This judgment of the Spanish left in considerable measure bases itself upon the left's understanding of the nature of the Spanish Civil War. These men who fought through those years know that it is a tempting and plausible error, but an error nonetheless, to conceive of that struggle in the simple, dogmatic terms of a Fascist-Communist war. They also know that to dismiss the Franco rebellion as a Nazi conspiracy is to distort the nature of the Civil War, to obscure the issues which persist today, and thereby to underestimate dangerously the forces still combating Spanish democracy. The Nationalist cause in 1936 was not a mere spearhead of Naziism. It mobilized the massed might of all the traditionally conservative and reactionary forces of the nation, particularly the Army and the Church. These forces welcomed the aid of international Fascism, while Berlin and Rome succeeded in exploiting them in their own grand international plan. But this magnificent opportunity for world Fascism would not have arisen if the Spanish Republic had been successful in confining and checking the forces of Spanish reaction. And those forces did not wither away when direct Fascist aid disappeared, or even when Fascism's grand international scheme was shattered in defeat. The battle against those forces was the decisive struggle which the Spanish Republic lost, and that is the struggle, as the leaders of Spanish democracy know full well, which must yet be fought to its final end.

Apart from all criticism of their former leadership, underground leaders within Spain shrewdly perceive in the Giral regime an inherent political liability which seems to have escaped most liberals abroad. They remember that even in 1936 the forces of conservatism in Spain were able to amass a popular vote which came close to marking an even split through the country. And they know that, a decade later, nothing drives these conservatives and moderates into Franco's wide embrace so swiftly as the memory of 1936 and the fear of civil war. By its very constitution, the Giral regime evokes precisely that memory and arouses that fear. It draws the deadly line of division precisely where it was drawn in 1936, and evokes all the passions and hates which then impelled a people to prey upon itself. If this is admitted to be the only answer to the Franco regime, then the Generalissimo is right in one important contention: his is the only alternative to civil war. And around him must rally the full conservative strength of Spain to fight the same fateful battle again.

All these circumstances have impressed on the leaders of the left an important political truth: it is clearer, simpler, and wiser to indict Franco as the dictator of 1946 than as the victor of 1939. The first finds himself engaged in the dangerous and difficult task of holding together a tenuous political alliance against a hostile people and a critical world. The second can rally about himself all who fought for his cause during the Civil War, who cannot escape from their own history as his friends, who are inexorably forced to fulfill their roles as his resolute allies.

For the underground forces of Spanish democracy, it becomes apparent that their triumphant achievement would be to offer the nation a clear alternative to the present Spanish regime which would not be an attempt to turn history back to 1936. This is the essence of their problem, and it is this which they have to date been unable to resolve.

In the search for a practical escape from their dilemma, leaders of the Spanish left have considered and debated the possibility of a Monarchic restoration: one that would guarantee essential human freedoms and assure a truly parliamentary government. Heated discussion of this issue in the councils of the National Alliance has been concerned less with whether this alternative is desirable than with whether it is possible. The question has not been whether a parliamentary government under a king who faithfully respected a fundamental Bill of Rights would be a welcome change. Obviously, it would. The critical doubt has arisen over whether a king would sincerely establish such a regime and, if he would, whether the reactionary forces behind him would allow him to do so.

Debate on this issue indirectly implicates the gravest and oldest problems of Spanish society. The year 1789 meant nothing in terms of experience to the Iberian peninsula. Spain met and faced the twentieth century with a society and political machinery more than a century behind the rest of Western Europe. Under the Monarchy and Dictatorship, she continued to maintain impervious isolation, while the economic revolution of the twentieth century shook the Western social order. By the time of the Republic, Spain was two revolutions behind Western history. From 1931 to 1936, she engaged in a valiant effort to effect both revolutions simultaneously. By 1939, both efforts were frustrated. Today two challenges remain to be met by the forces of Spanish democracy. They demand answers to these questions: Shackled by a totalitarian regime, should the Spanish left dedicate itself to trying to effect a political and social revolution simultaneously? Would reluctant acceptance of such a political solution as a restored Monarchy jeopardize all chance of carrying out the long-overdue social revolution?

To these questions, the National Alliance has made no unequivocal answer. Probably distrust of the Monarchic solution is keener and deeper among *moderates* than among the extreme left. This is not difficult to understand: in effect, moderate groups are afraid of losing their political identity and popular appeal under a Monarchy. The leaders of the extreme left have no such fear. For one thing, they do not renounce violence, as do the moderates, hence would always have an alternative course under a restrictive Monarchy. Moreover, under a monarchic-parliamentary system, they foresee moderate Republicans losing any popular appeal, with the masses of the disinherited and disillusioned swiftly turning their allegiance leftwards.

In this atmosphere of doubt and unsure purpose, for more than a year informal conversations have been held with Monarchist representatives (who have their own doubt and distrust of the purposes of the left). Enthusiasm has risen and fallen in quick cycles: in January of 1946, the conversations were warm with enthusiasm and hope; by April, they had chilled into icy hostility; by October, they were warmer again, with renewed possibility of an accord.

Two years after the defeat of Fascist armies in Europe, the political dilemma of Spanish democracy remains as stubbornly cryptic as before. The peril feared in any of four possible courses has created a boxlike political trap. To welcome the Giral regime would be to propagate fear of civil war, drive moderates to Fascist cover, risk another 1936. To renounce the Giral regime would be political madness, would allow the enemies of Spanish democracy to rejoice at public dissension. To welcome a Monarchic compromise would be to risk a course that might mean the death of the social and economic principles of the Spanish left. To battle against the Monarchy might be the quickest way of driving Monarchists to accept a compromise with Franco, resulting in perpetuation of Fascist tactics behind a new façade and entrenchment of reactionary forces more solidly than at any time in the last twenty years.

Viewed in this perspective, the task of routing General Franco has come to appear to many as scarcely easier in the political arena than in the military. For the leaders of Spanish democracy, this does not mean despair or fear. It means only pain and sorrow that the hope of escaping civil war seems steadily to grow more slender and remote. And for the great majority of them, this sorrow brings its own special grief in the knowledge that, if this be the only road to freedom, it may also, under the pitiless pressure of circumstance, become the road to Communism.

5

From the rugged and wretched underground up to the smooth, glistening surface of a scientifically enslaved nation, there rise the sounds and signs of a people in great toil.

In the tragic pageant of the emotions of a people, there mingle illusion and frustration, heroism and pain, hungry hope and choking despair. Darkness comes with night, black uniforms, censorship, prison cells, and death. Light comes from soft dawn on green hills and stony mountains and their secret dwellers, from exploding bombs and spurting rifles, from a little news of good cheer, from freedom's faithful flame itself.

Shadowy silhouettes show strange and various shapes. Stealthy figures move under the moon's light beside an isolated farmhouse, along the edge of a highway, or by the walls of a dimly-lit barracks. Beneath the same sheltering night, tired shoulders and head, under the light of a single dirty bulb, hunch over a clattering press which grinds out its smudgy, precious work. Bars on a window throw shadows on cold cement, a neat surface five feet square; and two eyes and a brain, both under their own shadow of pain, look out upon a world in which the sun sets with its fateful promise of another night of torture.

But these are not the silhouettes that will meet the casual eye. There is a more familiar profile to greet Madrid's gentleman of leisure who glances at the morning paper as he sips his coffee, smokes his cigarette or picks his teeth—or a half hour later in his day, glances at big posters as he carefully adjusts the buttons of his double-breasted gabardine coat. Here the silhouette that meets his calm and confident eye is steady, motionless, and grave: legs trim in military boots, abdomen only slightly protruding, receding chin lifted manfully, right arm fully outstretched, pointing—over the unseen multitude.

But this cannot be all.

No. This is not all. José and Pedro and Raimundo ,and Ernesto and Juan and Fernando and Julio and their comrades in the millions are all *free!*

Yes. They are free to read any newspaper they can buy, to hear any speech that can be delivered, to engage in any conversation that cannot too easily be overheard.

They are also free to enroll in the proper Falangist syndicate (if they want to work) and to accept the wages fixed by government decree (if they wish to be paid for their work).

They are free to mine coal, wash windows, mix cement, run errands, carry sandwich-boards, steer trolleys, pave roads, toss bricks, swear, cry, spit and sweat. For any of these but the last four, they will receive perhaps fifteen pesetas a day.

With these fifteen pesetas, they are free to spend two pesetas for rent, one peseta for clothes, and twelve pesetas for two meals each day.

Their wives and children, of course, are also free. All of them together, therefore, can share the enjoyment of one room without toilet or running water; soups mixed from beans and cabbage (a kilo of rice costs more than a day's wage), an occasional and not too fresh fish, infrequent chunks of brown bread, very rare glasses of watery beer or wine. They can get their clothing from charity whenever there is enough to go around. Naturally, they do not concern themselves with costly frivolities like shoes, meat, overcoats, towels, sheets, blankets, or soap. They do not need toothpicks.

Other people have a less clear, more quixotic kind of freedom. They can serve meals they have never tasted, grease cars in which they have never ridden, sell shoes that they have felt only with their hands, peddle tickets to a theater they have never entered, paint signs advertising wine they have never sipped, fix plumbing they have never used themselves, and sweep the floors of schoolrooms which their children have never seen. They also can say prayers which they do not expect to be answered.

What else can they do? Not many can flee to the mountains, because that is not the way to keep their families alive. Not a great many can write angry words for use in a political cause, because they would not be able to read them even if someone took the trouble to put them down on paper.

But they can murmur and they can talk. They can stand on street corners in not too conspicuous groups, they can lean leisurely against the side of a taxi, they can ask their friend, the taxi-driver, to come to their home in the evening and sit on the floor beside the big bed for a nice long chat. And wherever they talk, they can argue, declaim, rejoice, denounce, and invent—invent words, phrases, facts, whole wonderful facts, grand fables of things that should be happening, that must be happening, that their papers are afraid to report. . . . When Franco met his cabinet last night . . . The *Norte-Americanos* are going to . . . The last time Giron spoke to the workers in the cereal syndicate, they all . . . Did you hear what happened when Franco entered his box at the bull ring last Thursday? . . . Seven priests were shot in Oviedo last month. . . . Franco is burning seven candles in his chapel at the Pardo for the special intentions of . . . They say that there is so much white bread in Burgos that . . . They say that when the British Ambassador saw Martín Artajo he . . . They say . . . They say . . . say . . . say . . . say. . . .

Is the talk foolish and vain? Maybe—but is there anything else to do? What? Shake an angry fist every April 1 when the parade for the Glorious Victory goes by? Or just walk around with a clenched fist raised high?

Throw bombs? Whose bombs? Storm the Pardo? With what? What else? Write a letter to our newspaper?

Why get thrown into jail? Can we do more there than we can outside, enjoying this freedom? Jail? Who would serve our children their coarse beans and dirty fish?

What do THEY expect us to do? Is it true that THEY tell us not to keep him but not to shoot him?

Who said to "withdraw" him "peacefully"? *Que tontería!* What kind of language is that?

We've broken *our* relations with him. That was easy. We never had any to begin with.

What are THEY doing? Just talking? Just like us? . . .

Well, until they decide to do something, whisper, do not shout . . . *Viva la República!*

6

In the words of the manifesto of the National Alliance of Democratic Forces:

Only one course will make possible the salvation of Spaniards—that which returns to the people their liberties, that which permits the expression of the national will, that which allows the people to be the masters of their destiny. . . .

Spain is at the most tragic crossroads of her history. . . .

A nation without liberty is not a nation.

SPAIN AND THE DEMOCRATIC WORLD

9 SPAIN AND WORLD WAR II

OF ALL FASCIST STATES—either those born before the fateful autumn of 1939 or those later, equally monstrous creations of Axis occupying armies—only one did not take up arms in the Second World War to battle the United Nations. Only one great Fascist experiment in Europe did not elect to gamble its life on the success of a plan of conquest circling the great globe itself. And that Fascist State alone survived the final defeat of that plan in 1945.

Francisco Franco and his Falange had enjoyed only five months of triumph and power on the September morning when Nazi *panzer* divisions raced across the frontiers of Poland. Only the previous April had their day of victory been assured, partly because of the men, money, and munitions that had come to them from Nazi Germany and Fascist Italy (and despite the arms, men, and money with which Soviet Russia had sought to defeat them). But already on that September morning, as in the weeks, months, and years of world conflict that followed, they knew that one thing, one alone, must always take precedence over any demonstration of gratitude to their foreign allies: the exigency of their own survival, their continuing enjoyment of that precious, freshly won power.

From this spirit and resolve emerged a policy of foreign relations, devious, deceptive, and often defying logical interpretation except in terms of this transcendent purpose. With the same unscrupulousness, the same seemingly contradictory and conflicting tactics as those invoked on the domestic scene, General Franco's Foreign Office, through all the years of World War II, pursued a policy which has never contained more than two consistent elements: self-interest and anti-Communism. Since April 1, 1939, there has never been a time when the Franco regime has lost an opportunity to denounce and, in any possible way, to fight against Communism as an ideology and Russia as its national protagonist. All other aspects of Spain's foreign policy were reducible to this common denominator: a course of action that would permit the government to join in the expected feast of Fascist victory, yet also escape the famine of a Fascist defeat.

Any realistic review of the development of this policy must bear close reference to two fundamental principles. One is the necessity of distinguishing between words and deeds as bases for judgment. The second is the recognition of the particular character of the political regime following this policy.

Far from being faithfully expressed in words, the foreign policy of General Franco has often been concealed in words, often has been predicated on calculated conflict between words and deeds. In the year following the end of the European war, to cite one obvious example, the Spanish government's vehement official denials that it was harboring former Axis agents meant nothing beside the plain fact that the *Dirección General de Seguridad* was doing precisely that. In like manner, during the years of Nazi ascendancy on the European continent, there was no necessary or consistent correspondence between General Franco's fulsome oratorical tributes to Germany and the trade policies, for example, of his Ministry of Industry and Commerce in its negotiations with Berlin. This is not to say that the Generalissimo's oratory did not matter. It mattered a great deal when it conveyed, as so often it did, enthusiastic official endorsement of the mortal enemies of the democratic powers. But the words were important only in and of themselves, not as descriptions of a national foreign policy which was operating in distinct ways in a variety of spheres.

But even when the words are forgotten and the deeds alone are examined, Spain's wartime foreign policy still bore the marks of confusion and contradiction that could be explained only by the very nature of the Franco regime. That regime's distinct, independent, and often mutually hostile political forces, which frequently produced such sudden changes on the domestic scene, could not fail to bring clashing influences to bear on the formation of foreign policy. And these influences often succeeded in preventing that policy from being either rigidly defined or consistently implemented. While sympathetic Foreign Office officials in Madrid might be striving earnestly to meet the demands of Allied diplomats, Falangists in Barcelona might be distributing Nazi propaganda on the street corners; *Seguridad* police in a jail in Irun might be torturing a French refugee; and ex-Blue Legionnaires, enrolled in the service of German espionage, might be invading the American Consulate in Valencia to smash furniture and scream their hatred of the *yanquis*. All such things could, and did, happen simultaneously. The result has been that an enormous chasm almost always separated the intention and the performance of the Spanish government.

This fact could be construed as an excuse or apology for General Franco's foreign policy only by his blindest advocate. On the contrary, it has been a damning indictment of the very character of the Falangist State. No officials of that State found it difficult to implement policy when that policy was frankly pro-Fascist. The problem arose only when policy changed and practice persisted in its old ways. Even the pressure of expediency often had to surrender to the superior force of habit. And in its habits, its instincts, its impulses and its hopes, there could never be serious doubt as to the real character of General Franco's foreign policy.

2

Even before World War II officially started, the outlines of
Spain's policy had been made clear. At Burgos on March 27,
1939, Spain had signed the Anti-Comintern Pact, the protocol
of accession going into effect at once; and the German von
Stohrer, the Italian Campalti, and the Japanese Makoto Yano
felt that they could count on Spain in the days to come. In
the public press, in the months that followed before the beginning of World War II, this policy took the form of being
as violently anti-democratic as it was anti-Communist. The
United States became the target of the most vicious attacks.
Arriba (May 3, 1939) set the keynote for a hostile *Hispanidad*
policy in Latin America in an article laboriously headlined,
"End of the Spanish War Entails for South American Peoples
a Possible Change in Their Political Conceptions." The official
Party organ explained that this "change" would be brought
about "with damage to the democracies and consequent loss of
economic influence for the United States." [1] And the same
article assiduously followed the Nazi propaganda line in com-

[1] Similar sentiments were voiced by *Arriba* a year and a half later, when
its predictions of a changing Latin-American policy were denied by facts.
The cession to the United States by Uruguay of a naval base became the
occasion for the Spanish press (November 18-19, 1940) to unleash a venom-
ous anti-American campaign. *Arriba* angrily talked of "a Gibraltar of
America" and maliciously reported: "In all South America, anguish and
indignation are beginning to take the shape of positive acts of protest." It
described the event as not only the end of Uruguayan sovereignty but as
"an epitaph for neighboring nations." Simultaneously, the Madrid evening
paper, *El Alcázar,* screamed: "We must confront the Monroe Doctrine,
which was proclaimed in a moral climate far removed from the present,
the doctrine of the unity of the Hispanic World." The Spanish University
Syndicate (SEU) feverishly sent a telegram to "the students of America,"
protesting the "betrayal" by Uruguay. Simultaneously, radio broadcasts denouncing the action were beamed to South America (Falange National
Councilor Eugénio Montes gave an impassioned address), and on November 21, between 200 and 300 SEU students paraded in protest before the
American Embassy, heaved rocks at the American emblem, shouted "España
sí! Yanquis no!"

menting upon the rearmament program of President Roosevelt: "Since in the United States there has come to be recognized the profound bonds which unite the interests of international Judaism with the Yankee world, there begins to be seen clearly the object against which the colossal armament plans of President Roosevelt are directed: the Third Reich."

Similar fidelity to the Fascist gospel, before and in the first years of World War II, was expressed on every possible occasion by Foreign Minister Serrano Suñer, especially after his visit to Italy, in June of 1939. One especially memorable instance was Suñer's speech in March of 1941 on the occasion of the opening of a German press exposition in Madrid: "Today we joyfully salute the victorious effort of the German people to organize a Europe more just and more consistent with the past and present honor and glory of two peoples who, like Germany and Spain, have a right to the moral and geographic expansion of their greatness and freedom. *Arriba Alemania! Viva Hitler!*" All such official pronouncements were complemented by lavishly publicized meetings between Spanish officials and those of Nazi Germany: Suñer's trip to Berlin in September of 1940, the Franco-Hitler conference at Hendaye in October, and the almost simultaneous visit of Gestapo Chief Himmler to Madrid to teach the Spanish Security Police a few useful Nazi tricks.

Then there came General Franco's famous speech of July 17, 1941. . . . "The American continent cannot dream of intervention in Europe without subjecting itself to a catastrophe. . . . To say that the fate of the war can be changed by the entry of a third power is criminal madness. . . . The Allies have lost it. . . . In these moments . . . German arms are leading the battle for which Europe and our people have longed for so many years and in which the blood of our youth is going to be mingled with that of our comrades of the Axis, as a living expression of our solidarity. . . . Our Movement achieves in the world today an unsuspected vindication. . . ."

These public statements and actions did more than to set

the keynote of Spanish foreign policy for at least the first half of the Second World War. In themselves, they constituted an important kind of contribution to the German war effort which continued virtually to the day of Nazi surrender. Thus, in May of 1943, Franco's words had a different ring than two years previous: "We have reached what is generally known as a 'stalemate' in the struggle. For this reason, for those of us who view the conflict calmly, it seems senseless to delay the peace." General Franco's view of the war had changed in two years—precisely as had the attitude of Dr. Goebbels.

All this can be regarded, in a sense, as Falangist Spain's fulfillment of the Secret Cultural Agreement with Germany which had been signed at Burgos on January 28, 1939. Dedicated to assuring "spiritual and cultural co-operation" between Franco Spain and Hitlerite Germany, the agreement provided for exchange of professors, of students, of books, arrangement of expositions, opening of schools, currency facilities to carry on informational activities in each other's country, privileged positions for the language of each country in the school curriculum of the other, musical and theatrical exchange, motion picture co-operation—in short, the whole machinery by which Spain would serve as spokesman for the cultural and national interests of Nazi Germany. A simple illustration of the import of the entire agreement is Article 16:

> The signatory Parties will not permit the sale in bookstores or distribution by public libraries of those works which, through falsification of historical truth, are opposed to the other country, its form of government, or its leading personalities.

Although this "spiritual co-operation" was entirely verbal, it could serve somewhat different political purposes at different times. No one doubts, of course, the sincerity and genuine ardor of these rhetorical tributes to Fascism from the leaders of the Spanish State—so long as they were confident that a privileged role awaited them in a triumphant New Order. But as confidence in the inevitability of this New Order began to wane, the same public demonstrations of affection could serve a less obvious function: they could be used as substitutes for certain kinds of material "co-operation" which Germany wanted and which Spain (for sound reasons of self-interest) did not want to extend.

In the strict language of diplomacy, the status of General Franco's Spain veered away from "neutrality" only to the extent of proclaiming "nonbelligerence" in June of 1940—a policy which prevailed for more than three years until "strict neutrality" was reaffirmed in October of 1943. To perceive clearly and to appraise fairly the policies behind these words, it is necessary to review Spain's record of deeds and practices in three distinct spheres: the military, the economic, and the political.

3

The most flagrant military contribution which Falangist Spain made to the cause of Fascism was the notorious Blue Division—the "volunteers" from Iberia who, after September of 1941, were dispatched to Germany and to the eastern front to fight in the "crusade against Bolshevism." Officially sponsored by the Falange, with the public endorsement of the government and the special blessing of the Bishop of Madrid, the Blue Division's numbers reached a maximum in its first six months of some 17,000 or 18,000 men, and fell to a low of 3,000 to 4,000 just prior to its final withdrawal late in 1943. The military effectiveness of these men was negligible. They returned to Spain not with glory but with Russian loot and venereal disease: only as thieves and rapists had they left their mark on the Russian front.[2]

2 After it became politically expedient to try to bury all memories of the Blue Division, Gabriel Arias-Salgado, Vice-Secretary of Popular Education, developed the practice, in conversations with others and myself, of dismissing the Blue Division as a good-hearted gang of exceptionally virile men who did nothing on the Russian front but propagate their race. He found humor in the allegedly fantastic number of "Spanish" babies born

The anomaly of so many thousand Spaniards fighting along-side Germans in a war in which Spain was "neutral" or "non-belligerent" was defended by Falangist apologists on the grounds of the "two-wars" theory. It was the astounding contention of these officials that the only function of the Blue Division was to fight Russian Communists (who, it was alleged, would themselves invade Spain if they were allowed the chance) and no harm was intended thereby to befall the Western Allies fighting Germany (supposed to be in an entirely different war).

A slightly more plausible defense advanced by some Spanish officials was that the Blue Division represented the smallest possible military contribution to Germany which could have been made in the face of Germany's demands for outright participation in the war. Certainly, General Franco used the role of the Blue Division as an arguing point in conversations with the German Ambassador when the latter pressed for more "co-operation." But if such reasoning were allowed to justify the existence of the Blue Division, then any concession to Germany, short of declaration of war against the Allies, could be similarly defended as "the minimum concession" which Spain had to make to withstand German pressure. For a sovereign nation, it was an unimpressive defense.

The withdrawal of the Blue Division in the face of firm Allied pressure did not begin until the fall of 1943 and its remnants were not repatriated till the early spring of 1944. Even then a certain number of soldiers refused to return to Spain and continued to serve the German armies in behind-the-lines roles.

Spanish aid to the Axis in a strictly military sense did not end with the Blue Division. From the time of the fall of France until at least two years later, when Serrano Suñer was dismissed as Foreign Minister, the Axis could and did avail itself of

of Polish and Russian mothers. Because of this, he felt that the Blue Division should be regarded as nothing more than a bawdy kind of political joke.

valuable facilities in Spain. Axis agents operated with more than freedom in Spain: they had the collaboration in innumerable instances of the Spanish police and of the Falange in activities directed against the Allies at any point within their reach. This entailed espionage in Latin America and in the Mediterranean, sabotage of Italian warships (in the last year of the war), and systematic observation of Allied ship movements through the Gibraltar Straits.[3] In addition, Spain's unlawful occupation of the Tangier Zone following the fall of France in 1940 opened the way for the establishment there of a German Consulate serving as a key center for Nazi agents operating throughout North Africa.

On innumerable occasions in the first three years of the war, the Spanish government sanctioned the illegal entry of German war vessels into Spanish ports for repairs or refueling. The German Ambassador in Madrid had been able to cable Berlin in 1940: "The Spanish Government has agreed to the placing in readiness of German tankers in out-of-the-way bays of the Spanish coast for the supplying of German destroyers. . . . The Spanish Government has already shown similar obligingness in supplying German U-boats." [4] But at least from the beginning of 1943, such facilities ceased to be accorded Nazi vessels: despite a very few reported instances of this kind, the secret supply of German submarines and destroyers was no longer a policy of the Madrid government. This chronology, which followed the general pattern of changes in Spanish policy as the war progressed, should be emphasized as an illuminating commentary on the sincerity of the Franco regime's argument that it aided Germany only to combat Russian Communism. Needless to say, Nazi submarines in the Atlantic supplied at Spanish ports were not sinking Russian

[3] The Italian Consulate in Algeciras, on Spanish soil just across the bay from Gibraltar, had such a strategic view of the Rock that the Italian Consul developed the regular ceremony of inviting his Spanish friends to cocktails whenever an Italian air attack on the British base was scheduled.

[4] From official documents made public by the Department of State, May 4, 1946.

vessels. But more significant is the fact that much of the Franco regime's most flagrant aid to the Axis was extended in the years *between* the outbreak of war (September, 1939) and the German invasion of Russia (June, 1941)—at the time when the Russo-German pact was still in operation and when the only "Communist enemy" whom Spain could wound was Great Britain. In short, with the one obvious exception of the Blue Division, it can be said that Spanish aid to the Axis in all forms—military, political, and economic—was at least as flagrant when Russia was Germany's ally as when she became Naziism's intended victim.

In the last two years of the world conflict, Spanish military assistance to the other Fascist powers, with some few exceptions, reduced itself to a negative character. For sixteen months, Madrid refused to release promptly the five Italian warships and auxiliary craft which had entered Spanish waters at the time of the Italian armistice with the Allies. Only persistent protests (which involved highly technical questions of international law) brought their eventual surrender. Meanwhile, Axis agents continued their operations on Spanish territory long after the Spanish agreement of May 2, 1944, promising their prompt expulsion. Many of the most dangerous were forced to leave, but scores remained to plague the Allies till the very end of the war—and after. Finally, even after the liberation of southern France and the arrival of Allied armies at the Pyrenees, there was evidence that in a few instances Spanish nationals and Spanish vessels ran supplies from Spanish ports to German garrisons besieged on the French Atlantic coast. But the evidence on these trips was so slight as to suggest that they were extremely few, and in no case did such evidence implicate the Spanish government in these voyages, which were merely lucrative, private smuggling enterprises. The culpability of the Spanish government lay in its apparent inability to prevent these trips, detrimental as they were not only to Allied interests but also to its own efforts to gain favor with the United Nations.

Against this record of assistance to the Axis must be placed and measured certain services to the Allied cause which directly affected military operations.

Probably the most important affirmative assistance which the Spanish government rendered the Allies involved the passage of Allied refugees through Spanish territory to North Africa. Following the Allied armies' landings in French North Africa on November 8, 1942, the Nazi occupation of southern France precipitated a large and steady migration of refugees across the Pyrenees. The overwhelming majority of these were men of military age, including officers of the French and other United Nations armies who were seeking not merely escape from Nazi territory but also another chance to carry arms against the Germans. Enormous German diplomatic pressure was exerted in Madrid to prevent the safe passage of these men, but this succeeded only temporarily in forcing the Spanish government to insist that evacuation be effected via Portugal. By October of 1943 the Madrid government agreed to permit direct evacuation from southern Spanish ports. By the beginning of 1945, more than 25,000 refugees had used this avenue of escape to carry on their fight against Fascism.

This important fact must be qualified, however, by noting that the favorable policy adopted by the Spanish Foreign Office did not prevent local Spanish police authorities from inflicting on these refugees stern and frequently brutal treatment. This was a natural product of the comradely relations prevailing between German authorities and the Spanish police. Yet, during all the months of this migration, there occurred but one instance when local Spanish officials turned over a civilian refugee to German patrols on the French Pyrenees border.

Perhaps even more significant than this passage of refugees through Spain was the fact that in the year and a half between the Allied landings in North Africa and the landing of British and American armies on the beaches of Normandy, Spanish authorities also permitted the rapid transit through Spain of more than eight hundred United States Army Air Force personnel, as well as some seven hundred men of the Royal Air Force and other British military services. These were largely men who had been smuggled across the Pyrenees after having been shot or forced down in bombing missions over German-occupied Europe. This policy of the Spanish government was predicated on its decision to adopt the principle (theoretically neutral) of releasing without delay all belligerent military personnel arriving in Spain directly from enemy territory. Obviously, with German armies occupying all of France, this principle applied in practice to large numbers of Allied military personnel but to a wholly negligible number of Axis personnel. In addition to those who secretly crossed the French border, there were also some three hundred American Air Force men who landed in Spain either by mistake or in forced landings. Not only were all these men released, but there occurred no known instance when the security of secret equipment on these planes was violated by Spanish authorities: in many cases, the crews had failed to destroy such equipment and it was always taken over by the American Embassy without having been compromised.

On the issue of Spanish policy toward the military intelligence activities of the belligerent nations, while Axis agents systematically exploited Spanish territory for sabotage and espionage activities, Allied intelligence services were far from idle. An elaborate and competent British organization and an elaborate American organization (built largely around "oil observers" assigned to supervise the distribution within Spain of petroleum shipments received from Allied sources) worked assiduously from Spanish bases during the four years from the fall to the liberation of France. These Allied agents in Spain provided the most valuable source of information for the United Nations on all German troop dispositions in southern France.

When Allied armies in 1944 replaced the Germans on the Pyrenees, the viewpoint of Allied diplomats on the question

of refugees fleeing to Spain assumed a radically changed character. So long as German armies had been in occupation of
southern France, Allied missions in Madrid, in their representations to the Spanish Foreign Office, had stressed the "sacred"
right of asylum which a neutral country should grant all refugees. But the refugees now became German: about 1,500 German soldiers fled across the Spanish border to avoid capture
by the advancing Allied armies. At British and American insistence, they were swiftly interned by the Spanish authorities.
But the fact that Allied diplomatic representations for years
had based a case for their own refugees on the immutable right
of asylum did not strengthen the Allied position, at the end
of the war, in demanding extradition of "undesirable" Germans.

The first months of 1945 brought to the Allies several Spanish concessions of a military character, though none of these,
at such a date, could affect the collapsing Nazi cause. On February 19, negotiations which had been initiated by the United
States government ended in an agreement granting the United
States Army Air Transport Command over-flight and landing
rights in Spain, including the right to install military personnel and equipment at the Madrid airport and to develop
the Barajas field to suit the needs of its operations. At the
beginning of May, additional facilities were accorded the ATC
with the Spanish government's agreement to permit ATC
aircraft to over-fly Spanish territory on the Dakar-Casablanca
run, to install equipment and personnel at Cabo Juby and
Villa Cisneros, and to land at these points. At the end of the
same month, another important concession was made in the
granting of over-flight rights to unarmed American tactical
aircraft participating in the redeployment of men and equipment from the European to the Pacific theaters. For a period
of two weeks (as requested) these planes were allowed to over-
fly Spanish territory at will in direct flights from southern
England to Casablanca.

By this time, Spain had broken its diplomatic relations with

Japan, and even General Franco no longer believed it was "criminal madness" to think of the efficacy of American intervention in the European war.

4

In terms of economic warfare, Spain was a major battlefield through all the years of World War II.

As on so many other battlefields, here too German equipment and preparedness had given the Nazis an enormous initial advantage over the democratic powers. After the Nationalist triumph in 1939, the Germans had swiftly followed their political and military intervention with another kind of penetration deep into Spain's economy. The initial impetus came principally from the fact that the Spanish government had been placed in a debtor position by the extensive German aid received during the Civil War years. Huge Nazi credit balances had been built up in Spain on the basis of supplies furnished through the German clearing agency *Hisma*. To this there was added the value of 374,000,000 Reichsmarks which Berlin placed upon the services of the Condor Division. If this did not suffice for German purposes, in the political climate of 1939 and the years immediately following, the banks of Spain could be counted upon to supply any additional necessary credits. Despite the subsequent dissolution of *Hisma* at Spanish insistence, the first years of World War II witnessed a steady betterment of Germany's economic standing on Iberian soil. The fall of France necessarily produced closer economic relations with Germany than ever before, and with German troops on the Pyrenees it was a simple matter for the Spanish government to keep the "defenders of Europe" well stocked. The stocks included lavish quantities of foodstuffs, wolfram, iron ore. And at the same time that the collapse of France thus simplified overland shipments to Germany, Nazi submarines were harassing Allied shipping so successfully that Spanish trade with the Allies declined sharply.

But with all these advantages, Germany could not supply to Spain materials obtainable only from Britain or the Western Hemisphere—most importantly, petroleum. This dependence upon non-Axis sources of supply opened the way for the signing of the Anglo-Spanish war trade agreements of 1940 which extended to Britain authority over Spanish shipping. Crews, cargoes, and passengers passed under British navicert control, and, as an additional price for the opportunity to import from Allied sources, Madrid had to place a ban on the exportation of specified commodities to the Axis. Meanwhile, even during these blackest war years, Spain's pyrites, potash, and iron ore continued to be shipped to England.

By the summer of 1942, the diplomatic position of the Allies became strong enough to exact from the Madrid government approval for the initiation of a program of preclusive purchasing in Spain, designed to deprive Germany of some of the essential strategic materials which she had been gathering in such abundance in the Iberian peninsula. While permission to conduct such unmasked economic warfare did signify a substantial Spanish concession to the Allies, General Franco's negotiators also understood perfectly well that such warfare promised competitive bidding which would raise purchase prices on Spanish materials to an all-time high. Nonetheless this program fulfilled the Allies' purpose of keeping many millions of dollars' worth of Spanish goods out of German hands.

As the military course of the war plainly shifted, Madrid's economic policy veered progressively in the direction of closer co-operation with Britain and America. Significant signs of the times in 1943 were the Spanish government's exclusion of German participation in the Spanish *Iberia* Airways (in which German stock ownership had been heavy), and its agreement in principle to the American request for the granting of landing rights in Spain to American commercial lines. By the end of 1943, it was apparent to all diplomats in Madrid that Allied economic warfare was winning its main objectives: reducing

German credit balances in Spain, cutting German purchases of strategic products in Spain, and preventing Germany from using Spain as a funnel for supplies obtained outside Spain. This last objective had been achieved by the steady enlargement of the prohibitory terms of the war-trade agreements, supplemented by the Proclaimed and Statutory Lists and Allied treasury controls. Simultaneously, Allied preclusive buying had drastically raised the prices of materials Germany most needed, while heavy Spanish shipments to Germany during 1940 and 1941 had created a German overdraft in the Hispano-German clearing of some 180,000,000 Reichsmarks.

By mid-1943, Germany had fairly well exhausted its Spanish credits. This, of course, neither pleased the vehemently pro-German elements within the Madrid government nor the Spanish producers who had been growing monumentally rich, thanks to the competitive Allied-Axis purchasing programs. Hence the Spanish government extended to Germany the equivalent of 100,000,000 Reichsmarks—in partial payment of its Civil War debt.

But while this admirably served Germany's economic needs, not so satisfactory for the Nazis were two other measures which the Spanish government took at this time. First, it forced Berlin to deliver more than 150,000,000 Reichsmarks' worth of machinery, armaments, cereals and pharmaceuticals, as part payment on the German overdraft. Secondly, while Berlin had been contentedly viewing the Spanish Civil War debt as a sure economic asset, Madrid suddenly proclaimed further liquidation of that debt by presenting Germany with a claim of 220,-000,000 Reichsmarks for the services of the Blue Division and of Spanish labor in Germany. Thus the "volunteers" of the Blue Division, while joining Berlin in the hallowed "defense of Christian civilization," also performed another less glamorous but more practical service for the Franco regime.

All these developments had a result of real importance to the war effort of the United Nations: the German government, at the peak of the Russian campaign, struck a wartime low in its vital imports from Spain of hides, skins, and woolen cloth, as well as essential minerals.

The issue of Spanish shipments of vital raw materials to Germany has been confused by a voluminous amount of inexact or incomplete information that has circulated outside Spain. It is quite true that Nazi Germany obtained, for example, close to 500,000 tons of iron ore from Spain in the single year of 1943. This was deplorable, when the world knew that those half million tons of ore went directly into the support of a war machine bent on killing as many Allied soldiers as possible. But it is also true that this fact, standing alone, did not reflect the full extent or character of Spain's economic policy in World War II. In the same year of 1943, Great Britain obtained 925,000 tons of iron ore, almost twice as much as Germany. Also, in the same year, shipments of pyrites from Spain to Germany totaled 43,000 tons—while those to Britain and the United States came to 210,000 or almost four times as much. Fluor spar, needed by both the United States and Germany, in 1943 was divided thus: 15,000 tons to Germany and 18,000 tons to the United States. In this same period, Great Britain obtained 35,000 critically necessary tons of potash. The Allies were also able to corner the market on Spanish strontium and to purchase substantial quantities of mercury, even though Spain's supply of mercury was supposedly controlled by an Italian cartel. On the critical matter of wolfram shipments, the Allied purchasing program in 1943 acquired almost twice the quantity obtained by the Germans: a total of 2,770 tons, against a Nazi total of 1,445 tons.

While these statistics must have an important place in any fair judgment of Spain's economic policy, they must be weighed and appraised in relationship to other facts. The most important of these facts is that, although the entire Spanish economy depended upon the Western Hemisphere for continuing petroleum shipments, Spain persisted in trading heavily and profitably with the Axis. Secondly, while Anglo-American purchasing accounted in many instances for bigger supplies than went to the Nazis, the volume of Spanish trade with Germany nonetheless kept increasing on its own account. Thus, while Germany's acquisition of less than 1,500 tons of wolfram in 1943 was little more than half the Anglo-American total, it was more than 50 per cent greater than the German supply obtained the previous year, almost 500 per cent greater than the quantity received from Spain in 1941. Thirdly, Madrid had accepted and permitted the Allied preclusive purchasing program not from the least inclination to assist the United Nations but from its own need and desire to pile up a large dollar balance in its commercial relations with America. Finally, for every economic concession the Allies had to fight in a political environment that was almost unbearably pro-Fascist.

All these considerations led the United States and Great Britain, in November of 1943, to press the Spanish government with a series of critical demands. Set forth by Ambassador Hayes in an official Memorandum to Foreign Minister Jordana, these demands were: a complete embargo on wolfram shipments to Germany, the release of Italian warships and merchant vessels still detained in Spanish ports, the suppression of the German Consulate in the Tangier Zone, the expulsion from Tangier and from all Spanish territory of Axis agents, and the authorization for opening a direct radio-telegraph circuit between Spain and the United States. Weeks of negotiations on these points met with only exasperating Spanish evasiveness and procrastination, until the exportation of another 300 tons of wolfram to Germany in January of 1944 precipitated Allied use of its most formidable economic weapon: suspension of shipments of gasoline and other petroleum fuels to Spain.

While Spanish officials stopped shaking hands with Axis friends long enough to wring them in anguish before Allied diplomats, and while the press poured forth a torrent of self-pitying editorials about this "challenge" to Spanish "sovereignty," negotiations dragged and drifted till the compromise agreement of May 2 was reached. It was a compromise heavily favorable to Allied demands. Wolfram shipments to Germany, suspended since February 5, were to be resumed at the rate of a 20-ton monthly limit for May and June and a 40-ton monthly limit thereafter. In effect, this meant that in the four critical months preceding Allied landings in Normandy a meager total of 20 tons of wolfram could be legally exported to Germany.

But, despite the undoubtedly genuine efforts of the Madrid government to enforce the agreement (and despite also the stationing of British and American observers at key points near the French border), the venality of subordinate Spanish officials allowed German smuggling to get some 280 tons across the French border by the middle of August. To this, the Spanish government limply responded by canceling the authorized exportations for June and July. By this time Allied troops were on the Pyrenees, German armies were falling back toward the Rhine, and the issue was obsolete.

As for the other economic demands made by the Allies at the end of 1943, final authorization for the direct radio-telegraph circuit between Spain and the United States was obtained in the last month of 1944—after no less than fourteen years of successive attempts with the Monarchy, the Republic, and the Franco regime. And five months before, all the Italian merchant vessels in Spanish waters had been allowed to depart for Allied ports.

As the last months of the world conflict approached (and all feasible trade channels between Spain and Germany were severed), the economic objectives of the United States focused principally on matters of civil aviation. This first involved an attempt to sever the last remaining link between Iberia and Germany by forcing the suspension of the *Lufthansa* airline. The importance of this issue arose from the Allies' fear that such an avenue out of central Europe would be exploited for the escape of Nazi war criminals, Nazi assets or looted property. The American demand to suspend the *Lufthansa* was made in September, 1944. It was rejected by the Spanish on the grounds that such action could be taken only if some other means of communication, such as a Spanish or Swiss airline, were permitted by Allied authorities to link Spain with its nationals and its interests in Germany. Allied military authorities refused this request, and negotiations remained at a standstill until February of 1945. Then the Spanish government agreed to suspend the German airline if assurances could be obtained for the safe overland passage of Spanish diplomatic pouches between Spain and Switzerland. This was finally agreed to by the Allies and on April 17, only three weeks before the final Nazi surrender, the *Lufthansa* was officially suspended by the Spanish authorities. This belated burial of German civil aviation interests in Spain followed an important agreement between Spain and the United States, signed on the 2nd of September, 1944. Under its terms, the United States was accorded transit and landing rights in Spanish territory for American commercial planes operating over three independent air routes.

On May 8, 1945, official Victory Day in Europe, the Spanish government took formal possession of all German official and quasi-official properties in Spain. Following the declaration issued in Berlin on June 5, by which the major Allied powers assumed supreme authority over Germany and all German interests, discussions with the Spanish government began in Madrid for the transfer of all German property to Allied custody.

In the months which followed, the Spanish government made effusive public gestures of collaborating with the Allied authorities. In many instances, on the highest official levels, genuine and effective co-operation was extended in the complex work of uncovering and disposing of German assets, both Statal and pari-Statal. But in probably the majority of instances, especially in those depending upon the good faith of subordinate Spanish officials, German interests were protected and Allied efforts were stubbornly blocked. Both in Madrid and in key provincial cities, numerous cases arose in which Spanish officials helped their Nazi friends destroy important records or valuable equipment, conceal German agents, or bury private German assets in dummy Spanish corporations. In May of 1946, a full year after military victory, Allied authorities in Madrid had gained control over perhaps 50 per cent of an estimated $40,000,000 worth of official or quasi-official German assets, including property, gold, dollar currency, pesetas, stocks of morphine, and Nazi-owned corporations. An estimated $60,000,000 in *private* assets probably will never be recovered, thanks partly to Spanish connivance, partly to German preparedness for the day of defeat, partly to the immensely difficult legal problems involved.

From even this summary review of the economic aspects of Spanish foreign policy during the years of world conflict, certain conclusions emerge plainly. It is apparent, first of all, that the Franco regime's economic policy did not operate simply as an arm or instrument of German policy; on the contrary, it struck out and pursued its own independent course, in frequent conflict with German interests and objectives. German economic penetration into Spain's economy unquestionably assumed enormous proportions, but this penetration could not automatically dictate Spain's foreign trade policy, any more than could the vast British holdings of decades' standing in the Bilbao area or in the Río Tinto mines. Throughout Franco Spain's economic dealings, the simple standard of expediency and self-interest was the final ideal.

Yet it is equally apparent that, in these years, the Spanish government often betrayed its own inescapable *political* character by being unable or unwilling to serve its best economic interests. The merchant ships which sneaked from northern Spanish shores to supply besieged German garrisons on the French coast in the closing months of the war, the wolfram smuggled across the French border with the connivance of local Spanish officials, the German assets concealed with the aid of the rabidly Germanophile forces of the *Seguridad* . . .

all these instances testified to the inability of the Spanish regime, as a whole, to escape from its own political character even when expediency, if not salvation itself, demanded it.

While self-interest dictated policy, this immutable political character tended to dictate *practice*. Again and again, the unassimilated and heterogeneous character of the forces constituting the Spanish regime, while permitting the regime a certain suppleness and dexterity in domestic political maneuvers, made of its foreign policy a mass of self-defeating practices and mutually-contradictory purposes. So often the will to be self-interested was defeated by the habit of being pro-Axis.

5

Nowhere did the conflict and confusion of purposes and practices in Spanish foreign policy make themselves more manifest than in the strictly political sphere—precisely where Allied policy toward Franco Spain also was most beset with contradictions and anomalies. Military or economic issues were fairly clear-cut; objectives were easily definable, always tangible. But in the subtler realm of politics emerged all the bizarre and baffling complications that arise when a democratic and totalitarian power try to speak a common language. Beyond a certain point, the conversation becomes almost unintelligible.

Viewing from a distance the evolution of Spanish foreign policy away from its original unconditional Axis bias, probably three events seem to stand out prominently. These were: replacement of Serrano Suñer by General Jordana as Foreign Minister in September of 1942; public declaration of "neutrality" in October of 1943; and rupture of diplomatic relations with Japan in April of 1945. Yet, close inspection reveals that these events had little real meaning. In the first instance, Serrano Suñer's removal was dictated by domestic political considerations utterly unrelated to foreign policy. In the second instance, the Madrid government's official proclamation of "neutrality" was interesting only as an indication of the degree to which General Franco had come to believe that he could disappoint the Germans and get away with it; and it was a statement of utter political irrelevance, since Spanish soldiers in the Blue Division were still shooting at Russians on the Eastern front when "neutrality" was declared.

The Spanish Foreign Office announced the severance of diplomatic relations with Japan on April 11, 1945. The move followed official Spanish protests over the loss of Spanish lives and property in the Philippines during Japanese occupation. Had such a step been taken a year earlier, when American Ambassador Carlton J. H. Hayes had raised the question informally, it would have had some political significance. But in April of 1945, Nazi armies had been shattered, and the end of the European war was only a few weeks distant. In these circumstances Madrid's action was little more than a new expression of the old Falangist thesis that there were "two wars": in the European war, Spain was anti-Russian; in the Pacific, she was anti-Japanese. Japan, on the other side of the globe, provided a safe and convenient whipping post for Falangist propaganda, especially after her armies, driven from the Philippines, could no longer reach Spanish citizens or properties. Hence a diplomatic break was painless, and, from the Allied viewpoint, meaningless. The whole affair threatened to take on a ludicrous aspect when José Luis Arrese suggested to an officer of the American Embassy that he was prepared to lead a new Falangist Blue Division, this time against the Japanese!

While these headline-making events thus lacked real political significance, one true test of Spanish policy was the recurrent issue of diplomatic recognition of new foreign governments as they were made and unmade by the belligerent armies in the course of the war. From the outset of hostilities, the Spanish Foreign Office fretted and fidgeted over all the embarrassing questions raised by exile governments and puppet regimes. With a bland evasion of principle, it adopted the policy, wherever possible, of recognizing any and all governments. Thus, in the first years of the war, Madrid played the Axis diplomatic game by allowing the puppet states of Croatia, Slovakia, and Manchukuo to open diplomatic missions in Madrid. Yet at the same time, the Foreign Office refused to follow German policy toward occupied European countries. Throughout the war, the Allied governments-in-exile of Czechoslovakia, Yugoslavia, Greece, Norway, the Netherlands, and Poland were also allowed to maintain their own missions in the Spanish capital.

The particular problem of recognition which probably caused the Spanish Foreign Office most anguish was that of the French government. Here the usual solution was followed with a slight variation. Until September of 1944, Spanish authorities treated the Vichy regime as the legitimate government of France. But from the time of the Allied landings in North Africa, there existed in Algiers a Free French government which also claimed recognition for the Allies. It was a matter of immediate importance that some Free French representative be able to operate on Spanish soil, both to be of assistance to French refugees pouring across the Pyrenees and to gather important political and military intelligence from occupied France. The American Embassy applied heavy pressure on Madrid's Foreign Office, and General Jordana yielded with a secret agreement allowing a French representative to establish himself in Madrid in the guise of an American official. Two months later the Foreign Office agreed to *de facto* recognition of a Free French Liaison Mission in Madrid—while it nonetheless continued to recognize the Vichy regime as the legitimate French government. This continuing recognition of Vichy threatened to produce a most embarrassing situation after Allied armies had swept through northern France in the summer of 1944, yet it was still too early, in Franco's cautious judgment, to affront the Germans so firmly by recalling his Ambassador in Vichy. He managed dexterously to sidestep the issue by making Sr. Lequerica, Spanish Ambassador in Vichy, his new Foreign Minister and "forgetting" to appoint a new representative to Marshal Pétain. In September, it was the same ex-Ambassador to Vichy who, as Foreign Minister, authorized the Free French mission in Madrid to take over the prerogatives and premises of the dispossessed Vichy French Embassy!

Spain's light-footed diplomats had countless other unhappy moments. Not the least wretched days were those in September of 1943 following Mussolini's fall in Italy. While the Badoglio government established itself in Rome some months later with the support of Allied armies, the dissident Fascist regime in northern Italy claimed legitimate authority. The dilemma was made even sharper for Madrid's Foreign Office by a personal plea addressed to Franco by Hitler, asking for prompt recognition of the crippled Mussolini regime. The Spanish government at first refused and recognized the Badoglio regime as the legitimate Italian government. But this clean-cut decision did not last long. Over the vehement protests of the British and American missions, Madrid devised a new formula for evading such issues, recognized an "agent" of the Mussolini regime, and allowed him to establish a skeleton mission in Madrid. Rather plausibly, Spanish officials insisted that their extensive interests in northern Italy made it imperative for them to maintain some contact with local authorities there. But the serious direct result of their action was that the Italian diplomatic "agency" in Madrid quickly became a buzzing hive of Axis espionage and sabotage agents.

These successive matters of diplomatic recognition were the only political issues to arise, in Spain's wartime relations with the belligerent powers, which were almost always clear and simple, despite the frequently elaborate devices used by Madrid to evade too painful decisions. Other international issues of a political character, certainly all the major crises in Spanish relations with the democratic powers, contained so many hidden implications, unseen motives, or unpublishable purposes that world opinion rarely could form a reasoned judgment of them. Ideological controversy, the dictates of expediency on both sides, the secrecy of wartime diplomacy, and the compulsion to defer to military considerations—all these factors conspired to obscure simple political facts, and to force either Madrid's Foreign Office or Washington's State Department to appear before the public in roles for which they frequently received undeserved criticism or unearned commendation.

Public opinion in the United States—especially of the liberals and leftists who persistently denounced the maintenance of diplomatic relations with the Franco regime even during wartime—generally was loud in its acclaim of the Anglo-American decision to impose an oil embargo on Spain in February of 1944. This was the only occasion when the liberal American press applauded the State Department's policy toward Spain—for abandoning "appeasement" in favor of a "firm" or "tough" action against Falangist Spain.

It is true that the intentions of Washington at this time were admirable and that it had brought into play its strongest economic weapon. But the developments which followed were dismaying enough to lead any impartial observer to question the ability of the State Department to plan and execute any effective diplomatic offensive.

There was grave enough cause for such doubt. Washington had committed the singular and needless blunder of launching its offensive before co-ordinating its own objectives with those of the British government. Very soon after the oil embargo had been imposed jointly by Great Britain and the United States, it became apparent in Madrid that the State Department had failed to ascertain beforehand if both London and Washington were seeking the same thing. Both were equally anxious to force the expulsion of Axis agents from Spain and the closing of the German Consulate in the Tangier Zone. But on the most crucial issue of all—Spain's wolfram shipments to Germany—the British Foreign Office was by no means prepared (as was the State Department) to insist upon a total Spanish embargo.

Confusion and contradiction beset Allied negotiations in Madrid, which from the outset met more stubborn Spanish resistance than many had foreseen. As the weeks passed without a settlement, the Spanish Foreign Office began to see plainly that Ambassador Hayes and British Ambassador Sir Samuel Hoare were not equally insistent in their demands. While Hayes strove to convince Foreign Minister Jordana that the Allies would lift their oil embargo only in return for a total Spanish wolfram embargo, the word spread quickly through Spanish official circles that Hayes stood alone and that the longer Madrid held out the stronger would be the pressure of London upon Washington to accept a compromise agreement.

The contradictory strategies of Hayes and Hoare were only the logical consequences of different instructions from their respective governments. When the weeks of negotiations lengthened into fruitless months, the British Ambassador finally assumed an attitude that left little doubt that the British government was prepared to resume petroleum shipments to Spain on its own initiative if the State Department remained intransigeant. But neither the State Department nor London's Foreign Office would yield to the other's policy.

A personal transatlantic phone call from Churchill to Roosevelt was needed to resolve the dilemma. Churchill insisted that Franco and his Foreign Office would not retreat further under even sustained economic pressure. Reluctantly, Roosevelt acceded. A settlement was reached. When its terms were made public in Washington, the State Department ended the drama on a pitiful note, announcing to the world that it had accepted the settlement reluctantly and only at British insistence.

This was the art of diplomacy reduced to a crude craft indeed. The grand gesture of "getting tough" with Franco Spain had been long awaited and elaborately staged. But when the

United States and Great Britain, with the spotlight of world publicity upon them, moved to the center of the political stage and drew themselves up to their full and imposing height, they performed like amateur actors mumbling half-forgotten lines in a bad play. The occasion had been one of enormous opportunity, not merely to achieve certain immediate demands but also, by use of our most drastic economic weapon, to impress General Franco and his regime with evidence of Anglo-American determination to force them to yield to the principles, the practices, if necessary the dictates of a United Nations world. It could have been a chastening lesson. Instead, official Madrid could smirk at the spectacle of two of the United Nations unable to agree between themselves long enough to provide such a lesson. And, lest any of Spain's officials fail to see the bitter humor in the situation, Washington made certain that they all understood the cause for laughter by publicly proclaiming it.

This was one of the most striking instances in which world opinion could perceive only some of the more deceptive external aspects of Spain's foreign policy and relations with the Allied governments. There were many other similar occurrences, especially actions of the Spanish government itself, which defied quick and accurate appraisal from a distance.

A great deal of this difficulty arose from the fact that ideological inclinations and political (or military) purposes could not and did not operate on the same level. Thus, for example, in 1942-43 Spanish Foreign Minister Jordana crowned the *rapprochement* of Franco's Spain and Salazar's Portugal with the formal establishment of an Iberian Bloc, celebrated in elaborate diplomatic ceremony and with enthusiastic public declarations of enduring comradeship. In ideological terms, this development could be described accurately enough as the natural gravitation toward one another of two dictatorships and two totalitarian states. Thus described, the news should have been cheered by Berlin and Rome, mourned by London and Washington. This is precisely what did not happen. Jor-

dana's diplomatic action was not an expression of ideological
loyalty but a practical step in the re-orientation of Spanish
foreign policy—a step in the direction of the United Nations.
In the framework of world war and world diplomacy, Portugal's longstanding alliance with Great Britain and its close
historic ties to Brazil were, at the moment, more relevant facts
than Oliveira Salazar's stern suppression of all his political
opponents within Portugal. For the Spanish Foreign Office to
enter into a firm compact with this nation was to suggest a
new purpose motivating Spain's foreign relations: the decision
not to face exclusively toward Germany and Europe but also
to look toward the Atlantic and the Americas, and to emphasize all cultural, religious, and racial bonds with the Latin-
American countries. Virtually everyone of these countries was
at war with the Axis. This was the significant meaning behind
what appeared to be nothing more than the close embrace of
the Iberian peninsula's two totalitarian regimes. Berlin did
not fail to perceive it quickly: the formation of the Iberian
Bloc was followed only a few weeks later by the recall of Germany's Ambassador in Madrid. Even pro-Axis Spaniards conceded that his mission had been a failure and that one important contributing cause had been the creation of the new
Iberian entente.

In March of 1944 there came another of the frequent moments of diplomatic tension between Washington and Madrid.
It received little publicity but it again involved political
issues that were far from being transparently simple and clear.
The occasion for this issue was the Nazi coup d'état in Hungary which had resulted in the establishment of Sztojay's
puppet-Fascist regime. After a few weeks of hesitation, Madrid
decided to accord recognition to the Sztojay government and
receive the diplomatic credentials of a new chargé d'affaires
appointed by Budapest. As unfortunately happened more than
once, Washington responded with a policy which tripped over
a flat conflict in its own objectives and sprawled in diplomatic
confusion on the door of the Spanish Foreign Office. In the

first place, the State Department reacted with understandable indignation at this latest Spanish deference to Berlin's wishes. But in the second place (and *at precisely the same time*) Washington instructed the American Ambassador in Madrid to enlist the aid of the Spanish Foreign Office in an important mission of mercy: to use the facilities and immunities of the Spanish Embassy in Budapest to save Jews, as well as other religious and political minorities, from the harsh persecution promised by the Sztojay regime working under Nazi orders. This humanitarian service was agreed to and undertaken by Madrid: acting upon instructions from Foreign Minister Jordana, the Spanish Embassy in Budapest issued visas and "letters of protection" which saved the lives of hundreds facing Nazi deportation or execution. As for the American request that the Spanish government also break relations with Budapest, the Foreign Office explained with logic that it could scarcely be asked to do this and at the same time use its diplomatic mission in Hungary to protect the hunted and the persecuted.

In the whole history of Allied wartime relations with the Spanish government, probably no single issue arose which contained so much concealed political dynamite as the famous Laurel incident. By October of 1943, the redirection of Spanish foreign policy away from its initial totally pro-Axis policy was becoming slowly but plainly evident. Suddenly, without a moment's diplomatic warning, all evidence to this effect seemed to be contradicted and erased by the news that General Franco's Foreign Office had dispatched a congratulatory telegram to the new head of the Japanese puppet government in the Philippines, Sr. Laurel. The brazenness of the deed was excelled only by its patent stupidity. On top of Washington's deep suspicions (later well confirmed) that many Spanish citizens and members of *Falange Exterior* were serving as Japanese agents in the Philippines, this official action was intolerable. In Madrid, the American Embassy at once expressed its outrage and indignation. In Washington, speculative discussion included the serious possibility of a diplomatic break with Spain. In plain fright, the Spanish Foreign Office rushed to the press an emphatic statement that its message had been a routine diplomatic courtesy in no way implying any intention to recognize the Laurel regime. It was a pitifully weak explanation for such a gratuitous public compliment to the Philippines' arch traitor.

But this tense diplomatic situation, on its surface, bore no suggestion of a crucial underlying political question which had nothing to do with the virtually academic issue of Spanish diplomacy in the South Pacific. The far from academic matter was the danger that General Jordana would be driven from the Foreign Office before the storm which the incident had raised. As Foreign Minister, Jordana had unqualifiedly accepted personal responsibility for the message to Laurel. But every diplomat in Madrid was firmly convinced that the message had been deftly slipped through or past his office without his understanding of its meaning (perhaps even without knowledge of its existence); and that this had been the treacherous work of a notoriously pro-Nazi career diplomat in the Foreign Office who was chief of the Diplomatic Cabinet.

The German inspiration behind the message was plain, but its purpose was nothing so transparently simple as the felicitation of a Philippine Quisling. The cannily conceived objective had been to place Jordana in a deadly political crossfire. For more than a year he had been harassed and badgered by all the Falangist and Germanophile elements within the Franco regime, battling every step in his policy that suggested a change favorable to the United Nations. He had survived these remorseless attacks principally because General Franco believed that he could perform an essential service: to placate and to conciliate the United States. If the Laurel message succeeded in raising American wrath to the diplomatic-breaking point, Jordana's labor would become bankrupt. Germans and pro-Axis Spaniards, who had been unable to force his removal for his Allied sympathies, might now use a different kind of ammunition to destroy him for his failure to have won reciprocal sympathy.

It was a consummately adroit maneuver. In the weeks of critical tension following the Laurel note, the German Embassy in Madrid clearly saw itself within reach of its greatest chance to reverse the new direction of Spanish foreign policy. If Jordana could be ousted, it would not be a difficult matter to convince General Franco that it was impossible successfully to appease the United States and that only an unqualifiedly pro-Axis policy could pay political dividends. Within Spanish government circles, the motivation and secret purpose of the whole maneuver were betrayed to all by the fact that Falangist Minister José Luis Arrese assumed the lead in denouncing the "failure" of Jordana and demanding his removal. But the envoys of Naziism did not rely principally on Arrese or his fellow-Falangists to destroy Jordana but upon inexorable diplomatic pressure from the United States!

Wisely, American policy avoided the trap so temptingly baited. Diplomatic dismay and anger were made unmistakable to Madrid's Foreign Office, which was left in no doubt as to the grave jeopardy in which it had placed relations with the United States. But instead of pressing for a humiliation of the Spanish government which could have taken only the form of the ignominious dismissal of Jordana, American tactics left Spanish officialdom chastened and nervous. Then, immediately seizing advantage of a moment when the Foreign Office would be psychologically off balance, the American ambassador submitted a list of American demands having nothing to do with a Philippine traitor but of much more urgent moment: an embargo on wolfram, release of Italian warships, expulsion of Axis agents from Spain and Tangier.

Although these demands were not met until the following year (and only after the Anglo-American oil embargo), this American strategy in November of 1943 bore the best marks of a sure sense of timing and of intelligent diplomacy. If Anglo-American plans for the subsequent oil embargo against

Spain had been prepared with comparable intelligence, a much quicker and more decisive victory would have resulted. In the full course of America's wartime policy toward Spain, no paradox was more striking than the fact that it was fumbling and ineffectual when (at the time of the oil embargo) it seemed to be daring and determined, that it was alert and perceptive when (at the time of the Laurel incident) it seemed to have ended in failure.

6

In Madrid, the morning of Sunday, November 8, 1942, came with a chill beneath an overcast sky.

Precisely at nine o'clock, the dramatic scene was enacted in the private study of the Pardo. Four men were present. Generalissimo Francisco Franco stood by his desk. Before him was the American Ambassador, Carlton J. H. Hayes, his tall figure and broad shoulders dwarfing the Caudillo, his eyes tired and shadowed from a night of great tension and little sleep. Beside Franco stood his Foreign Minister, General Jordana, in martial dress, even slighter in frame than his Chief of State. And completing the group was the official Spanish interpreter, Baron de las Torres: serious and solemn as the occasion demanded, yet, with his burly figure, round face and big mustache, unable to avoid the suggestion of the bass in a barbershop quartet.

On the wall behind General Franco were two photographs. They were of Hitler and Mussolini.

The American Ambassador handed a document to the Baron de las Torres. It was a letter, in English, addressed personally to General Franco. The interpreter translated the phrases carefully:

Your nation and mine are friends in the best sense of the word. . . . You and I are sincerely desirous of the continuation of that friendship for our mutual good. . . . I believe the Spanish government and the Spanish people wish to maintain neutrality and to remain outside the war. Spain has nothing to fear from the United Nations. I am, my dear General, your sincere friend.

The letter was from President Roosevelt. The occasion for it, the motive for its words of friendly cheer, was expressed in the statement: "I am sending a powerful army to French possessions and protectorates in North Africa."

General Franco listened patiently, expressed his pleasure and acceptance of the President's assurance that this military action was "in no shape, manner or form directed against the government or people of Spain." As he listened and as he spoke, American and British soldiers were sloshing up North African beaches, their warships firing successive salvos against coastal defenses and enemy vessels, their planes bombing Vichy French installations from Casablanca to Algiers. The first great offensive of the United Nations was under way, and upon its success depended the fate of World War II. Its own success depended, in large measure, upon the actions of Spain's totalitarian regime, upon the outcome of that memorable Sunday morning meeting in the private study of Spain's dictator.

Many months later, General George Marshall, in his Biennial Report, wrote of the critical moment of the North African offensive:

> The combined air forces, other than carrier-borne and a few transports and heavy bombers, had to be funnelled through the single restricted field at Gibraltar, which could have been put out of action in less than half an hour. There was no choice but to accept this hazard.

That fatal half-hour never materialized.

It had been at the end of September when Ambassador Hayes was secretly notified that the American and British Combined Chiefs of Staff planned an early invasion of French North Africa—military history's most spectacular and daring amphibious enterprise. He confided the news to only those officers of the Embassy, including myself, whose work would have to be co-ordinated in preparation for the vital test ahead. Diplomatic and propaganda preparations were carefully conceived to complement each other. On the diplomatic level, the Embassy prepared to win the confidence of the highest Spanish officials, generally to reassure them in the spirit of President Roosevelt's subsequent letter to General Franco. The prescription for propaganda was somewhat different: unceasingly to emphasize the swift Allied conversion of war potential into war might, and to stress—suggestively but with not too plain an insinuation—the destructive power of Allied long-range bombing against any enemy.

In the weeks both immediately preceding and following the first North African landings, Allied nerves in Madrid became raw and frayed. In the Embassy staff were many Foreign Service officers who had been rushed, smuggled or bombed out of their previous posts—Warsaw, Amsterdam, Belgrade. Many grimly readied themselves for the nightmare to descend again, this time on Madrid. In the last days before the critical one arrived, Washington indicated that it was just as nervous as Madrid, perhaps even more pessimistic over the chances of winning the bloodless war in Spain. Warning came from Washington in neat cryptic fashion. It was a secret code message which merely called the Embassy's attention to a certain paragraph in the standard Foreign Service regulations. But it was the paragraph stating the procedure to be followed when an Embassy must be vacated in emergency flight from advancing enemy armies.

Then, on the afternoon of Saturday, November 7, both the British and American Ambassadors received the coded cable which was their pre-arranged signal: THUNDERBIRD NOVEMBER EIGHT TWO AM SPANISH TIME.

Perhaps one intangible factor was among the most decisive in determining the final outcome—the fact that Spanish officialdom, in the tense days preceding THUNDERBIRD, was even more nervous than anyone else. For weeks, the fear had been haunting and growing in government circles that Britain and the United States might remember Wellington's peninsula campaign and choose Spain as their military highroad into Hitler's European fortress. In part, this fear was the product of diligent Nazi propaganda, which had broadcast the rumor that the Allies might strike at Spain. This was the most notable of several instances in which Nazi propaganda was conceived clumsily and with fatal miscalculation of its psychological effect. The very fear which Nazi officials sought to cultivate in the minds of Spanish officials, far from impelling the latter to assume a truculent attitude toward the Allies, helped to create such a state of nervousness that President Roosevelt's assurances, as well as news of the North African landings, brought a sense of relief so welcome as to approach sheer gratification.

It was at 2 A.M. on the morning of November 8 when, as the Allied North African landings actually began, Ambassador Hayes phoned a sleepy General Jordana to say that he must see him immediately. Carrying the President's letter and seeking a quick audience with General Franco in order to deliver it, the Ambassador was received by a Foreign Minister in bathrobe, pajamas, and a state of fear-worn nerves. When it was apparent that Franco could not be reached until morning (he was on a hunting trip), the agitated Jordana urgently begged to be allowed to know the contents of the Ambassador's message. For a half hour, in his homely attire, Spain's Foreign Minister pattered in his slippers up and down the floor, struggling with his worst fears of imminent disaster. Finally, the Ambassador decided to allow him to see the President's message. Poor Jordana smiled happily, sank back in his chair, and sighed with relief, "Ah! Spain is not involved."

By Monday, November 9, the Spanish decision was taken. The press of the nation carried on its front pages (under government orders, of course) the text of the American guarantees that Spanish sovereignty would not be violated. General Franco's military Cabinet had already resolved their policy: no action would be taken to impede Allied operations, no facilities would be granted either belligerent (*i.e.*, Germany), no belligerent forces (*i.e.*, German forces) would be admitted on Spanish soil. The Spanish government's decision was communicated to the German Embassy without even being requested. Subsequently, on more than one occasion, the German Embassy asked for a reversal of this decision, but they must have known themselves that, once taken, it was irrevocable. On December 7, Ambassador Hayes could take pride in advising President Roosevelt that the Spanish Foreign Office had officially and categorically assured him that the Government was "determined . . . to resist *forcefully* any attempt by *any* foreign power to invade Spanish territory."

But it was not within the power of either Allied Embassies or the Spanish Foreign Office to decide or to know whether such an invasion would be attempted. This was the great uncertainty. Two days rarely passed in succession without Madrid being jarred by new rumors that Nazi forces were massing on the Pyrenees or thrusting across them. Preparations had to be made for the worst eventuality. In the Embassy, confidential files were burned, code books readied for quick destruction, stores of gasoline laid in the basement to prepare for a motor race to Gibraltar against Nazi forces that might come down from the north. The advance of Allied armies in North Africa could not ease the situation. On the contrary, it might urge Nazi strategists more than ever to execute a drive through Spain, overwhelming Gibraltar, cutting Allied supply lines by sea, and springing into North Africa to attack the Allied rear.

Why did not the Germans strike? Military historians may conclude by agreeing with Hermann Göring that their failure to do so was perhaps their fatal blunder of the war. But, despite all the possible gain from such an offensive, the prospect offered many deterrents and grave risks. With the Allied nations sufficiently strong to mount such an offensive as the North African invasion, German armies, already spread thin in many places, would have had to assume an enormous additional responsibility in the whole Iberian peninsula with its long, jagged coastline. At the same time, the German general staff could not be certain that the Allies were not hoping and prepared for a Spanish battleground on the continent. Nor could the task of seizing and occupying Spain be an easy one. Transportation would be a grave problem: Spanish railroads, of different gauge from the French, were badly disorganized, and rolling stock was scarce and antiquated. Supply would be another difficult matter: there was not enough food in Spain to allow an occupying army to live off the land, and lines of supply into France, which could pass the Pyrenees at only a few well-known points, would be easy targets for Allied bombs. Finally, Spain's internal political situation held promise of trouble for any occupying army, especially a German one. Even if the Spanish Army under the government's orders did not itself battle a German invasion, the appearance of Nazi forces could quickly set off nation-wide explosions in a country rife with hatreds and superlatively skilled in the art of guerrilla warfare. Though Allied military strategists had decided not to follow Wellington's example, the German general staff might well have recalled Napoleon's experience in Spain.

Reverting for a moment to the last days and hours that preceded the most critical moment in the Allies' wartime relations with Spain, it is interesting to record how three ambassadors passed their time:

Ambassador Hayes was busy, I know. He was uninterruptedly planning and conferring with his colleagues and advisers, working with even more than his characteristic industry and resolution. He was preparing for a dramatic meeting that would take place beneath two handsome photographs of Adolf Hitler and Benito Mussolini and that would contribute so materially both to the destruction of those men and the opportune disappearance (two years later) of their pictures.

Ambassador von Stohrer was bringing his dramatic diplomatic career to an unhappy end. His first mission to Madrid as a young Embassy secretary during World War I, it will be

recalled, had ended with his implication in a crude plot to
assassinate the then Prime Minister Romanones. Now, on the
Thursday evening before the fateful Sunday, at a banquet at
his Embassy, he vigorously disputed the assertion of a Spanish
guest that an Allied invasion of North Africa was near. The
following day he not only reported this conversation in a
dispatch to Berlin but also added his own conclusion that all
German intelligence sources in Spain agreed that such an invasion would not take place. Before his dispatch reached
Berlin, it had.

Ambassador Hoare, "to maintain an attitude of unconcern,"
spent Saturday afternoon shooting wooden pigeons with a
Spanish friend. His sporting companion was the eldest son of
a former Prime Minister—the now aged Count Romanones.

7

Like the whole of Franco Spain's foreign policy, its conduct
toward the Allied offensive in North Africa has been the object of the most contradictory interpretations. Two such interpretations, diametrically opposed, deserve analysis.

The most determined critics of American wartime policy
toward Spain advanced the theory that Spain's military inactivity in 1942 followed a German design. Madrid was supposedly given the assignment by Berlin of waging a ruthless
war of nerves, keeping Allied strategists alarmed over the possibility of a Spanish attack through Morocco. The tangible
result of this war of nerves (it has been alleged) was that General Mark Clark and his entire U. S. Fifth Army had to station themselves on the Spanish Moroccan frontier, thereby
gravely weakening the forces that could be thrown against
the Germans in the Allied drive toward Tunis.

This interpretation of history, for all its seeming plausi-
bility, suffered from acute ignorance of the facts. First, while
all estimates of Spanish troop-dispositions at a given date may
be inexact, the forces in Spanish Morocco, generally calculated

to have been around 150,000, did not represent even one-quarter of the strength of Spain's standing army; nor was this fraction extraordinarily high in wartime for an area where Spanish forces were traditionally heavily concentrated, an area of crucial strategic importance to Spain at all times. Secondly, following the success of the Allied landings, these Spanish troops were not reinforced or increased in any obvious menace to the Anglo-American operations. But most important of all is the fact that, even had the Spanish government been the friendliest of democratic states, only the most credulous and careless military leaders would have depended upon Spain to protect the Allied flank, plunged exuberantly ahead to the east, and blandly disregarded the continuing threat of a successful German drive through Spain. This, not Spain's Moroccan armies, was the threat against which Allied leaders and the American Fifth Army had to guard. The Nazi decision could have come with devastating speed, with heavy German forces rushing across the Pyrenees and airborne units stabbing deep into southern Spain. Gibraltar was as vulnerable to assault from the landward side as had been Singapore. As an elementary precaution against such a dangerous attack, the Allies had to adopt military measures which only the most inventive imagination could attribute to a Spanish "war of nerves."

A far different appraisal of Spanish policy in the autumn of 1942 was that which subsequently was propagated, with tireless zeal, by officials and apologists of General Franco's regime. This interpretation was based on the contention that the Spanish government, having acted from the purest motives of a pacific and neutral foreign policy, had imposed a heavy debt of *gratitude* upon America and Britain—gratitude that Spanish armies had not attacked the Allied forces. This exquisitely Fascist argument was repeated to Allied representatives in Madrid by Falange propagandists and Spanish officials with such monotonous insolence that it eventually wore indignation down to the level of sheer boredom. The American and

British Ambassadors, for months, had to listen to this extraordinary dialectic. The Party press broadcast it to the nation with fanatical persistence. At one meeting with the government's press and propaganda chief, I was subjected to it once too often. I angrily retorted that his argument amounted to the assertion that a man living in a civilized community should go around thanking his neighbors for not burning his home or stealing his wife; and I asked the foolish question, "What standard of political morality is that?" But the answer was too plain: a Falangist standard.

This was no mere conversational gambit employed by Spanish officials for the benefit of Allied diplomats. It was the sincere belief of these men and the most striking revelation of the principles inspiring their policy and actions. In the following summer of 1943, one of General Franco's closest friends told me of a conversation he had had only a few days earlier with Spain's Chief of State. He had asked: Did the Generalissimo not worry over what might happen to his regime in the event of a United Nations triumph? Not at all. What would be the Caudillo's policy toward a world of victorious anti-Fascist nations? What would he do? With magnificent equanimity, General Franco replied: *"Pasar la cuenta"* ("pass the bill"). The "bill" for what? For two signal "services": keeping the Germans out of Spain after France's 1940 collapse, and taking no military action against the Allied offensive in 1942!

A fair summary judgment of Franco Spain's role in World War II must take account of a variety of considerations. There was the undeniable importance of the Spanish government's decision in 1942. There was the extraordinary and easily deniable Falangist claim to Allied gratitude for that decision. And there was this very significant fact: that decision would never have been in doubt had not the character and conduct of Spain's totalitarian regime so plainly marked it as a danger to the United Nations from the start of the war.

I believe that a reasoned and unimpassioned analysis of all these facts leads to one conclusion: what rightly has been most shocking to the peoples of the United Nations was not what Franco Spain did for the Axis cause so much as its unmistakable desire to do more. I have said before that the words and the deeds of General Franco's regime had to be distinguished and kept separate in their respective spheres. But between the sphere of words and that of deeds, there lies a third sphere from which must come the evidence for final judgment: the sphere of motives and intentions.

General Franco made clear the spirit and intent animating his policies in his own personal correspondence with Hitler:

"I would like to thank you, Der Führer, once again for the offer of solidarity. I reply with the assurance of my unchangeable and sincere adherence to you personally, to the German people, and to the cause for which you fight. I hope, in defense of this cause, to be able to renew the old bonds of comradeship between our armies. . . .

"I consider, as you yourself do, that the destiny of history has united you with myself and with the Duce in an indissoluble way. . . . Our Civil War, since its very inception and during its entire course, is more than proof. . . . We stand today where we have always stood. . . . You must have no doubt about my absolute loyalty to this political concept and to the realization of the union of our national destinies with those of Germany and Italy. . . .

"I want to dispel . . . all shadow of doubt and declare that I stand ready at your side, entirely and decidedly at your disposal, united in a common historical destiny, desertion from which would mean my suicide and that of the cause which I have led and represent in Spain."

It should be recognized that there is some justification in the argument of the Generalissimo's apologists that even these glowing words sound like the speech of a man who does protest too much in his fervent plea, "You must have no doubt. . . ." Published correspondence of Hitler and Mussolini from these same years has revealed that the German and Italian leaders entertained the deepest suspicions of General

Franco's willingness to share their military burden. The only known secret military protocol between the Spanish and German governments, signed on February 10, 1943, did not signify any serious concession to Nazi pressure: "The Spanish Government . . . declares that it is determined to resist every entry by Anglo-American forces upon the Iberian Peninsula or upon Spanish territory outside of the Peninsula." A written protocol was scarcely necessary to assure that Franco's armies would fight in such circumstances. And by December of the same year, German Ambassador Dieckhoff already was protesting to the Spanish Chief of State the "danger" which Berlin saw in several Spanish concessions to the Allies.

But while these are facts, they do not, by any process of logic, warrant the conclusion that General Franco was craftily misleading political friends whom he had no desire to assist. His rhetoric was deceptive, not because its promises were insincere, but because circumstances which General Franco could not control prevented their fulfillment. His protestations of loyalty were expressions of the most genuine desire, not only to help those with whom he was "united in a common historical destiny," but also to share the booty which a generous destiny might bring. And the fact that he escaped the consequences of the destruction of that destiny, by the armies of the United Nations, can be considered a tribute to the elusiveness of his political tactics but *not* to the integrity of his political principles.

Even in the moments when the promise of Axis military triumph seemed brightest, General Franco's regime could not fail to see the hazards in joining the fray. Few of the Caudillo's official lieutenants were deceived by their own public speeches on the strength and security of their government against domestic challenge. The war fatigue of the Spanish people fortunately prevented that challenge from becoming an open and militant threat; but if the Madrid government decided to call for a foreign war, the people, confronted with an inescapable choice, would certainly have chosen a civil war. And these political circumstances were reinforced by compelling economic facts. Not only did the nation lack the resources to fight on a major scale for any length of time, but its economy was also plainly dependent on the Western powers for supplies of petroleum essential to national recovery.

While the risks of war were so strikingly apparent, the possible rewards seemed agonizingly uncertain. Substantial territorial gain could come only from the French possessions in North Africa claimed by empire-minded Falangists. But the chances of winning any such reward were made confused and doubtful by the complex game of Latin politics which Adolf Hitler was playing. In the war's first years, especially after June of 1940, the Führer was fascinated by the possibility of converting France (through Vichy) from a former enemy into a genuine and active ally. This intriguing scheme prohibited any thought of slicing off French Morocco and delivering it as a bribe to Madrid. At this same time, Il Duce would have welcomed such an action—not from any interest in Spanish territorial ambitions, nor from an urgent desire to see Spanish armies take the field, but from a keen anxiety to see Hitler fail in his courting of France, lest the influence of a friendly Vichy rise to challenge that of Rome within Axis councils. By the time when it became apparent that Hitler's dream of winning France was a vain one, British and American armies were invading the very territory which might have been used to reward Madrid for entry into the war. And even though Berlin might have then been willing to promise a specific territorial reward for Spanish military co-operation, the position of Rome had been drastically revised. Since there was no longer any political danger of French ascendance in Axis councils, there was no longer any reason to toss valued French territory to Spain—when Italy itself might be able to claim it. In this tricky and treacherous cycle of Latin politics, Madrid could find no moment to seize when the enormous domestic risks of war could be outweighed by the certainty of greater foreign gain.

For these reasons, Francisco Franco was never able to fulfill his hope "to renew the old bonds of comradeship" between his armies and those of Naziism.

Instead, he managed to divide and dissolve that "common historical destiny" shared by Madrid and Berlin and Rome— and, for a time at least, to escape "my suicide."

10 THE PRESENT AND THE FUTURE

Historians of tomorrow, seeing clearly through the fog and smoke that cloud and confuse today's ideological struggles, may conclude that the main practical difference between a "democratic" and a "totalitarian" state is that the latter never commits suicide.

If they reach this conclusion, they almost certainly will cite, as a supreme example of this distinction, the relations between the Spanish regime of Francisco Franco and the Western democracies after the triumph of the democracies in the Second World War.

I hope that, by the time they are printed, this judgment and the following pages may have become academic and obsolete. They can be made so, next week or next month, by measures taken by the United Nations, the Department of State, the British Foreign Office, the French Quai d'Orsay. These measures would mean the abandonment of a policy which, if it cannot be called dead, at least has come to look alarmingly lifeless—a thing without pulse or purpose.

Perhaps, too, in the weeks and months immediately ahead, events may come to pass within Spain that will profoundly affect the attitude of the entire democratic world toward unhappy Iberia. But, today, the signs of serious change in Madrid are nowhere to be seen. A few new actors to take their roles

274

in the same tragic drama would be perhaps an interesting, but scarcely a serious, innovation.

None of those possible and generally unforeseeable events, however, either in Spain or within the United Nations, can affect the transcendent importance of the issues implicit today in the democratic world's relations with the present Spanish State. Were the Western powers to change their views, a new policy could be carried through to a just and successful conclusion only under the inspiration of a true understanding of those issues—a public opinion that is informed, honest in motive, and clear in purpose. And were the Spanish people suddenly to be visited tomorrow by some quick, miraculous kind of political redemption, the issues of today, confronting the democratic world, might be evaded, but they would not be solved. By such a miracle, we, of that democratic world, might be spared the pain and trouble of meeting those issues—*this* time. But it would be a dangerously illusory kind of reprieve. For these issues are not transient, nor incidental, nor peculiar products of an isolated diplomatic question. They happen to be the issues upon which may depend the survival of the democratic world—or its suicide.

2

Time, varying circumstances, and changing objectives conspire to make of a nation's foreign policy something whose very adaptability may be its highest merit or whose inflexibility may be its gravest weakness. Consistence in a nation's diplomacy is neither a necessary evil nor a necessary vice: it may signify either firm fidelity to essential principle, or the most pernicious lingering of traditional habits and inhibitions.

In the decade which has passed since the outbreak of the Spanish Civil War, American policy toward Spain has evolved through three stages, each marked by distinct problems and objectives. The first period was that of the Civil War itself and our conduct toward the embattled Spanish Republic; the second, our wartime policy toward the regime of General Franco; and finally, our policy since the end of World War II.

In the first stage, American policy was so shortsighted and irresolute that it may be marked, as Sumner Welles has said, the cardinal blunder of the Roosevelt administration's international relations. It was, of course, the nightmarish product of the pretty dream of the Western powers that the forces of Fascism and Communism, left to battle each other, would end in mutual destruction. Only a thin margin of thought separated this hope from the deliberate scheme of fortifying Fascism to check Communism. And this, like all dreams, tended to ignore the obvious in its fanciful distortions of the obscure. The obvious was that to turn whole areas of the world into arenas for Fascist-Communist combat was to abandon all such areas to the moral, if not political, control of the victor in each clash. Since the Western powers wanted neither to be victor, their scheme was remarkably well devised to defeat their own purposes. Spain, with the Western powers' "non-intervention" policy, made this defeat plain, but too late.

The second stage in this decade's American policy toward Spain—the policy of 1941-45—has been a subject for debate conspicuous for giving off more heat than light. The heat was generated by popular indignation over the maintenance of any diplomatic relations with a regime based upon and identified with the principles of our Fascist enemy on the fields of battle. And although the flames of public wrath were undoubtedly fanned by Communist groups for their own purposes, the genuineness and sincerity of much of this righteous anger have been above such suspicion.

Unfortunately, good intentions have rarely sufficed either to constitute a sound foreign policy or to justify its indictment. It was an unhappy coincidence that the outbreak of World War II, which awakened so many to the tragic implications of the Spanish War just concluded, itself created circumstances in which it would have been incredible folly to have tried suddenly to change those implications.

The angry attacks of liberal and left-wing American opinion upon the State Department's wartime Spanish policy arose from misconceptions and careless judgments which were almost as grievously wrong as other, very different misconceptions which had dictated Washington's policy in 1936. In essence, these attacks called for a righting of wrongs at a time when only a greater wrong could result. A good many of the more shrill indictments of the American liberal press seemed to ignore even the fact that proper timing is an elementary law of sound foreign relations. Because American policy toward Spain had committed an egregious blunder before 1939, and because the regime that resulted was as repugnant as most liberals had feared, were not good reasons for adopting a policy that would have driven this regime into the open war of the Axis powers upon the United Nations.

Many critics have contended that such considerations of "expediency" could not vindicate a policy. But in time of war— and the most fateful war in which the United States was ever involved—even the most pious critics did not argue that it was their government's responsibility to do the *in*expedient. Survival itself is generally conceded to be expedient, and "survival" was no overstatement of the issue in World War II.

Endless examples attest these simple truths. If the purest ideological considerations had been allowed to prescribe the conduct of America's wartime foreign relations, then liberal opinion, which since the end of World War II has been so critical of British imperial policies, should have been just as articulate on that subject in 1940. If it had, it would have served the ends of Nazi propaganda perfectly. Similarly, pure political justice might have vindicated Britain's dispatch of an expeditionary force to help Finland repel Russian invasion— yet how grateful the world has been that that force never sailed! And in 1941, after Hitler's armies began their invasion of Russia, how just was the wrath of American liberal opinion when conservative groups raised ideological issues to question the giving of military aid to Soviet Russia!

The motivating forces behind Washington's wartime policy toward Madrid were plain and inexorable. The Department of State followed the orders of the Joint Chiefs of Staff. The American Ambassador in Madrid followed the instructions of the Department of State. The supreme and overriding objective of Washington was to keep Spanish armies out of the war and Axis armies out of Spain. The American mission was not assigned to Madrid by the State Department for the purpose of arguing with General Franco over the virtues of democracy. That might have been its objective had the Chief of the Spanish State been known to be the kind of person easily impressed by either political virtue or political argument. Its purpose was to assist the war effort of the democratic powers: to help allow them to demonstrate their own vitality in triumph over their menacing aggressors. A militantly hostile Spain might have seriously delayed that triumphant demonstration.

Certainly, the anomaly of negotiating and dealing with such a regime as the Spanish government, while our armies were battling its German counterpart, was bitter and painful. American officials in Madrid probably had reason to appreciate this fact even more keenly than political commentators in New York. But the necessity which forced American policy into such a position dated from the sad years of 1936-39; it was not arbitrarily decreed in 1942. It is true that, in 1942, by a righteous display of diplomatic anger, we might have salved our political conscience for what we had done or failed to do in 1936. But this was precisely the capricious kind of self-flagellation which would have given joy and heart only to our most mortal enemies.

In this, as in so many aspects of Spanish history under the Falangist State, democratic leaders within Spain perceived the realities of the situation with far greater clarity than most of their ardent sympathizers in the outside world. They knew, of course, that Nazi triumph in World War II would enslave them as surely as all other freedom-loving peoples, and that it would loom menacingly closer if German armies slammed

shut the western door to the Mediterranean, sealing it as an
Axis lake. They knew that their own position, tragic as it was
under the Falangist State, could only be made more desperate
under a German occupation that would wed Falangist tyranny
and Teutonic efficiency. And they knew that it was precisely
against this grave chance that Allied diplomacy was stubbornly fighting. That made it their battle too.

If "expediency" was a shallow kind of invective with which
to attack this policy, "appeasement" was no truer a description. The word "appeasement" derived its political meaning
from the Munich era—from the pathetic attempts of a frightened pre-1939 London and Paris to satisfy Nazi Germany's
insatiable appetite for conquest. These were the acts of weaker
nations designed to placate a vastly stronger nation—concessions exacted under the menacing threat of superior force.
The wartime relations between Franco Spain and the United
States could not be described in those terms. Certainly, American policy suffered abuses, met reverses, received public insults
—and it adopted an attitude of toleration and patience in the
pursuit of what it considered to be its own essential objectives.
Madrid was the scene of continual "appeasement" in the exact
sense—but it was the Franco regime which (pursuing its own
selfish ends) had to appease alternately both German and Allied pressure. Once the chance to share in a Fascist victory was
lost, Madrid had to face the threat of German armies on the
Pyrenees and the threat of Anglo-American economic sanctions. Under these conflicting menaces, the policy of the Franco
regime could correctly be described as one of attempting
double appeasement.

Following the defeat of Fascism on Europe's battlefields,
American policy toward Spain entered its third and present
stage. This has been the period of long-range verbal artillery—
the series of public official denunciations of the Franco regime
beginning with the San Francisco Conference. In August of
1945, the communiqué of the Potsdam Conference barred the
Spanish government from membership in the United Nations

on the grounds of "its origin, its nature, its record and its
close association with the aggressor states." The following
March came the Anglo-French-American note calling for the
"peaceful withdrawal of Franco . . . and the establishment
of an interim or caretaker government." There followed the
debate in the United Nations Security Council, meeting in
New York, on the Polish call for severance of diplomatic relations with Madrid. And, as this is written, the General Assembly of the United Nations is preparing to take the issue over
from the Security Council.

If the proper criterion for judging the merit of a foreign
policy were merely the intention motivating it, American policy toward Spain in this postwar stage would be a thing of
beauty. If the test be its efficacy in producing results, then it
must be considered also a joy forever—for Francisco Franco.
From the American viewpoint, this policy, conceived in error,
has ended in bankruptcy.

As a general principle applicable to all statements denouncing the Franco regime from abroad, it can be said that probably the worst way to urge democracy upon a foreign country
is that way which permits the nationalistic sentiments of a
people to be mobilized into a hostile legion. No statesman
with any knowledge of the resources of the Franco regime
could believe that it could be shaken by nothing more lethal
than adjectives. Any sober statesman must also know that a
series of verbal denunciations, holding up a foreign government to public scorn, serves only as a pretext for the chief of
that government, through a controlled press and radio, to
identify his own personal salvation with the protection of
national "honor" and "sovereignty." In the spring and summer of 1946, all the rhetorical attacks from London, Washington and Paris upon the Franco regime only served to provide
the Caudillo with the political opportunity to make a series
of speeches throughout Spain, arguing passionately that the
country, not he as its leader, was the object of attack. As a
result, every political observer and diplomat in Madrid, more

than a year after Allied victory in Europe, agreed that the democracies' diplomacy had immeasurably strengthened the position of General Franco.

Another consequence of the war-of-words policy, equally adverse, has come in the Generalissimo's own personal determination to retain power in the face of such challenges. His publicly announced and reiterated reaction can be summarized in the two words: "Quit pushing." It has been a reaction which the least advanced student of Spanish popular psychology should have anticipated clearly. Ironically, this result has been achieved by precisely the kind of diplomatic nudging and needling whose purpose was to bring political change in Spain, quietly and peaceably, by "convincing" Franco that he should surrender power.

In addition to supplying Falangist propaganda with useful new material and fortifying Franco's personal obstinacy, American policy has been defeating itself in a third important respect: by strengthening the very alliance of political forces around Franco which it has sought to weaken. The public indictments of the Spanish regime have insistently stressed its *origins* instead of its *practices*. Thus the Potsdam Communiqué assailed "its origin . . . having been founded with the support of the Axis powers"; and the Tripartite Note of March, 1946, stressed also aid of Germany and Italy to the Franco cause "in its rise to power."

There are two distinct types of indictment which can be leveled against the Franco regime. They need not and should not be confused. One condemns it as the victor of 1939; the other indicts it as the dictatorship of 1946. The first denounces its birth, the second its life. And—this is the important distinction—the first tends to unite all forces ever associated with Franco and the Falange, while the second tends to divide them.

This distinction arises naturally from the history of the last decade in Spain. From the Civil War in 1939, General Franco emerged with the firm support of the Spanish Army, the Spanish Church, the nobility, the wealthy, and a fair proportion of the country's modest middle class. All of these groups, but especially the first two, have been inseparably identified with that military victory and, to the present day, defend its justice. Yet since that day of victory, despite the dexterity of Franco's political maneuvering, fragments—often substantial ones—of these groups have become disappointed or disillusioned, have seen the terrible political tyranny of the Falange, have begun to suspect (if dimly yet) that the Generalissimo himself may be a political liability, and have come to understand (again, dimly) the simple fact that the Spanish people cannot and will not live without their freedom. All such groups of moderate, wavering opinion could have been effectively influenced by indictments of what the Franco regime has done *since* 1939— but they cannot renounce the very creation of that regime because they shared in it. Consequently, indictments based upon 1939 and before relentlessly drive these forces back into the roles of allies of Franco, force them to conclude that their own salvation is inextricably linked with that of the Caudillo. The result is plain: the most intransigeant elements within the Franco regime have been armed with the argument that peaceful change is impossible since the Civil War must, in effect, be refought.

Nor has this line of diplomatic attack gained in consistency what it has lost in effectiveness. As a Madrid lawyer (a moderate Republican) argued to me a few weeks before I left Spain: "Why do not the United Nations or the United States indict this regime for what it has done since 1939, both to its own people and in its foreign policy? You weaken your own position when you indict it for having won the Civil War, because your own government then recognized it as the legitimate Spanish government. Why bother trying to reverse that decision and give the Falangists an easy argument with which to reply? Surely you do not have to go back to 1939 to find your evidence against this man and his regime."

Again the mocking irony reappears. Washington and London have publicly proclaimed that their most cherished purpose is to avoid another civil war in Spain. They have repeatedly refused to adopt measures which (allegedly) would precipitate such open strife. And yet they have insisted in stating their indictment of the Franco regime in terms of the Civil War itself. With the most pacific intentions, they have announced a policy which draws a line across Spain precisely along the scar of 1936.

The firmest and most complete statement of the Western powers' Spanish policy came on March 4, 1946, when the governments of Great Britain, France, and the United States released their Tripartite Note. This remarkable diplomatic document declared:

The Governments of France, the United Kingdom, and the United States of America have exchanged their views with regard to the present Spanish Government and their relations with that regime. . . . So long as General Franco continues in control of Spain, the Spanish people cannot anticipate full and cordial association with those nations of the world which have, by their common effort, brought defeat to German Naziism and Italian Fascism. . . .

There is no intention of interfering in the internal affairs of Spain. The Spanish people themselves must, in the long run, work out their own destiny. In spite of the present regime's repressive measures against orderly efforts of the Spanish people to organize and give expression to their political aspirations, the three Governments are hopeful that the Spanish people will not again be subjected to the horrors and bitterness of civil strife.

On the contrary, it is hoped that leading patriotic and liberal-minded Spaniards may soon find means to bring about a peaceful withdrawal of Franco, the abolition of the Falange, and the establishment of an interim or caretaker government under which the Spanish people may have an opportunity freely to determine the type of government they wish to have and to choose their leaders. . . .

The question of the maintenance or termination by the Governments of France, the United Kingdom, and the United States of diplomatic relations with the present Spanish regime is a matter to be decided in the light of events and after taking into account the efforts of the Spanish people to achieve their own freedom.

As an expression of beatific intentions, this statement was impeccable. As a declaration of policy, its principal flaw was that it made no sense.

In Madrid, in the days following the issuance of this Tripartite Note, my Spanish Republican friends, even the most ardent and impassioned, showed a restraint and courtesy characteristic of their people. Whenever I met them, they all began with a pleasant remark to the effect that they were glad that we had publicly declared the desirability of the Caudillo's "withdrawal." Then they faltered and stumbled in an effort to find something else to say. It took a little coaxing and encouragement to bring them to the frank admission that they could not understand what the three great nations were trying to say. Once that reluctant confession was made, they warmed to the discussion. . . . "Withdraw" General Franco? Splendid idea. How? . . . Do it peacefully? But if he does not want to be "withdrawn," then what? . . . Does anyone seriously believe he wants to depart? Then what should the Spanish people do? Wait for another Tripartite Note to suggest the route the Generalissimo should follow into his peaceful retirement? . . . "No intention of interfering" in Spanish affairs? That sounds strangely like democratic policy toward the Civil War, out of which Franco battled his way to power. And if the democracies have no such intention, why are they issuing a note urging the Spanish people to change their own government?.

I could not answer these questions. I still do not know how an intelligent response could be given to any of them on the basis of declared American policy.

After this undecipherable expression of intention by the Western powers, the initiative in the United Nations' diplomatic offensive against Franco Spain passed to eastern Europe. It came with Poland's plea to the Security Council to condemn the Spanish government as a threat to world peace and to force the severance of all relations with Spain.

Although this new line of attack at least had the virtue of calling for a clear and unequivocal policy, the Polish indict-

ment suffered from several grave handicaps. First, the very fact
that Poland sponsored the charges (while Great Britain and
the United States demurred) played conveniently into the argument of Falangist propaganda in Spain that Russian Communism was the true source of inspiration for all foreign criticism. More serious was the fact that Poland's indictment
seemed to be predicated on the belief that the truth was not
enough. It had to be improved upon by invention. Accordingly, the Polish delegate to the Security Council spiced his
critique with some of most ludicrous charges ever unsmilingly
presented to a presumably serious international meeting. The
purpose of these charges, designed to bring the Spanish case
under the Council's jurisdiction by showing a threat to world
peace, was to cast Franco Spain in the role of a potential military aggressor, pressing frantic research on the atomic bomb
and menacing the French border with a huge mobilized army
ready to strike across the Pyrenees. Estimates of Spanish armed
forces on the Pyrenees, carried by the American press, raced
madly past the 400,000 mark.

While an indictment framed in these terms produced a fan-
tastically distorted picture of Spain, its effect within Spain was
to tend to discredit the integrity and accuracy of the grave and
unanswerable charges which others aimed against the Franco
regime. When the temporary leader in the United Nations'
diplomatic offense was discovered to be apparently carried
away by his own inventive imagination, the propaganda machine of the Spanish State gratuitously was handed ammunition with which to ridicule all opposition and criticism, both
the passionately serious and the unintentionally comic.

While the Polish charges themselves produced this dismal
result, the contrary attitude taken by the British and American delegates in the Security Council also played the game of
Falangist propaganda. Although the British and American
representatives were obviously pained and embarrassed by the
Polish delegate's indiscriminate mixture of fact and fancy,
their refusal to consider serious diplomatic action against the

Franco regime made it simple for Falangist propaganda to depict them as defenders of that regime. Most firmly, the American and British delegates insisted that any recommendation by the Council to the General Assembly, calling for a diplomatic break with Franco Spain, should *not* include any time limit upon such action. Logically, this looked to the people of Spain like evidence of great Anglo-American anxiety to avoid any measure that would bring too sudden or too drastic a change in Spain.

These have been the consequences of a policy which has been a curious compound of fear, vacillation, bold and empty words. Had the enemies of General Franco, both in eastern and western Europe, conspired to stage a political farce with the secret purpose of fortifying their foe, they could not have written a more effective drama, nor cast their characters with greater skill, nor executed their roles with a finer sense of timing.

3

Does Spain matter?

Should the American people fret or fight over the political future of the people of Spain?

Should the Department of State's overworked peacemakers concern themselves with the tactics and practices by which a totalitarian regime continues to inflict itself upon 25,000,000 Latins in a country which took no formal part in the Axis war upon the rest of the world?

Is there any need for the grocer or druggist in Tulsa or Dubuque to worry because a druggist or grocer in Bilbao or Barcelona "got himself shot" by a color-blind dictator for being a "Red"?

Many will answer these questions in the negative. In 1932 these same people dismissed the Manchurian incident as some remote Oriental scrapping of little consequence. In 1935 they welcomed the possibility that Mussolini might also make Abyssinian trains run on time. In 1936 they liked the way

Il Duce commemorated Good Friday by raping Albania. In 1937 they approved the way in which some sensible Spanish generals were restoring order in Iberia. In March of 1939, they thought that Czechoslovakia was a pretty cheap price for peace. In September of 1939, they scratched their heads in perplexity. Something had gone wrong.

For all other people, Spain does matter—today even more than a decade ago. Questions of ideology or political sentiment need not enter at this moment. What happens in and to Spain matters for several simple, solid reasons:

Because the United States, Spain, and Latin America form a historic and geographic triangle, and plane geometry tells us that each angle in a triangle is affected by changes in the other two;

Because the Iberian peninsula means the western gate to the Mediterranean;

Because Spain is the land bridge between Europe and Africa;

Because Spain occupies a vital place in a map of the air routes of the world;

Because in the turbulent world of 1947, on a European continent still tragically unsure of its political and economic future, a potentially explosive Spain is a danger spot of the first magnitude;

Because Soviet Russia knows Spain to have been the scene of a critical Communist defeat and believes that it can be made the scene of a resounding Communist triumph;

Because, in the confronting of East and West in today's political councils, in their respective appeals to the trust and confidence of the peoples of the world, Spain is a festering sore on the conscience of the Western powers.

I believe that these facts justify the statement that, in deciding their country's relations with Spain's totalitarian regime, the American people must make a judgment of critical importance and of the greatest urgency.

The postwar policy of the Western democracies, the policy of our State Department, has registered utter failure in its announced purpose of speeding political evolution in Spain. This fact alone might not be all-decisive, if certain other purposes of that policy, perhaps almost as important as the immediate removal of Franco, had been achieved. These other purposes have been two: to avoid the risk of civil war in Spain, and to deprive Communism of any chance to win ascendancy in Iberia. What has converted the State Department's failure into a disaster has been the appalling fact that its policy can only hasten the likelihood of civil war and facilitate the rapid growth of Communism in Spain.

On this fiercely alien soil of Spain, Communism is spreading principally from the same cause which permitted both it and Fascism to thrive in the crucial years of 1936-39: because the Western democracies have failed to evolve and express a clear, purposeful policy that would free Spain's democratic forces from the deadly Fascist-Communist crossfire in which they have been placed. Even though all the world has seen the tragic folly of the Western powers' pre-1939 foreign policies, the assumptions and preconceptions that inspired that policy have persisted to dictate action (or rather, inaction) today. The result, for Spain, cannot fail to be the same today as it was before: to leave only Fascism and Communism as the mighty combatants in an isolated political arena.

In this arena, the growth of Communism has been natural and easy. The most elementary and patent facts of Spain's political life have made it so: the Spanish people's overwhelming opposition to their present regime; the Communist boast that Russia alone is battling for the overthrow of that regime in the international councils of the world; the desperation of Socialists, left and moderate Republicans who have always looked to the Western powers as their models, their inspirations, their friends. It is true that the vast majority of Spanish people have been as emphatically anti-Communist as they have been anti-Fascist. But from the latter position there has been and will be no retreat, even under the most savage pressure.

From the former position, the people are being slowly driven under the relentless pressure of political circumstance.

Every month, every week, every day, the prestige and power of Spanish Communism are growing. Soviet Russia is not achieving it. We—the Western democracies—are doing it. Our policy has left the forces of Spanish democracy without support, with little reason for hope, with no sure knowledge even of our political purposes. Thus disarmed, they cannot be expected to battle successfully the Communist contention that only the Communist Party counts upon tangible foreign aid, that only Soviet Russia is determinedly anti-Fascist, that only Communism can be the instrument of Spain's liberation.

With the haunting, approaching specter of Communism there comes nearer, too, the shadow of civil war. Sooner or later, in peace or in war, the Spanish people can and will rid themselves of today's totalitarian tyranny. American policy toward Spain has recognized precisely this certainty and has cited it to vindicate its own strategy of "masterly inactivity." But this policy also, with astounding illogic, professes to be an escape from the danger of civil war in Spain. In the absence of drastic action from abroad, there are only two possible ways by which the regime of Francisco Franco could be liquidated: by suicide or by civil war. It will not be suicide. It will, if necessary, be civil war. This will not be a new or novel experience for the people of Spain. Political statisticians fond of citing the number of dictators who have ruled Spain, as reason for more dictators, forget the equally high mortality rate of Spanish tyrants. The policy of refraining from "interference" in Spanish affairs will not succeed in perpetuating indefinitely the Franco regime. It can merely postpone its death, and help to make it a bloody one. That happens to be precisely the eventuality which our policy is supposed to avoid.

Subject to certain contingencies, one conclusion is plain. If Spain does matter to the United States, if we wish to see the Falangist State destroyed, if our national interests would not be well served by a Communist Spain, if we hope to help the

Spanish people escape another civil war, for their sake and that of the world, then it is time to do something a little more impressive than issue verbal manifestoes, and to speak phrases that make more sense than to instruct "patriotic Spaniards" to seek out and "find means" to effect a "peaceful withdrawal" of General Franco.

4

If the democracies of the West were to abdicate their present policy toward Spain, they could choose between several others.

One policy, which could at least claim to be coherent, consistent, and intelligible (as our present policy cannot), would frankly confess that we renounce Spain as an issue of political warfare, that we will define our foreign policy without reference to ideological controversy, and that we are prepared to accept and deal with any *de facto* regime on earth. Cynical as this policy would be, it would be plainly superior to the present one. It would abandon the folly of stating ends, the means to achieve which we are unwilling to employ. It would remove the democracies from the less than honorable position they have assumed—the position of appearing to covet the cheap luxury of declaring noble political purposes without having the courage to assume obligations or to run risks in the achievement of those purposes. It would be a policy that the peoples of the world could understand.

It would also be, however, a policy that would shock and dismay most peoples of the world—and against which the conscience of the American people would rebel. Only its logic, but neither its morality nor its efficacy, would be superior to the present policy of delivering solemn, safe international sermons.

Sermons without sanctions is one thing. Sermons with sanctions can be something quite different. In the latter direction lies the only real hope for the Western democracies to develop a worthy and constructive policy toward Spain.

Such a policy would entail: an end to the fatuous banalities about not "interfering" in Spanish affairs; a categorical statement that overwhelming evidence convinces all democratic peoples that the Franco regime is not a decent neighbor in the society of nations; and support of that statement with action. Such action would entail some or all of the following measures. First, an ultimatum to Madrid from the Western democracies that their diplomatic relations will be severed by a specified date unless the Caudillo and Falange are supplanted by at least an interim regime promising to consult and respect the will of the Spanish people. Secondly, a supporting declaration of similar character by the greatest possible number of the nations of Latin America. Thirdly (if necessary), an ultimatum, either to precede shortly or to coincide with the diplomatic break, announcing economic sanctions to be imposed before a specified date. Fourth (if necessary), the imposition of sanctions.

With what speed would this course of action bring an end to the Falangist State? It is probable that the first two steps would suffice to bring results within the specified time limit. It is virtually certain that the third step—the threat of economic sanctions—would suffice. It is absolutely certain that the Spanish government could not survive a period of economic sanctions for longer than three to four months.

With the launching of this prearranged line of attack, what succession of developments might be expected? Obviously, the reasonable hope would be that the political forces within Spain, especially the Army and secondarily the Church, without which the Franco regime could not stand, would realize, at last, that the men, the practices and the institutions of the Falangist State were liabilities with which they could no longer be identified, liabilities under mortal and inescapable fire, liabilities which must be liquidated from within to escape the serious consequences that so plainly threatened the nation from without.

I describe this as a "reasonable" hope. The reasons are important. Both the Spanish Army and the Spanish Church have always placed their own interests above the interests of any political regime with which they happened to be identified. Their interests antedate, and have no necessary dependence upon, the Falangist State—once they see plainly that the transient privileges which that State has bestowed on them can no longer be defended. Moreover, these are the elements in Spain most anxious to avoid another civil war. *If they are brought to know from the outset* the full extent to which the Western democracies are prepared to go in destroying the Franco regime, they will see from the outset the risk of civil disorder that lies ahead, should Franco and the Falange entrench themselves for a long siege. In this way, under the impact of determined foreign pressure, these groups' own fear of civil war, instead of encouraging them in their defense of the Falangist State (as it has in the past), could be converted into a force opening the way for change.

From the viewpoint of the democratic powers, the policy outlined plainly suffers from being purely negative in character. From this weakness, I can see no practical escape. There could be only two possible alternatives. One would be a positive recognition of the Giral group of Republican exiles: this would be utterly disastrous because of that group's uncertain following within Spain, because such an action would revive the most passionate hatreds and fears of the Civil War itself, and because it would effectively place the democratic nations in the role of dictating acceptance of a specific regime to the people of Spain. The other positive alternative is a purely theoretical one: the sponsorship by the democratic powers of a truly representative government of national coalition, established in exile and composed of members selected from the exiled leaders of the Spanish Republic, democratic leaders within Spain, liberal Monarchists, and certain anti-Franco military leaders. Such an action by the democracies would have the advantage of allowing them to seize the political initiative, as distinct from the policy of adopting only negative measures and awaiting their consequences. But it would raise intricate, if not insoluble, controversies over the choice of representative leaders; and, as much as a recognition of the Giral regime, it would constitute a usurpation by foreign powers of the right of selection which can belong only to the Spanish people themselves.

While I do not believe that any informed democratic observer of Spain can doubt the need for the democratic powers to take a bold and constructive course of action to end the Franco regime, I also feel sure that no advocate of such action should (or needs to) ignore or conceal its risks and uncertainties. One such risk is the hardship that would be inflicted on the people of Spain, and even the chance of civil strife, if economic sanctions had to be applied and did not bring quick results. Another and very different kind of risk would come with too quick and too superficial results: the dismissal of Franco and the apparent dissolution of the Falange by conservative forces allied to the present regime, who would then fail to permit real political freedom in Spain by the perpetuation of their own privileges behind a new, if less repugnant, façade. And a third risk comes not from Spain but from Communist pressure in all parts of the world—a pressure upon the Western democracies to refuse to accept any political evolution in Spain judged by Communists to be insufficiently sweeping and hence "undemocratic."

But, in recognizing these dangers, we must at the same time realize that they are largely the consequences of the failure of the Western democracies themselves to take firm political action at an earlier time, at precious moments of psychological advantage which were allowed to pass. At least three such moments were missed: the time of the removal of German troops from the Pyrenees and their replacement by Allied forces in 1944; the weeks immediately following the surrender of Nazi armies in Europe; and the month after the electoral victory of the Labor Party in England. On all three occasions, the spirit and stamina of the Falangist State plunged to the levels of fear and near despair, as the leaders of the State expected an imminent political offensive from the Western powers that would be relentless and irresistible. No such offensive came. Falangists and the most fanatically Fascist followers of the Generalissimo recovered their political poise. In happy astonishment, they stared at clear political skies, clean of any suggestion of coming storm. And in the shining daylight of this delivery from fear, they mounted the political platforms of the nation to deliver their hastily drafted speeches about "Evangelical democracy" and "organic democracy" and "Christian democracy." Because those moments of psychological advantage were lost by the Western democracies, the task of the democracies has become unquestionably more difficult and hazardous. But that fact makes it nonetheless necessary, nonetheless compelling.

Against the course of action which I have outlined, against any action designed to weaken, by deed rather than the word, the Franco regime, many arguments have been advanced. Some have been naïve, some hypocritical, some based on a rigid refusal to know the facts, and some which are serious and need at least brief mention and answer. I believe the four arguments that follow are the most important.

1. The United Nations cannot take action against the Franco regime under the terms of its charter without evidence that it is a threat to world peace. Such evidence does not exist. And if the United States and the Western democracies take action independently, they betray lack of faith in the United Nations organization and impair its prestige.

It is perfectly true that only distortion of the facts can depict Franco Spain as a menace to international peace and that, therefore, the United Nations Charter cannot be literally cited in collective action against Spain. But it is not true that the Western democracies would weaken the structure of the United Nations by changing their own policies toward the Franco regime. The issue of Falangist Spain dates from years before the birth of the United Nations organization and arises from the policy of the democracies toward Spain throughout those years. Only an anxiety to throw off the burden of making their own decision could induce the Western powers to insist that the United Nations accept and inherit the legacy of their mistakes. And only an incautious or irresponsible friend of the United Nations could insist that the young organization must accept such responsibilities to demonstrate its worth.

2. No foreign power should "interfere" in the sovereign affairs of the Spanish nation.

This argument raises an essentially false issue by slurring two key words: "interference" and "sovereignty."

In a real sense, there is no possible way by which the United States can fail to "interfere in" (in the sense of influence directly) the domestic affairs of Spain. Our government's maintenance of customary diplomatic relations with the Franco regime cannot be considered a "neutral" position without political significance within Spain. It may well be our State Department's desire and intention to have its policy so considered—but the Falangist State itself will not permit it. Instead, Falangist propaganda systematically has exploited the fact of diplomatic recognition and every suggestion (true or false) of American accord with Spain, not as perfunctory diplomatic relations, but as effective American endorsement of the Falangist State.

The concept of "sovereignty," whether or not it is a dangerous and obsolete one, cannot possess clear political meaning in a country such as Spain today. When a considerable majority of the people of a nation deny the very legitimacy of their government, and would welcome its destruction, it is not unreasonable to question the authenticity of that government's claim to be the custodian and defender of the nation's "sovereignty." And, since the Franco regime rose to power by force of arms and with considerable foreign aid, its righteous citation of the principle of "sovereignty" conveys a suspiciously new and sudden reverence for legal rights which somehow fails to be utterly convincing.

3. A policy of political and economic sanctions against Franco Spain will precipitate civil war in Spain.

Such a policy runs the risk of civil war. The present policy of the Western powers promises the eventual certainty of civil war. Between the two policies, choice should not be difficult.

And in measuring this risk, certain factors should be kept in mind. One is the fact, which I have already mentioned, that the most powerful groups around Franco are anxious, in their own interests, to escape civil strife; and once these groups understood the full scope of the action planned against the Franco regime, they themselves would be the most anxious to escape the full impact of that action in its most drastic form. Another pertinent consideration is the fact that it is Falangist propagandists who insist most loudly that the Western democracies must not dare take action against their State unless they wish to bring on another civil war. After several years of its reiteration, this argument sounds like the crudest and weakest kind of political blackmail.

4. The fact that Communist parties and "front-organizations" throughout the world advocate political and economic action against Spain is clear proof that such action would serve only Communist purposes and ends.

To begin with, this contention (which seems to me the most infuriatingly specious of all these arguments), despite its superficial simplicity of logic, conceals two unproven presumptions. To deduce that a given course of action will serve Communist ends merely because Communists advocate it is to assume, first, that Communist parties are seeking what they say they seek, and secondly, that they are correct in their own assumption that a certain course of action will achieve their ends.

I cannot subscribe to the increasingly popular belief that Communists are possessed of an infallible insight enabling them to assess precisely the consequences of any given political action. And I fail to see why judgments determining American foreign policy should try to exploit vicariously this mythical insight by accepting and applying a Communist criterion (in reverse) to determine our own national interests.

Moreover, I do not believe that either Soviet Russia or informed Communists anywhere in the world are really anxious to see the Western democracies force the overthrow of the Franco regime. The ideal circumstances for the growth of Communism in Spain are those that prevail at this moment. None more advantageous can be conceived for the simple reason that, under these circumstances, Spanish Communists believe (with considerable reason) that they stand an excellent chance of effectively dominating all the forces of the Spanish left. Why, then, should Communist and Russian spokesmen all over the world publicly advocate action by the Western powers against Franco Spain? First, because they know (as does the whole world) that Washington and London are firmly opposed to such action and may even stiffen in their resistance to it under Communist pressure advocating it. Secondly, because, without serious danger that the policy they advocate publicly would be adopted by Great Britain or the United States, Communist leaders and Russian statesmen can publicly charge the Western powers with tolerating the vicious vestiges of Fascism, and can arouse suspicion among all peoples that Western "democracy" is shallow, insincere, hypocritical, and ineffectual.

Finally, I believe that this argument betrays an acceptance of the dangerous, unscrupulous and irrational standard that what Communists advocate is *per se* error, what they denounce is *per se* truth. While such a standard of judgment produces patent absurdities, it can effectively result only in a foreign policy which embraces and endorses all political forces which claim to be anti-Communist. Statesmen who conceive of foreign policy today in these terms should never have permitted the hanging of Joachim von Ribbentrop, for he was their oracle. At least they should ponder the end to which he came.

5

Let us have no easy illusions. For no country, certainly not for a nation so complex as Spain, can any quick, vicarious political redemption be won. It is right and true to say that only the people of Spain can define and build their own political future. What we can do is help strike off the chains today preventing them from finding and following their own path. But theirs is the path to find and follow.

When no sure prediction can be made about the political fate of a single European country, let us say ten years from today, certainly none can be made for Spain. Spain is not going to develop a sound and virile democracy in a month or a year, no matter what action other powers of the world may take. Other powers may again, as they have in the past, destroy her immediate chances of developing such a democracy. But none can build that democracy for her.

The best evolution within Spain for which we can hope and work may appear to be a difficult and, at times, disappointingly inconclusive one. Today, the chancelleries of the Western democracies may meticulously draft a list of their ultimate desired objectives: utter abolition of every vestige of the Falange Party; end of the military rule of Franco's dictatorship; his disappearance from any public office; re-institution of a legitimate judicial procedure, with full amnesty for all political prisoners and complete abolition of the Franco regime's special punitive courts; institution of the rights of free press and free assembly; and provision for free elections upon which may be based a truly representative parliament. . . . But while we envision such goals, we would deceive only ourselves if we were to assume that they would all be achieved with brilliant speed. We, the people of the Western democracies, should be mentally prepared to view conditions that will certainly fall far short of perfection—just as our statesmen must be ready to deal on a peremptory *ad hoc* basis with un-predictable, changing political circumstances.

And even if all the specific political goals of which we might conceive today were suddenly realized by the Spanish people, these achievements in themselves would not guarantee a sturdy, enduring democratic society. This can only be the long labor of a people who have spent more than a decade under the dark night of civil strife and domestic tyranny . . . a labor which cannot be performed by well-wishing statesmen of foreign countries, which can only be the collective work of the teachers in new Spanish schools, of workers in free labor unions, of peasants on land that is their own.

Today, with the help and the faith of the democracies of the world, this great work can be begun. From the dirty huts along the Guadalquivir and the green pastures of Guipúzcoa, from beneath the Moorish arches of Cordova and out of the damp caves hidden in the Guadarrama, from the slums of Barcelona and the prisons of Madrid, across the crusted, sun-baked plains of Castile, there may soon come the men able and ready to build a free, good society.

11 THE END OF THE BEGINNING

AS I WRITE these final lines, the second day of the Prince of Peace since the end of the Second World War is almost here. Not far distant is the second anniversary of the Day of Victory of the United Nations.

The United States Navy Department has just submitted to the Bureau of the Budget a record-breaking peacetime budget of $5,900,000,000 for the 1948 fiscal year. News dispatches from the nation's capital explain to us that the Navy is especially interested in a strong submarine force and in the full-scale of development of "guided missiles."

In Moscow, the Russian Foreign Office has just announced that no foreign correspondents are to be permitted to make radio broadcasts to the world beyond Soviet frontiers.

In Bucharest, a fresh style of political vaudeville known as the "Rumanian elections" has just been staged. The Communist-dominated government bloc has triumphed according to schedule.

In London, a Socialist government has made clear to the British people that the peacetime production of civilian goods must yield priority to the urgent need of maintaining the armed forces of the nation at their peacetime peak.

In Athens, King George II has returned to the throne of Greece, to the apparent satisfaction of Great Britain. But in

300

the north of Greece, Communist guerrilla forces, sweeping through the valleys of the barren mountain ranges, have brought strange new gods to Mount Olympus.

In a New York delicatessen store on West 58th Street a Ukrainian delegate to the United Nations was shot in the leg during a holdup. The chief Ukrainian envoy declared that it was a political assault. Some blocks away, in the Waldorf-Astoria Hotel, the Foreign Ministers of Soviet Russia, Great Britain, France, and the United States were earnestly debating the authority which the governor of Trieste shall exercise over the city's police forces.

In Buenos Aires, President Juan Perón has had the satisfaction of receiving newly appointed ambassadors from both the United States and Russia, after successfully demonstrating that his kind of government can even survive an occasional popular election.

In Hiroshima, there is still a reminder.

In this world, the democratic peoples again may ask themselves: Can our relations with Falangist Spain, in these last years and today, seriously affect our destiny?

Certainly there can be no doubt that the history of American relations with the government of Francisco Franco has brought to us several important and useful lessons on the ways, the problems, the perils in our relations with all other peoples and governments of the world. From these lessons we can profit.

We can learn, here as elsewhere, that there exists no common language by which a democratic and a totalitarian state can speak to each other and perfectly understand one another. We can also learn, from the wartime history of our relations with Spain, that a wise and mature public opinion avoids the temptation of passing judgment, too quickly and without sufficient information, on those many diplomatic issues which rarely are so simple or uncomplicated as they may appear at first inspection. A politically mature democratic people realizes that it is not the privilege but the duty of the leaders of their foreign policy frequently to act on these issues without giving complete public explanations. And when such a people does decide and express its judgments on the policies of either their own or of other nations, it will seek, weigh, and carefully distinguish between words, deeds, and motives.

We can also wisely remember that the democratic cause in a foreign country is not always best served by its most voluble and enthusiastic advocates in our own midst. The most just and honorable cause can suffer grave damage inflicted by advocates whose uncontrolled zeal carries them into the realm of exaggeration and fancy, of invention and misleading rhetoric. Thus have some too anxious friends of Spanish democracy, insisting that Spain's underground forces have possessed far greater strength than has been true, only succeeded in helping to blind the democratic world to the dangers which surround those forces in Spain. Others, who with equal passion have insisted that the Franco regime was merely the synthetic political product of an Italo-German conspiracy, have only induced their audience to forget or to underestimate the real battle which Spanish democracy has yet to fight—the battle against its indigenous Spanish enemies, the still powerful and entrenched forces of oppression and reaction. The grave harm done by exhortations of this kind cannot be atoned for by the good intentions of those who make them, for the road to democracy or to peace must be paved with a harder surface.

While these considerations have real meaning and importance, they all are, in a sense, secondary issues. For, in the development of a national foreign policy they serve only as cautions and warnings, not as incentives or objectives.

Spain—its problem and its tragedy—confronts us with a trial and a test of the fundamental principles which must inspire and animate our relations with all other peoples of the world. It challenges our very understanding of the world in which we live. This fact, in the final analysis, explains why Spain matters to the American people.

Today the peoples of the world know that the United States,

the triumphant achievement of the liberal-capitalist age, has the most impressive and productive industrial machine of all history. They know that it is capable of turning out the world's best cars, cheapest washing machines, shiniest refrigerators, biggest buildings, swiftest planes, and the atomic bomb. They do not yet know, however, what are this nation's exact motives and objectives in the world at large, this nation which, in this fifth decade of our century, professes to be the Western world's greatest champion of democracy.

Perhaps the most appalling illusion which afflicted the Western world in the 1930's was the belief that the truth and virtue of its philosophy were so manifest that a peculiar and mysterious perception on the part of all peoples, even of the politically uneducated, would compel them to scorn and reject the pretentious promises of Fascism. The history of the last decade should have sufficed to make clear to us that not all peoples of the world have been convinced of the integrity of our intentions or the imperishable merit of our political doctrine. Had all peoples been so convinced, the democratic world would not have had to wage six years of war against Fascism. Nor would it today be speculating on its own chances for salvation in the face of the challenge of Russian Communism.

Today the Western democracies can become the victims of no illusion more vain or dangerous than that which insinuates the false confidence that some divine and immutable destiny has decreed the immortality of their faith and has promised to defend it for all time against all mean and savage forces of this earth.

For a very simple reason, neither peace nor security could come to the democratic world when Nazi generals signed their surrender at Rheims. There are no armistice terms applicable to a war of ideas. Nor is there any weapon of war so powerful that it can destroy beliefs, erase suspicions, change cynicism into faith or doubt into trust.

We cannot then believe that what we have, for these many years, called "Fascism" could ever have felt a bayonet thrust between its ribs or have swallowed a capsule of cyanide to end a life of shame.

Nor can we believe that the greatest or most dangerous underground hides in the Bavarian mountains. For it is not there. As arms have been smuggled into obscure caves, as looted Nazi funds have been buried and concealed in dummy corporations, as fleeing Fascists have sought refuge in once neutral nations—so, in like manner but with deadlier effect, have ideas been smuggled into men's minds across the frontiers of reason. So has the poison of Fascism been sold in bottles marked with innocent labels. So has the virus of the disease spread to men and to places remote from the original source of infection.

Out of this underground, from this legacy of ideas and emotions which could not be destroyed on a field of battle, there has come the sound of old words. They are echoing, hollowly yet enticingly, in the great political chambers of the capitals of the democratic world. The echo says: Let Us "All" Unite to Save Ourselves from "Communism."

The memory of truculent Fascism's insidious exhortations is still too fresh and clear for this plaintive appeal to succeed in dictating the policies of the democratic world. But, unfortunately, the memory is not vivid enough to prevent this plea from frightening the capitals of Western democracy into the same inaction and passivity which marked their policies before the Second World War. Thus, their judgment of every concrete problem in their world relations takes on a familiar and uniform cast:

Dare we shake the foundations of the Spanish regime of Francisco Franco—or would this action aid the forces of Communism?

Dare we press China's Generalissimo Chiang Kai-shek to effect democratic reform of his military dictatorship—or would this action aid the forces of Communism?

Dare we amend and modify the imperial system of colonial

possessions of the Western powers—or would that aid the forces of Communism?

No two of these questions—or of the long list which could be added—involves identical political factors. But the significant fact is that, with equal agony in struggling to confront all these issues, democracy is gripped by *fear*. And it is precisely that fear which marks a democracy that is in retreat and in mortal danger.

All those political questions which begin with the words, "Dare we . . . ," can be translated into one transcendent question: Dare the democracies be democratic?

If this courage is lacking, if the champions of democracy are so cynical of their own faith that they are afraid to come to the aid of their disciples in distress, lest they become "Communists," then the political warriors of the democratic world can spare themselves the trouble of girding for battle with the forces of Communism. The war is already lost.

Today, in Spain, it is being lost. The Falangist State is anti-Communist. The people are anti-Falangist. The majority of the people are also seekers of democracy and believers in personal freedom. But to aid these people, to undermine the Falangist State, might this not aid the forces of Communism? Nothing, therefore, can be done. No formula for action can be found. No honest statement of principle or purpose can be made.

This is Munich—not in the world of power politics, but in the world of political ideas.

As in Spain, so in the rest of the world. Why? Because the peoples of the world cannot be won to a political faith whose apostles themselves despair of its own efficacy. Because the peoples of the world cannot understand, much less embrace, a gospel whose preachers are not only uneloquent but also inarticulate. Because the peoples of the world know that the forces of democracy are afflicted with a fatal creeping paralysis if their practical policies signify a total abdication of their own principles—an abdication forced by nothing more glorious or compelling than the fear that their own principles may be exploited by their enemies. And because neither preachments nor armaments but the plain convictions and beliefs of the peoples of the world will decide the life or death of the democracy of the Western world.

Certainly, this democracy faces no challenge so grave as that of Communism. Certainly, the Western democratic nations confront no issue as decisive as their relations with Soviet Russia. But if the democracies' preoccupation with these challenges (instead of inspiring a clean resolve to fulfill democracy's own promise for all peoples) becomes an hypnotic fascination that merely freezes them into immobility, then neither challenge can be met. If the world vision of the democratic nations becomes so narrowed that it can focus only upon that one-sixth of the globe's surface under Russian dominion, and so intense that it cannot perceive and develop clear democratic policies and practices in the rest of the world, then the remaining five-sixths of the world will be lost to the Western democracies, not by defeat, but by default.

There are two roads to suicide. The first is that which starts from the giddy heights of unreasoning assurance that we live in one world which, despite occasional errors and caprices, is innately, eternally and invulnerably democratic. This is the road of the blind. The second fatal road starts from the dark abyss out of which comes the despairing cry that democracy can offer no greater hope to the peoples of the world than that which is contained in denunciation of Communism and a totally negative struggle against its claims. This is a hope and a struggle no more inspiring, no more elevating, than those of Fascism itself. And this is the road of the coward.

Either of these paths is easier to follow than a third, because survival always entails a greater struggle and a greater sacrifice than suicide.

For the American people, this third road starts from the clear understanding that democracy's battle for existence is *never* completely won. It advances to the realization that the durability of a people's peace depends upon all people's understanding of its terms and their faith in its promises. It comes to the realization that, in this age of profoundest revolution, the United States can serve neither the world nor itself by transforming itself (a nation born of revolution) from a young, daring and progressive country, into a citadel or an arsenal for the frightened and besieged forces of reaction and despair.

Only if inspired by these convictions, can we look back upon battles already fought, sacrifices already made, with the right to believe that the struggle has been worth the pain.

We have fought not to win, but to be able to continue the fight. That is the way the history of democracy is written.

INDEX

PRODUCTION NOTES

DESIGNER: *Maurice Serle Kaplan*

TYPES: *Linotype* Baskerville *with display in* Orplid

TYPESETTING, ELECTROTYPING, PRINTING, AND

BINDING: *Quinn & Boden Co., Inc., Rahway, N. J.*

DATE DUE